Y0-AFJ-848

Collective Goods Neglected Goods

Collective Goods Neglected Goods

Dealing with Methodological Failure in the Social Sciences

Herbert J. Kiesling
Indiana University, Bloomington

World Scientific
Singapore • New Jersey • London • Hong Kong

Published by

World Scientific Publishing Co. Pte. Ltd.
P O Box 128, Farrer Road, Singapore 912805
USA office: Suite 1B, 1060 Main Street, River Edge, NJ 07661
UK office: 57 Shelton Street, Covent Garden, London WC2H 9HE

British Library Cataloguing-in-Publication Data
A catalogue record for this book is available from the British Library.

COLLECTIVE GOODS, NEGLECTED GOODS:
Dealing with Methodological Failure in the Social Sciences

ISBN 981-02-3846-0

Printed in Singapore.

Preface

I can remember clearly as a first year graduate student hearing Professor Herbert Fraser remark that economic methodology was that part of the discipline which became of interest to economists only in old age, the obvious implication, even to a neophyte student, being that economists in the prime parts of their careers — those actually doing the real work — had better things to do with their time. I remember the twinkle in Herb Fraser's eye as he delivered this wisdom (sometimes within hearing of other faculty members who enjoyed the humor but did not demur), and while I did not even know what methodology was at the time, I remember thinking Fraser's remark was likely delivered tongue-in-cheek.

Tongue-in-cheek statements, as we all know, typically have a grain of truth in them, and later, when well into my own active career, I began to wonder. As a student of tax analysis and government policy making, I only gradually came to appreciate that statements similar to Fraser's remarks often betray more than just humor; they point to essential elements of what Dierdre McCloskey has termed the "rhetoric of economics," that is, how economists organize their persuasive efforts, where "persuasion" is considered in the broadest possible way. Persuasion depends importantly upon what persons choose to include in their investigations, or as McCloskey would put it, their "conversations."

I have come to believe, over the last half of my active career, that economics in particular, but other social sciences (and moral philosophy) in addition, have made major mistakes in the present century by omitting two important types of concerns from their "conversations," and that this has led to great social harm. (I speak of the mainstream, or dominant, traditions in the social sciences and moral philosophy; it would not do to talk of any academic discipline as a single entity.) First, social scientists have refused to include collective goods (or goals) within the domain of analytical concern (economics, psychology, moral philosophy), or have done so only selectively (sociology and political science.) Secondly, social scientists and moral philosophers, with few exceptions, have refused to collect data in depth concerning human subjective beliefs, opinions, and historical recollections. To an important extent the errors overlap, in that one reason always given for the non-inclusion of collective goods is the alleged difficulty of gathering data for collective good demands, data which would require quality interviewing techniques if it were gathered correctly.

These mistakes are methodological in nature, and so related to the realm of "rhetoric" discussed by McCloskey, although I must admit that thinking of them in terms of the McCloskey framework leaves me uneasy, for the simple reason that many economists seem to have misinterpreted McCloskey's rhetorical arguments as being "just" about persuasion with regard to arguments narrowly conceived (such as political stances), and so have not given them proper importance by incorrectly considering them "unscientific." Still, many of the points made by McCloskey in recent years (see especially the 1994 book) provide a context for my own criticisms. McCloskey speaks of how economists and psychologists "spurn whole classes of evidence," for example, and her criticism of logical positivism and empiricism helps greatly our understanding of the reasons for the neglect of the collective and subjective.[1]

In no way would it be correct to consider my pointing to these mistakes an original contribution on my part — there is nothing new under the sun — although perhaps I may be somewhat unique in pointing specifically to the consistency with which collective goals have been excluded outright in economics, psychology, and moral philosophy, and mishandled elsewhere. And while any number of writers have pointed to the absence of attempts to gather subjective data in one discipline or the other, I am not aware of any who have pointed to the consistency in which attempts to gather quality subjective data have been avoided in *all* the social sciences, as well as in moral philosophy, over the entire

[1]McCloskey (1994: 101). To the extent that McCloskey is part of a postmodernist movement that holds that "anything goes," as alleged by Blaug, I would however be in disagreement with Blaug (1998a: 29).

twentieth century. The twentieth century has been the century of specialization, and persons concentrating on one discipline only (more normally, a small slice of a discipline) have failed to notice the immensity and sweeping nature of these problems.

I can also note with satisfaction that, in recent times, there is a large and increasing number of serious academic writers who are noticing and writing about substantial portions of these issues. Any number of writers have pointed to the unfortunate split between the study of marketplace efficiency and moral concerns in economics, as well as the excessive narrowness in viewpoint of mainstream economists more generally. Perhaps the most noteworthy of these has been Amartya Sen. Others that readily come to mind include Mark Blaug, Allen Buchanan, Amitai Etzioni, Robert Frank, Robert Goldfarb, William Griffith, John Maloney, Dierdre McCloskey, Howard Margolis, Patrick Larkey, Wassily Leontif, Patrick O'Sullivan, Deborah Redman, and Lionel Robbins. Writers adopting critical stances in other disciplines besides economics include Elizabeth Anderson, Joseph Bessette, John Glass, John Goldthorpe, Rollo Handy, Seymour Sarason, Barry Schwartz, M. Brewster Smith, Sybe Terwee, James Wertsch, and Frederick Wertz. There are many others. One could undoubtedly add most feminist social scientists, as well as many young methodologists. In the late 1950s, the fine novelist, C.P. Snow, pointed out the seriousness of a problem of "two cultures" among the intelligentsia, where "Scientists" and non-scientists "had almost ceased to communicate at all, who in intellectual, moral, and psychological climate had so little in common that instead of going from Burlington House or South Kensington to Chelsea, one might have crossed an ocean."[2] Mancur Olson, the important early writer about collective goods, has recently argued that the study of efficiency issues is not nearly enough to explain the success or failure of newly developing nations. The magazine writer John Cassidy pointed out how the recent winner of the Nobel prize in economics, William Vickrey, quickly dismissed his prize-winning 1961 paper as "one of my digressions into abstract economics," going on to say, "At best, it's of minor significance in terms of human welfare."[3] Newspaper reporters in articles covering annual meetings of the American Economic Association

[2]Snow [1971 (1959): 14].

[3]Cassidy (1996: 51).

often comment on how arcane and unrelated to the real world are many of the sessions. There are numerous critics in other disciplines too, as further discussed in Chapter 4.

Due to the pervasive nature of the two methodological errors which provide the subject matter of the book, the narrative stretches over a sizable range of subject matter, and so the book is meant to be of interest to a broad class of readers: those in the social sciences and moral philosophy, historians, journalists, the law, interested persons in the general public, and perhaps even some political leaders. I have tried to make the discussion in the book accessible to all these readers. Perhaps with the natural bias typically possessed by authors, I consider the message of the book to be of great enough social importance to merit a fairly broad level of interest and concern.

Again, I must acknowledge my great debt of gratitude to my colleague, H. Scott Gordon. I first began to be interested in broader social concerns many years ago when Scott gave a lecture in one of my graduate courses on the subject of justice and equality. Professor Gordon is wiser than I on many of the issues discussed below, and his comments have been a constant source of help over the years. I should point out, however, that Scott and I are not always in agreement, and specific instances of this, in particular with respect to the place of subjective data and of ethical naturalism, will appear in the pages below. Others who have been helpful in various ways have included Robert Bish, Keith Caldwell, Christopher Clague, Dean Dudley, Allen Grimshaw, Francis Feddersen, Helen Hollingsworth, John Kennedy, Pat Larkey, Tom Lyon, Michael McGinnis, Roger Noll, Ron Oakerson, Dong Mayhard, Mancur Olson, Julie Pedroni, Claire Robertson, Bertina Rudman, Karl Schuessler, Eugene Steuerle, Dennis Young, and James Wertsch. I owe a profound debt for editorial help I received from Bob and Marcia Kern, who proved once and for all that friendship need not stand in the way of perceptive and incisive editing, and also to Donna Snow Robinson, who edited the entire manuscript. I also owe a deep debt to my three in-depth interview respondents who, unfortunately, must remain anonymous.

My greatest debt over the years devoted to the writing of this and my previous book is due for the support given me by my wife Iris and two children, Scott and Stephanie, all three of whom have been wonderfully perceptive about many of the issues discussed in the book, and from whose comments I have benefited a great deal. Scott is an academic linguist in his own right, and so has been able to give me a number of useful comments relating to his field, especially for the material in Chapter 7. I would like to dedicate this book to them.

And finally, the psychologist Seymour Sarason dedicated his 1981 book, *Psychology Misdirected,* as follows: "To John Dewey, Prophet with Honor," thus capturing a bit of the admiration I also feel for one of the truly towering intellectual presences of the modern era. Perhaps I flatter myself to think that this book may have met with his approval.

Contents

Introduction

Positivism recommends phenomenalism, that is, looking at the outside of things, behavioralism...[But] in a social science, after all, behavioralism is silly, because it throws away the evidence of introspection.

Dierdre McCloskey
Knowledge and Persuasion in Economics, 1994

In the early and mid-nineteenth century, when *laissez faire* served as an intellectual model for social order, few intellectual historians should have expected a theory of public goods to parallel the development of the theory of private goods. But why was such a theory absent later?

James Buchanan
The Demand and Supply of Public Goods, 1968

It has become conventional among students of fiscal policy...to dissemble any underlying social philosophy and to maintain a pretense of rigorous objective analysis untinctured by mere ethical considerations...Having been told that sentiments are contraband in the realm of science, they rigorously eschew a few proscribed phrases, clutter up title pages and introductory chapters with pious references to the science of public finance, and then write monumental discourses upon their own prejudices and preconceptions.

Henry Simons
Personal Income Taxation, 1938

> ...for constantly I felt I was moving among two groups — comparable in intelligence, identical in race, not grossly different in social origin, earning about the same incomes, who had almost ceased to communicate at all, who in intellectual, moral, and psychological climate had so little in common that instead of going from Burlington House or South Kensington to Chelsea, one might have crossed an ocean.
>
> C. P. Snow
> *The Two Cultures and the Scientific Revolution*, 1959

It has not been difficult in the twentieth century to talk about the "marvels of scientific progress." From the automobile at the beginning of the century to the computer chip toward the end, the successes of science have been spectacular. But when people are speaking of the successes of science, typically they are referring to progress in the natural, or "pure," sciences. Progress in the *social sciences* is mentioned far less often. I believe that there has not been nearly enough attention given to why this is.

I believe that the social sciences in this century have made serious methodological mistakes and so failed to exploit potential well within their reach. To be sure, it must be admitted that social science has one major disadvantage *vis-a-vis* the natural sciences — the controlled experiment. But on the other hand, they have a major advantage that the physical sciences do *not* have: subjects who are able to communicate their feelings, beliefs, and personal histories. A leaf or a molecule cannot talk and tell an investigator all about its history and observations, *but a person can*. This is the advantage that the social scientists have, by and large, failed to exploit, very likely because of misguided attempts to be exactly like the natural sciences. As a result, the social scientists — economists and psychologists in particular — have seriously neglected one whole class of human activities: those dealing with collective goals.

I became interested in this mistake many years ago as a student of how economists analyze taxation, an interest which resulted in the publication of a book, *Taxation and Public Goods* (1992).[1] In the writing

[1]Kiesling (1992).

of that book, I became convinced that the problems I had found extended much farther than the economic analysis of taxation, a conviction which led to the present effort. Given the similarity of thematic material in the two books, it should be useful if I reproduce briefly the main points from the earlier book.

How Economists Evaluate Policy

The procedures used by economists for evaluating social policies such as taxation, which led to my dissatisfaction, can be illustrated as follows. Let us suppose there are n dimensions to the goodness quality of a social policy. Just as an example, let $n = 10$, but in practice the number of dimensions are determined by social goals important to society members. While all ten of these dimensions are important aspects of the policy in question, there is one that assumes key importance and that indirectly affects the prospects of the other nine: the dimension dealing with the efficiency of resource use or how the policy might affect the amount of total material product that society can obtain from its scarce resources. Let us further suppose that the other nine dimensions are considered by economists as being "ethical" in nature and, thus, outside of the range of issues that they will deal with directly. But, since all ten dimensions are interrelated in complex ways (all use resources for one thing, but there are many others), this presents a serious difficulty for complete evaluation.

While this difficulty is widely recognized among economists, they have taken the position that they need not deal with it directly. Instead, they adopt a compromise using one of two approaches. First, they assume the position that others, whether practitioners of other academic disciplines or properly chosen social and political decision-makers, should be given the task of dealing with the non-efficiency dimensions (we might call them the "justice" dimensions). But this does not mean that the economists have been able to rid themselves of the nine justice dimensions since there are interactions between them and efficiency. In order to deal with the non-efficiency dimensions, economists have adopted one of two approaches. In the first of these, the attempt is made (in theory anyhow) to charge the social decision-makers with the task of providing unanticipated (by society members) transfers of wealth ("lump-sum" transfers) in order to obtain a situation close to what is considered "best" in the justice dimensions. This gives them, presumably, an approximately correct starting point in terms of social justice concerns. Having gotten this far, economists can now apply their tools to find the most efficient policy. If this policy changes the situation with respect to the justice dimensions (as it must, because of all the interactions that exist), then further lump-sum transfers will be required.

While the suggested procedure of lump-sum transfers might work in a perfect world (although even then there would be difficulties), it is completely inadequate when we descend to reality. There are at least two reasons; either one is sufficient to show inadequacy. The first reason is that in practical application it would not be possible to come close to the ideal arrangement for the non-efficiency social goals, and in the absence of knowing how far away society is from the correct point, no ethical judgments are possible. We know that in the real world the justice dimensions do not get addressed by economists, or at least do not get addressed very much, and so the required lump-sum transfers are never forthcoming. In effect, the other dimensions either get neglected entirely, or else they are only partially included on an *ad hoc* basis. Theoretically, addressing the justice dimensions in partial fashion does no good whatsoever. Thus, if the lump-sum redistribution is only able to take society a fraction of the way toward the correct point for the non-efficiency dimensions, we are at a loss to assess the ethical value of this relative to economic efficiency. Suppose the lump-sum adjustment took society one-third of the way to the correct point, or one-half, or nine-tenths. Could economists still concentrate single-mindedly on efficiency, or if not, what are they then supposed to do? Policy analysis needs to be more systematic than this, and the neglect of some goodness dimensions in favor of others amounts to ethical bias directly.

The other approach (the second reason) often used by economists to deal with the non-efficiency dimensions involves defining and using a proxy dimension for representing "equity," that is, for representing all of the justice dimensions. The proxy often chosen is a measure of income distribution, where more equal distribution is considered better, although in taxation the proxy is often some concept of equal sacrifice (see below). The problem with this approach is obvious: it is not possible to represent a number of dimensions — many in conflict with each other — with a single proxy. In my earlier book, I gave this proxy variable approach the name of "two-dimensional Paretianism," so-called because simple Paretianism in economics (one-dimensional Paretianism) is the name given to maximizing efficiency in the market sector only (arriving at the point where no one can be made better off without someone else being made worse off.)

Illustration from the Area of Taxation

The major part of the earlier book was taken up with an extended discussion of how the problems just described impinge upon the economic analysis of taxation. Therefore, a brief summary of the main points should serve as a useful illustration of those problems. I can also use it to show how those problems were mostly avoided by the classical utilitarians.

In the nineteenth century, many economists still believed in the viability of utilitarianism for arriving at policy decisions. While few, if any, economists believed in the full cardinal utility which would be required for rigorous mathematical interpersonal utility comparisons, they presumably believed that some intellectuals could make judgments concerning how much utility was forthcoming as society members advance toward or away from their social goals ("principal agent utilitarianism," Chapter 1). Using this approach, they could easily incorporate *all* important social goals into their analyses and the problems discussed above would be side-stepped. Whatever we might say about the wisdom of giving social science experts such power, the utilitarian approach at least solves the problem of the undue neglect of the non-efficiency dimensions of human welfare.

However, as economists moved into the twentieth century, problems developed with the classical approach. As the mathematical rigor of the discipline increased, economists became increasingly disenchanted with the viability of the classical approach because of the impossibility of making precise interpersonal utility comparisons. As time went by, this gave rise to the problems I have described. One tradition for dealing with non-efficiency dimensions had already been growing in the late nineteenth century, having been started by John Stuart Mill at mid-century — the "equal sacrifice" idea. According to this, each taxpayer should give up equal amounts of utility somehow defined, usually as a proportion of his or her utility, with utility increasing with income as a decreasing function.[2] Morally, this is a one-sided approach, or at least one-sided in addition to the standard economist's goal of marketplace efficiency, as it uses one dimension in the moral (or justice) realm to stand for many. The only personal characteristic of concern to the policy-maker is income (or wealth); nothing is said concerning such other personal characteristics as how the income was earned or special needs or other aspects of personal situations. Such social considerations as the degree of wealth disparity are not even taken into account, at least those where any attention is paid to the *reasons* for the wealth disparity (such as earned versus inherited). The tax policy this "equal-proportional sacrifice" idea translates into depends upon the degree to which the analyst thinks marginal utility declines with income (or wealth). If the decline is steep, highly progressive taxation is called for; if gradual, only mildly progressive rates should be applied.

The equal sacrifice notion continued well into the twentieth century, even up to the present, although since the 1950s it has been quite weak. The 1950s were important, I believe, because of the publication in 1953 of a short monograph by two law professors, Walter Blum and Henry Kalven, called *The Uneasy Case for Progressive Taxation*.[3] They graphically demonstrated that the "technical" arguments that economists traditionally had been giving for justifying progression in taxation were really based on nothing beyond ethical opinion. This, along with the demise of the formal use of utilitarianism for purposes of policy design more generally, had a great effect on tax analysis. It has caused economists to retreat into a cocoon of dealing only with egoistic motivation and market tradable goods, or what I have termed "single-dimension Paretianism." This took economists out of the business of making judgments in the "ethical" domain at all, a development that has been accompanied by a considerable lessening of progression since the 1950s.

[2]Thus, persons receive more utility from additional dollars obtained at lower income levels than at higher. The further assumption often made was that the utility-income relationship was identical over all individuals.

[3]Blum and Kalven (1953).

A second way that has been used in the twentieth century for dealing with justice considerations has been to simply use the income or wealth distribution as a measure of justice, and to presume that if either of these (income in particular) were made more equal, the policy was a good one justice-wise. Again, this allows one variable to stand for many and is very clumsy: there can be many good or bad reasons for a more equal income distribution. A variation on this which has been used by mainstream tax economists over the past half century has involved invoking the concepts of "vertical equity," the equitable treatment of unequals, and "horizontal equity," the equitable treatment of equals, where "treatment" in both instances is denominated in terms of income. The vertical concept is again impossible to deal with in terms only of income because there can be any number of reasons for income differences. The idea behind the horizontal measure is to leave two taxpayers in the same relative position after the tax change as before. This fails too. The fundamental problem is the extreme dependence which the concept places upon the idea that the initial distribution of income was correct. This, in turn, can be viewed as some combination of two positions taken by economists: either a rather polyannaish acceptance of the status quo, or a ramification of the attempt by economists to split issues of economic justice narrowly, conceived in terms of income alone, away from all other justice concerns.[4]

In the earlier book, I discussed a number of common social justice goals of likely importance to most Americans and showed how they fared with respect to contemporary tax laws. Some do well. The United States

[4]From time to time, the problem gets pointed out in the academic journals, but that tends to be as far as it goes. One good example is a 1989 paper by Kaplow, who pointed out that there was no normative basis whatever for the horizontal equity approach (Kaplow, 1989: 140–143). But when the author submitted a paper to the same journal suggesting that indices could be constructed to represent justice ideas more precisely — differences in tastes involving the work-leisure choice, differences in ability, and differences in initial entitlements — the referees rejected the paper outright on the basis that my indices could not be represented by proper mathematical axioms (whatever that means) and that, while the implied policies represented by my indices probably ought to be pursued, they are unacceptable to economists because they would give rise to "horizontal and vertical inequities in the conventional use of the term," thus in so many words explicitly admitting that the conventional equity measures used in the taxation literature were not only worthless, but quite capable of giving (and likely to give) incorrect signals.

(US) tax system rates reasonably high with respect to the goals of rewarding ability, rewarding effort and ability together, and promoting overall market-sector efficiency. But the US tax system does not do well in furthering the social goals of not unduly rewarding luck (inheritance), of rewarding effort where ability is lacking, of providing for various serious social needs, of providing provision for the realization of lifetime potential on the part of the disadvantaged, and for dealing with the considerable widening of the gap in income and wealth (the latter especially) that has occurred in the last three decades.

The Philosophy of Social Science Context: Overview

When I began to turn my attention from problems of over-narrow perspective in tax policy analysis to the operations of economists more generally, and to some of the other social scientists, it became obvious that these problems fit into a much broader context of thinking which extended across the social sciences (and even moral philosophy) and which had a long history. This material, involving the philosophy of social science, will be discussed farther along, but a brief sketch of its basic importance is also required in these introductory comments.

Let us suppose that a candidate social scientist wishes to find some dependable scientific principles or "laws" about what causes humans to put up umbrellas. After some observation, he posits the proposition that the "cause" behind the unfolding of umbrellas is the existence of a rain shower. The rain is the "cause" of the opening of umbrellas.

This seems a reasonable conclusion, but could a second student of the phenomenon, attempting to exercise the care typified by "pure" scientists, ask whether there might be more depth to the problem. How is "cause" to be defined? Is it an inevitable relationship, where the first event must lead to the second event without exception? This is the definition normally employed in the physical sciences. But then the conclusion reached is somewhat more shaky if there are instances when a rain shower does not lead to umbrellas being put up (assuming they are being carried; explaining why some persons do not carry umbrellas requires another explanatory proposition which may not have a straightforward cause-and-effect explanation). Perhaps it was the sun that was associated with the umbrella going up, or perhaps the person simply did not raise his or her umbrella for some other reason not readily apparent.

There are now two possibilities. The first is for our candidate scientist to feel that his explanatory scientific proposition is good enough if it explains the actions involved "most of the time;" the second is for him to search further for explanations of *why* a person might not have raised his or her umbrella in the rain, perhaps by administering a questionnaire or by sitting him down and interviewing him in some depth in the attempt to ascertain what the psychological circumstances might be which caused this individual not to raise his umbrella.

This very simple example can be taken fairly far as a basis for explaining developments in the philosophy of social science over the last three or four centuries. The dominant tradition has been that stemming from following the first alternative given above, although the second alternative has become increasingly important in recent decades.[5] Hollis defines the first tradition as one that deals with "explanation," the second as preoccupied with "understanding" (and, thus, explanation too). O'Sullivan terms the first tradition the "objectivist-behaviorist" approach, where an attempt is made to view humans as "things" whose actions can be explained objectively. He terms the second tradition the "subjective-interpretive" approach, where an attempt is made to understand the actions of persons as stemming from motives operating to achieve individual goals. In the following pages, I attempt to sketch the main tenets of each approach, including strengths and weaknesses. This is not the book for a close investigation of issues in the philosophy of social science; the interest is rather in issues involved in the study of social policy. The reader can obtain further useful background in Hollis (1994), O'Sullivan (1987), and Gordon (1975).[6] On the other hand, what is thought about the philosophy is often closely related to what one feels it possible to accomplish in

[5]Both approaches date back to Greek philosophy. Since the seventeenth century, the objective approach has been the important one, especially in Anglo-Saxon social science, although subject to increasing criticism in the last two or three decades. The subjective approach was important in Europe since the early part of the nineteenth century. See O'Sullivan (1987: 60 ff).

[6]O'Sullivan is a sympathetic exponent of the second approach; Gordon is on balance an opponent of the second approach, and Hollis is more neutral, leaning perhaps towards some sympathy with the second approach.

policy analysis. In this introduction, then, for each approach I first give a list of summary points and a few further comments, all done in the briefest possible manner.

Objectivist Approach: Summary Points

1. A central tenet of the more traditional, or objectivist, approach is that the empirical data to be used in social science must be obtained only through direct sense experience by third parties (a view going by the name of "empiricism"). This stance is in obvious imitation of what occurs (or is thought to occur) in the physical sciences, and many followers of the empiricist tradition over the years have strongly believed that the methods used in the social and physical sciences should be identical.
2. Science, whether social or physical, is to be made up of objectively testable propositions using data as described above *only* (all other data are put into the ethical domain), and which are to be kept separate from all ethical involvement. Ethical disputes are to be handled in some other way, perhaps through the political process.
3. As time goes by, a greater and greater percentage of human actions will be explainable by phenomena which are externally observable.
4. While motivation is important in social science, it is possible to establish motivation for purposes of science (as opposed to ethics) by using common sense ideas gained from introspection and shrewd observation of human actions. It includes the idea that there are philosophical reasons why human psychology is not trustworthy enough to yield any other reliable data on human motivation.

Comments, Objectivist Approach

It would seem that there are any number of phenomena in the world besides those which are directly observable and could be useful for science. On the other hand, it is usually true that the observable are the more measurable. But limiting data to the observable will strongly limit the amount of explanation that can take place in many instances. My umbrella example above was somewhat favorable to objectivist methods. Hollis gives another, perhaps more realistic example, in which the researcher is trying to establish whether a young male French voter who works in a large factory will vote communist. The investigator cites studies which show that young workers in large factories have in the past voted Left with a probability of between 0.60 and 0.70, and in those areas where the Catholic Church has a strong influence the probability is even somewhat higher: in the neighborhood of 0.80. The church being strong in his town, we therefore predict that M. Rouget (a particular worker) will vote communist. But the chance of error is large, at least 20 percent, unless we know more about M. Rouget.

Another reservation to the older approach is that it is often easy to demonstrate that humans are moved by motivations which are non-selfish (see Chapter 6). Also, while it is not possible to explore all aspects of human psychology and to trust the outcomes completely, it may be possible to do well enough to yield useful policy-making models where specific motivations are not necessary, or where broadly shared values may be relevant, or where we deal only with single decision-makers.

Finally, because of their empiricism, their suspicion of altruistic motives, and their distaste for exploring inner psychological states empirically, objectivists tend to be hostile towards the inclusion of collective goods demands (motives for attempting to achieve collective goals) in their social science modeling efforts.

Subjective Approach: Summary Points

1. All human actions stem from motives felt from within, and the only truly accurate reality in human affairs is that which results from human cognition based upon their having reflected upon their own conscious states. From reflection upon themselves and their activities, humans come to know with certainty that: (i) they are doing something; (ii) what they are doing; (iii) why they are doing it; and (iv) that they are always free to choose what they are doing at present.[7] Human action is caused by persons taking actions to further their own goals

[7]O'Sullivan (1987: 183).

and intentions. In doing this, at the moment of choosing they have absolutely free choice. A given outside force (for example, the influence of the Roman Catholic church for M. Rouget) may influence such choices strongly, weakly, or not at all. Even if the outside influence is strong, it is never total.

2. The ethical values held by individual humans can be treated as facts and incorporated into social science. (Value judgments on the part of scientists are to be avoided entirely, just as in the objectivist tradition.)
3. Rationality judgments are impossible to ascribe *a priori* since it must always be assumed that an individual knew his objective and was choosing what he considered to be the best way of reaching it (Chapter 2).
4. The empirical testing of human beliefs, intentions, and motivations is of central importance, and the way in which humans use language to convey these things is a key concern in such testing.

Comments on the Subjectivist Approach

The subjectivist approach is more ambitious and satisfactory for explaining human actions in that all human objectives, selfish or otherwise, are included into consideration. In practice, this makes the actual building of explanatory models somewhat more complicated. But the way in which the objectivist approach introduces simplification is through ethical bias (by systematically excluding one entire group of important concerns), and there should be ways of reducing complication without introducing such bias.

The area in which subjectivism is most readily attacked is that involving empirical implementation, especially given the deep reservations held by many objectivists with respect to finding foolproof methods for looking into the inner psychology of other humans, a problem often termed the "other-minds problem." How can one mind truly know what is in the mind of another? Whatever the philosophical subtleties of this problem, what it comes down to in practice involves the degree to which one can trust the results obtained through interviews and polls. In

Chapter 6, I argue that there are reasons why respondents can often be assumed to be cooperative, and it could be that this problem is much less troublesome in practice than it may be in pure theory. It is a problem that should be at its worst in the area of cultural anthropology when an anthropologist attempts an explanation of a society with a theretofore unknown language, and with cultural folkways completely at variance with anything that has been seen before. As Hollis points out, even in situations of this kind, such as in the initial exploration of the Zande peoples by Evans-Prichard, it seems as if the other-minds problem was satisfactorily overcome.[8]

A Note on Individualism and Aggregation in Social Science

Another aspect of social science methodology which must be mentioned is discussed in detail by Hollis in his 1994 book. It is the degree of social aggregation considered important by the analyst. Some writers, such as Durkheim, have taken a relatively holistic approach, while others, such as most economists (including myself), consider it important to begin with the individual. Thus, Durkheim argued that "social facts," such as religious background, were of determining importance, while individualists would start from individual behavior or motives and proceed from there, but without ignoring such outside social influences as religion. (A subjectivist may build religious training into what he knows about an individual's motivation.) Neither approach would leave out the other entirely.

Economic Science in Methodological Context

Even a cursory view of the methodological context is enough to yield considerable insight into why some of the problems I noticed in tax analysis are present. Only concerns observable from outside a person by third parties are included in consideration. Inner states are to be avoided, and the motivation design which results from this, "cognitive rationalism,"

[8]Hollis (1994: 230).

pays attention only to the instrumental pursuit of selfish individual goals. It is not practical to study the inner psychology of persons because of the "other-minds problem." As already mentioned, all of these beliefs are the kind of thing that causes social scientists to exclude collective goods, or social goals, from their analytical concerns.

Many years ago, when I first began to find taxation analysis wanting, I was puzzled that economists were ignoring criteria stemming from collective goals. Others found this puzzling as well. Professor James Buchanan had trouble understanding it, and once remarked that while intellectual historians might have been able to explain a theory of public goods to be absent in the nineteenth century age of *laissez faire*, "why was such a theory absent later?" (see the epigraph). Modern economists have not neglected collective goods in the sense of studying their characteristics; indeed, there is a large literature. But most of these discussions have the secondary purpose of showing why such goods are too unwieldy for economists to use in their analysis directly. Is this correct? The time has come to review the nature of this important class of human goods and to see what it is about them to cause economists and some other social scientists (and even moral philosophrs) to neglect them rather summarily.

Collective Goods

Description of collective goods

First, a note on terminology. What I term "collective goods" in this book have often been termed by economists as "public goods." To my mind, these two terms mean exactly the same thing, but over the course of my career I have gotten the impression (which could be incorrect) that sometimes economists use "public goods" to infer goods potentially delivered by the government. If this is a possibility, the label of "collective goods" is the broader, more inclusive one, and it is the one I have chosen to use. Another term for "collective goods," perhaps more understandable still to members of the general public, is the term "social goals," meaning those goals held in common by groups of individuals. The latter term is also used at numerous places in the text.

The basic qualities of collective goods are established in the following quotations.[9] The first is from a paper by the Italian economist, Ugo Mazzola, published in 1890:

> The utility of most public goods is complementary and indivisible. The services of law and order, public health, etc., are contributory causes to private satisfactions. But although their consumption produces individual satisfaction, the quantities consumed by each individual cannot be divided up and measured.[10]

The other quotation is from the opening paragraph of the first paper on collective goods written in English by Howard Bowen and published in 1943:

> Social goods...are not divisible into units that can be the unique possession of individuals. Rather, they tend to become part of the general environment — available to all persons within that environment (e.g., education, protection against foreign enemies, beautification of the landscape, flood control). Consequently, these goods cannot easily be sold to individual consumers and the quantities available to different individuals cannot be adjusted according to their respective tastes. The amount of the good must be set by a single decision applicable jointly to all persons.[11]

Both quotations point to the key quality of collective goods: receipt of a good or service by a number of people in common. Collective goods are goods accruing to groups as groups. However, the emphasis in the two statements is somewhat different. Mazzola speaks of indivisibility in consumption, a demand characteristic, while Bowen's emphasis is on the fact of common supply. The supply side characteristic is central: if there exists a set of stimuli that must be experienced in common, all who experience this set have no choice but to "demand" it in common

---

[9]These duplicate material presented in Kiesling (1992: 9–10). Buchanan (1968: 192) gives credit to Francesco Ferrara, who wrote in the 1850s and 1860s, for the first discussion on the idea of collective goods.

[10]Mazzola (1890: 171–172), quoted in Kayaalp (1988: 20).

[11]Bowen (1943: 27).

with all other people who receive it at the same time. A collective good is supplied in common to a number of individuals who are powerless to influence it once it is a *fait accompli.* And unlike what is true for individual goods, the consumption of a collective good by one person does not lessen the amount of it available to the others to whom it is being supplied.[12]

Given the central importance of common supply for defining collective goods, we need only focus on what kinds of phenomena are provided in common to groups of more than one person. This is not a difficult task, at least conceptually. If a sorority chapter or dormitory has a reputation for giving good parties, all members of the sorority or dormitory share in the prestige forthcoming from the fact. If a town makes a pretty park available, all potential users share in its benefits. The quality of crime prevention in a city or state or nation is a widely shared good. The common defense is an obvious shared good, the prototypical example often given in textbooks. Deterrence of nuclear war is a public good shared by every person on the earth. Examples are endless; the key nature of the operational concept is obvious and well-known. Any shared experience is a collective good.[13]

In sum, collective goods, like all economic goods, deal with human goals, in this instance, *social* goals. A collective good is advancement closer to a collective goal. Also, as with all economic goods, collective goods of interest to economists and other social scientists are those so valuable people are willing to give up money or other scarce resources for them. In addition, collective goods of interest in the analysis of social policies are those which, to some extent, are under human control, for which human choice is possible. Our definition for *collective goods* is

[12]This has been termed by economists as the "non-rival" property of a collective, or public, good. A good, such as an apple, which when consumed by one person is not left for consumption by others is termed "rival" consumption good. Another property possessed by most, but not all, collective goods is the property by which it is not feasible to price it to individuals, known as "non-excludability." See Musgrave and Musgrave (1989: 43).

[13]The word "good," whether used in an individual or collective context, is used in the generic sense typically used by economists, which means that it can also mean "bad." A "good" is movement towards a goal; a "bad" is movement away from a goal. In discussing a "good," we are in effect discussing the goal itself.

then: *shared experiences, due to factors potentially subject to human control, and considered important enough to merit the expenditure of scarce resources.*

We can point out a few other characteristics of collective goods by comparing them with individual goods. Individuals may be said to deal with individual goods using more self-centered motives than they do with collective goods, although this is a tricky proposition. It is easy to think of individual good purchases which stem from altruistic motives and collective good demands which stem from selfish ones.

Other arguable differences exist with respect to tangibility and the ability to access benefits. Apples, rakes, automobiles, for example, are tangible, and if a person pays $9.95 for a rake, we can reasonably assume that his benefit was at least that amount. Some individual goods, such as the visit to the psychologist, are not tangible, although we can still attribute benefit. While many collective goods are tangible, their benefits are often less so. A submarine or 1,000 miles of interstate highway are tangible. The benefits of the highway may be fairly tangible: the number of passenger miles or freight ton-miles travelled, but the defense deterrent benefit of a submarine is more ephemeral. Many collective goods are highly intangible. The benefits are hard to measure, but important to the successful group experience, such as institutional arrangements, beneficial norms, and ethical values which promote group welfare. (It is with respect to this last class of collective goods that my criticism of social science methods is strongest, particularly with regard to economics. These are the collective goods which have been most "neglected.")

Empirical difficulties with collective goods (especially for empiricists)

It is readily apparent that it is more difficult to deal with the demands for collective goods empirically than for individual goods, although it seems dubious that this justifies ignoring them entirely.[14]

[14]The reader is reminded that the term "demand" is used here in the standard way used by economists, that is, to mean all of a person's wishes about the desirability of consuming a good, negative as well as positive. In addition, the implied meaning is that of "effective demand," which means demands for which a person would be willing to make money payment.

Assuming, as we must, that social sciences are built on a foundation of individual actions, there is an important fundamental difference about the ability to gather demand data for individual and collective goods which lies behind many of the problems discussed in this book. The act by which individuals obtain individual goods, whether by purchase, barter, or whatever, and whether the good is tangible or intangible (an automobile or visit to a psychologist), can be *observed* by other individuals. The objectivist or behaviorist methodological approach works out fine for individual goods. In addition, it is not prohibitively difficult for us to attribute a person's apparent benefit of an individual good; this is done simply by noting his opportunity cost, or the item (often a sum of money) given up by him in order to get the item he traded for.

With collective goods, on the other hand, the situation is much different. While it is possible to observe how much of a social good is purchased by a *group*, it is not possible to observe how much of it is purchased by an *individual* on the basis of his or her own wishes. A nation may purchase a submarine or 1,000 Head Start teachers, but a given individual may have preferred that his group purchase no submarine or 2,000 Head Start teachers. Some kind of subjectivist approach is needed to get information on individual demands for collective goods which is then used as the data for the additions required to obtain group demands.

It is also difficult to attribute individual *benefits* for collective goods. As already mentioned, collective goods involve the fortunes of more than one person at the same time but are viewed through sets of individual eyes. This means that there are two distinct viewpoints operating at the same time in the same person, sometimes involving conflicting goals. For data collection purposes, this situation can be difficult for us to sort our way through.

The benefits forthcoming from collective goods depend upon the nature of the demands they satisfy. The nature of demands persons have for collective goods (or the nature of the goals individuals entertain on behalf of groups) may or may not involve non-selfish motivation, but often there is an other-regarding component. An example of a collective good demand which is almost entirely selfish might be a church member's demand for a religious education building where he considers that his own children will receive benefits from the building greater or equal to the amount he will need to pay. The same demand would be other-regarding if the person's individual benefit would be less than his planned payment: persons with no children who vote for a school tax increase in their school district would be an example. They are obviously receiving benefits which arise from other-regarding motivation, from the consumption of others. But a student of collective goods delivery often has a difficult task keeping track of which collective good benefits arise from selfish motivation and which from more altruistic motivation.

Another problem, perhaps even more daunting, exists with respect to the financing of collective goods. Since all group members automatically share a collective good, no behavioral device exists for ascertaining how much a unit of collective good is worth in the eyes of an individual consumer. But if social scientists resort to the other alternative available, they find themselves faced with a problem which may cause a built-in bias. There is an incentive for persons to refrain from cooperating in the financing of collective goods even when they value them positively. Since everyone in a group receives a collective good willy nilly, when an individual is asked for an assessment of how much a collective good is worth to him or her, if that person has the least suspicion that the answer may affect the amount he or she will be asked to contribute to its financing, there is then a definite incentive to dissimulate. This difficulty is widely understood and known by the name of "free-rider problem." Samuelson captured the problem quite well in his 1954 statement of the theory of public goods.

> (I)t is in the selfish interest of each person to give *false* signals, to pretend to have less interest in a given collective consumption activity than he really has...(T)his fundamental technical difference...[goes] to the heart of the whole problem of *social* economy: by departing from his indoctrinated rules, any one person can hope to snatch some selfish benefit in a way not possible under the self-policing competitive pricing of private goods.[15]

Not only are there passive reasons for not cooperating in the financing of collective goods, there are reasons for actively failing to cooperate,

[15]Samuelson (1954: 388–389; emphasis in the original).

for engaging in dissimulation with respect to one's own demands for such goods. The free rider problem has sparked the universal concern of economists and other social scientists, and has given rise to a voluminous literature which will be further discussed in Chapter 6.

To repeat once more the crucial point (it is difficult to overemphasize it), a behaviorist, while able to study a person's demands (wishes) for individual, or "private," goods, has no way to do so for a person's demands for collective goods. Subjective data gathering techniques are required.

What are the Prospects?

The problems discussed in the following five chapters have been often taken seriously on the basis that collective goods are extremely difficult to work with empirically. Researchers must find out about persons' mental states; an "other minds problem" exists. As I see it, the problem can be broken into two parts, the first having to do with problems involving polling and interviewing, the second with problems involving combinations of introspection, empathy, and scholarly inquiry.

There is no doubt that an "other minds problem" exists when it comes to polling and interviewing. Respondents are free to dissimulate or refuse to cooperate in either approach and, as discussed in Chapter 7, researchers who think they can arrive at scientifically "objective" polling methods are probably fooling themselves. I have encountered researchers who have used interviews from time to time in their own work or that of their students — betraying a reasonably open-minded approach towards research — and have told me simply: "I do not trust interviews." And polling methods are not free from other minds problems either. Besides the problem of undependable respondents, both polling and interviewing are beset with possible interviewer bias problems (Chapter 7).

On the other hand, one wonders whether the picture must be unrelievedly dark. After all, writers and scholars have used poll and interview information to wide advantage in recent years. Below, I will present arguments for the usefulness of poll and interview data for the attitudes persons have toward social goals and, in particular, simple and useful information about *which* social goals are generally important to group members. It doesn't seem right that when scientists find themselves faced by a problem, even a large problem, they should stick their heads under the covers and merely ignore it. Attacked head on, it may seem smaller than at first thought.

While it is undoubtedly true that there is a greater chance for error in obtaining facts from questions about events that occurred to individuals in their childhood than there is, say, in measuring the pressure behind a flow of liquid, I am at a loss to see why this means that the data gathered from interviews should be barred from scientific inquiry entirely. An integral part of scientific methodology is accepting the possibility of error, and sophisticated statistical techniques exist for dealing with error. Journalists, historians, clinical psychiatrists, and psychologists depend heavily on the personal recollections of interviewees and consider the comments of non-hostile respondents as being highly dependable and useful. Even if respondents make errors in their own recollections of their personal history, it is such history *as presently viewed* which is of key importance in the determination of their current beliefs and values, in any event. A trained in-depth interviewer can cross-check respondents' answers against one another. It seems likely that many respondents are cooperative enough to overcome the (often highly remote) possibility that their answers will make a financial difference to themselves. It would appear that what goes as the "other minds problem" among philosophers is finding out *with certainty* the inner workings of the psychology of other human beings. It is quite possible for a student of policy to admit this is true and still obtain psychological data for samples of humans which is adequate for useful policy studies. These points are further explored in Part 2.

Having said all this, I still do not believe that it would do to take an overly Pollyannaish view of the "other minds problem" for polling and interviewing techniques. I suspect that many of the newspaper reports of results in the many polls that seem to pervade the modern political and social scene are often more slanted than reporters indicate when they report margin-of-error statistics. I did some interviewing of my own to gain some feeling on all this, reported on in Chapter 7, and while I have a strong feeling that the responses I report for the three ladies I interviewed at length are truthful and accurate (we can't know for sure, although they cross-check quite well), few respondents in the population at large are as intelligent and socially motivated as are the three respondents I interviewed.

There is a second way the problem of mental states can be approached, however, which is merely to establish which social goals are generally of importance based upon introspection, empathy, and scholarly investigations. A great deal can be accomplished through this approach, enough to render wrong the judgment that behaviorists apparently make that "other minds problems" are serious enough to justify neglecting collective goods altogether as evaluative criteria. (In this, economists are inconsistent because introspection and empathy are precisely the approaches they have used to obtain the motivation which powers standard economic theory, that of "cognitive rationalism.") As a good illustration of this, I would again ask the reader to consider my findings with respect to tax analysis reported in my 1992 book. I was able to show that a great many important taxation issues were overlooked simply because tax economists refuse to specifically consider social goals which are surely important to large groups of Americans. Merely working out the tax ramifications of such social goals as having a fair reward structure or allowing persons to realize their lifetime potential is highly educational — I would consider it essential — both for decision-makers and for members of the population as a whole. The "other minds problem" cannot be given as a valid reason for neglecting such goals because it is simply too obvious on the basis of straightforward common sense that such goals are important to most Americans and, indeed, most humans.

For most (if not all) policy problems, large or small, it will not be difficult for researchers to work out the sets of social goals which are of fundamental importance to that particular problem. Having done this, economists and other social scientists can then be asked to use their expertise to compute the trade-offs as the group tries to use the policy in question to advance toward its various goals. (More in Chapter 6.)

Social Science Without Prejudice

The issues involved with maintaining a value-neutral social science can be simply and briefly stated. In the course of human affairs, there are two occupational groups specifically charged with furthering human welfare:

the political decision-makers and the social scientists.[16] It is the task of the decision-makers to resolve situations where some persons will become better off and others worse off, while it is the task of the social scientists to advise the decision-makers on how best to reach whatever goals they may have. But social scientists may not exert influence concerning welfare conflicts between persons; that is the job of the decision-makers. If it so happens that social scientists do exert such influence, they are not being value-neutral.

We can restate all this as follows. The human welfare that the decision-makers and social scientists are charged with furthering can be represented in terms of humans moving toward their goals and moving toward more important (to them) goals before moving toward the less important ones. Important to human welfare, then, are the goals that individuals consider (at all) important and the importance (or weights) individuals place on each goal. Each individual can work his own welfare problem out for himself, but the *social* problem involves how the respective welfare of individuals are to be weighted and this is the task, as already indicated, of the decision-makers (and only them).

If social scientists were to influence the interpersonal weighting process illegitimately, how would they do so? There are two possibilities. First, they could illegitimately influence which social goals were chosen as being (at all) important. Secondly, they could illegitimately influence the weights placed upon the social goals that have been chosen for consideration. So now we can posit a very simple rule for what the role of the ethically neutral social scientist should be: it is a regime where all values given either to the weights placed on social goals or the identification of the goals themselves are supplied by, and only by, the group's (for example, society's) properly chosen decision-makers. The social science experts may explore and obtain information on how advances towards and away from goals are technically related to each other, but *they may supply no weights concerning importance.* Let us call this THE RULE.

Let me now provide some examples of actual social science situations from recent experience where the simple rule just enunciated has been

[16]For the purpose of this simple illustration, I assume the activities of groups such as the natural scientists and engineers are performed at the behest of the decision-makers.

violated. When economists and most scholars in the "public choice" tradition admit one class of goals into their analysis and summarily exclude others, they have illegitimately assigned zero weights to the latter, contrary to the RULE. When moral philosophers exclude all ethical goals from their discipline which were not derived through pure reason on the part of moral philosophers — for example moral values held in fact by large sub-sets of some society — they have illegitimately assigned zero weights to the latter, contrary to the RULE. When professional psychologists confine the analysis of individual psychology to each individual's own thought processes and to behavior testable in laboratory settings, and neglect individual psychological beliefs due to social influences and testable in other than laboratory settings, then they have illegitimately assigned zero weights to the latter, contrary to the RULE. Finally, if political scientists or sociologists provide analyses of social issues where they place more emphasis upon some social goals for goodness criteria than for others, in failing to assign equal weights to all social goals they have failed to follow the RULE. Or if they fail to include some important social goals as evaluative criteria entirely, they have illegitimately assigned those criteria zero weights, thus breaking the RULE.

The substantive discussions that follow are divided into two parts, one dealing with failures (Chapters 1 to 5) and the other with suggestions for what might be done to deal with them (Chapters 6 to 7).

I believe it fair to say that most students of social science would agree that economics is the discipline that has grown to assume the most influential role of the social sciences in terms of public policy-making. In many ways, economics has been quite successful, but the time has come to look beyond its successes and carefully observe its failures and how the latter may assume social importance. The situation of economics, including something of the historical context, is discussed in Chapter 1.

A concept of crucial importance in any science is that of *causation*. In the social sciences, if, as I argue, a proper methodology deals with the subjective, a key part of causation is that provided by human motivation. In this respect, economists have tended to make two assumptions: first, that for some areas of human experience the scientist can divine with certainty exactly how persons are motivated (that they will pursue their own material self-interest in identifiable ways, the approach known as "cognitive rationalism"); and second, that it is impossible for the scientist to attribute motivation for any other area (for example, areas involving ethical belief). I consider both contentions incorrect and Chapter 2 is devoted to a discussion of rationality and motivation in which I attempt to show why.

Important to the objectivist view of social science methodology that has been predominant over the last three centuries has been the idea that the empirical data used in social science must be restricted to facts that can be observed through direct sense experience by third parties. What this has meant is that the realm of emotion has been relegated to a secondary role in human affairs, a monumental error of great social significance, particularly since emotional training is the key foundation for ethical belief and compassion for others. Chapter 3 is devoted to an explanation of why emotion is not only "rational," but also, as the basis of important social goals, of key importance for human motivation and, therefore, for policy analysis.

Even though economics has arguably been the most influential of the social sciences, this does not mean that the other social sciences are unimportant. In Chapter 4, I deal with the question of whether, and the extent to which, the mistakes discussed in Chapters 1 to 3 are also present in the other social sciences.

In Chapter 5, the final chapter of Part 1, I query whether the mistakes discussed in Chapters 1 to 4 have been socially important by adversely affecting the way in which the delivery of actual collective goods are evaluated.

Turning to my suggestions for what ought to be done, in Chapter 6 I present a detailed discussion and justification for the methodological approach I suggest in this book for dealing impartially with all human goals and doing the appropriate empirical work.

Objectivist social scientists, in rejecting subjectivist approaches, invariably use as their trump card the argument that it is not possible to gather accurate data with respect to the thoughts, feelings, beliefs, and personal histories — that is, the subjective psychological existence — of humans. The principal objection given by such writers is that the interviewer simply has no way of verifying that what the interviewee tells him is the truth. They believe that any data gathered about subjective states should be limited to that which can be gathered from "objective" queries on public opinion polls. In Chapter 7, I present arguments meant to refute these positions, both by citing the work of others and by presenting data from a small number of in-depth interviews I conducted to throw some light on the degree to which it is possible to cross-check statements made by respondents in different contexts.

The book ends with a brief postscript.

Part 1

Methodological Failures

The first part of the book — five chapters — deals with the major methodological mistakes I believe have been made in the social sciences and moral philosophy in this century. The first has been the failure to include collective goals properly into either analysis or policy evaluation. In two disciplines, economics and parts of psychology, the neglect has been almost total, while in the others it has been selective. Most of the discussion in Part 1 deals with aspects of this neglect of collective goods.

One ramification of the neglect of collective goods, but perhaps also a cause of it, has been the refusal by social scientists and moral philosophers to empirically investigate individual beliefs, attitudes, and experiences in depth. Some attention is given to this second failure in Part 1 too.

Chapter 1

Collective Goods and Economic Science

(W)e should discuss whether economists ought to consider distributional issues at all...(S)ome argue that discussion of distributional issues is detrimental to objectivity in economics and economists should restrict themselves to analyzing only the efficiency issues of social issues.

This view has two problems. First,...the theory of welfare economics indicates that efficiency by itself cannot be used to evaluate a given situation. Criteria other than efficiency must be brought to bear when comparing alternative allocations of resources.

...In addition, decision-makers care about the distributional implications of policy. If economists ignore distribution, then policy-makers will ignore economists.

Harvey Rosen
Public Finance, 4th edn., 1995

The position which I have labeled as objectivist or behaviourist has had a long history in the human sciences...Its central conviction is that the human sciences can progress in their understanding of man only by rigorously following the same methods as the natural sciences. For this purpose, man must be treated only as another object in nature subject to efficient causal natural laws: as a sophisticated and complex organism but nothing more. All references to subjectivity, to human consciousness, freedom, and intentional activity must be banished since such subjective states are strictly unobservable and so can have no place in a rigorous human science...

Patrick O'Sullivan
Economic Methodology and Freedom to Choose, 1987

Economics is widely recognized as the most sophisticated of the social sciences, with methodology closest to that of the physical sciences. Its achievements over this century, both theoretical and applied, have been outstanding. But impressive as these achievements have been, they have come in areas of human activity which, for the most part, exclude collective goods, a fact which I believe now stands as the discipline's most important failure. As the twenty-first century opens, it is time for this failure to be addressed.

The story behind this neglect of collective goals in economic science is long and interesting. In part, it involves a widespread misconception about the ability to discuss matters in the ethical domain without being "ethical;" without engaging in value judgments and giving political or ethical advice. Remarkably, this distinction between examination and advice has not been understood. While economists are to be commended for their efforts to maintain a value-free science and to avoid contact with the ethical domain, unfortunately their failure to maintain the distinction between objective analysis and ethical argument has led to mischief.

In the long evolution of the discipline of economics and its eventual neglect of collective goods, there is one great turning point. This was the complex of developments in the 1870–90 period which has come to be known as the "marginalist revolution." Before that time, the boundaries of economic science, or as it was then termed, "political economy," were amorphous and economists were quite willing to discuss matters outside of technical concerns dealing with material wealth. With the introduction of more rigorous and mathematical methods in the 1870–90 period, economists became more sure of where the boundaries ought to be placed, and more willing to exclude areas where such mathematical rigor could not be readily applied. It could be, also, that this new tendency on the part of economists toward narrowing their scientific concerns was reinforced by a methodological tradition in English scientific philosophy known as "empiricism" (see below).

As we view the historical developments in economic science with respect to how economists viewed the limits of their professional concerns, it becomes apparent that there is a parallel, but highly related, story that needs to be told dealing with the subject of utilitarianism. The fortunes of utilitarianism and developments concerning how economists view their science have been, and still are, closely interwoven. Again, the marginalist revolution was important. Developments from that period having to do with the increases in mathematical rigor had profound effects upon utilitarianism as it was viewed by professional economists and this, in turn, had important effects upon how they viewed their science.

In sum, the events begun in the marginalist revolution culminated in a rather complete and sharp delineation by economists of the limits of their professional concerns. If we were to divide all human goals (with economic implications) into an A-domain and a B-domain, with the former referring to market-tradable goods and the latter all other goods, we could say that after the marginalist revolution, and no later than the 1930s, economists restricted their analytical concerns only to the A-domain and not the B-domain, or in most instances, not to any interactions between the two domains. Economists also made vigorous and plausible attempts to justify these developments, attempts which many have thought, and continue to believe, to be successful. But there are at least four lines of argument as to why these economists are incorrect. The attempt to maintain such a separation fails, and much of this chapter is devoted to developing the four lines of reasoning as to why this is so. Given the parallel importance of utilitarianism in these developments, some separate discussion of that topic will be necessary as well.

Economic Science Before the Marginalist Revolution

While students of economic science down through the ages have always had the study of material wealth as their central focus, before the present century there also existed a second approach dealing with broader social issues. Amartya Sen terms these two approaches the "engineering tradition" and "ethics tradition," respectively. Both can be traced to the Greeks. Aristotle characterized economics as dealing largely with wealth.[1] Household management, the major part of the subject of economics as the Greeks saw things, is in large part concerned with material wealth. Adam Smith described political economy as "the essence of the nature, reproduction, distribution, and disposal of wealth,"[2] and of course we have the title of his major work, *The Wealth of Nations.* McCulloch, in

[1]Sen (1987: 3).

[2]Smith (1976: 678–679).

his *Principles of Political Economy* (1825), defined political economy as "the systematic inquiry into the laws regulating the production, distribution, consumption, and the exchange of commodities or the products of labour."[3] Other earlier writers who viewed political economy in this way and, in addition, felt that policy judgments were to be avoided included Senior and Cairnes.[4] Many other examples could be given, but the point is too well-known to require further documentation.

The ethical tradition also traces back to Aristotle in the *Nichomachean Ethics* where, as described by Sen, he held that:

> ...The story of economics, although related immediately to the pursuit of wealth, is at a deeper level linked up with other studies, involving the assessment and enhancement of more basic goals. "The life of money-making is one undertaken under compulsion, and wealth is evidently not the good we are seeking; for it is merely useful and for the sake of something else."[5]

Sen adds that there were two aspects to Aristotle's approach: first, that of "the problem of human motivation (as) related to the broadly ethical question 'How should we live?'"; and second, a view that the central concern of economics is social: "though it is worthwhile to attain the end merely for one man, it is more god-like to attain it for the nation or for city-states."[6]

In more modern times, many economists before this century took a keen interest in matters of justice and distribution, often including them directly into their analytical concerns. There is no better example than Adam Smith, who was seldom afraid of gazing broadly over the whole human experience, having extended discussions of such topics as education and religion in the *Wealth of Nations*, not to speak of the material in his "other" book, *The Theory of Moral Sentiments*.[7] Smith's friend,

---

[3]McCulloch [1870 (1825): 9].

[4]Senior (1827), Cairnes (1888: 39–42).

[5]Sen (1987: 3). The inner quotes are the words of Aristotle quoted by Sen from Ross (1980).

[6]Ross (1980: 2) cited in Sen (1987: 4).

[7]According to Daniel Bell (1981: 55–56): "When Adam Smith is using the word *nature*, his idiom and content are classical (i.e., ancient) philosophy. Nature implies a *telos*, a purpose immanent in the form of the object, which is the task of men to realize. Natural

David Hume, was also not shy about discussing moral issues, including his perceptive treatment of the subject of sympathy. Of the nineteenth century writers, the most important presence is John Stuart Mill, whose writings were full of discussions of social justice issues.[8] Maloney has made a survey of economists writing at the latter part of the century with respect to their inclinations to include value judgments of political or ethical questions as part of their craft. Of the dozen economists he discusses, at most only three believed in scrupulously avoiding the moral domain (Jevons, Cannan, and Marshall).[9] He shows also how members of the press and public expected any economist worth his salt to take ethical positions routinely,[10] and states that words such as "positive,"

liberty is not the state of nature of Hobbes, a mechanistic world driven by appetite, murderous self-interest, and aggrandizement. It is a world — otherwise *The Theory of Moral Sentiments* makes no sense — where men strive for disinterested moral judgments (what Aristotle called *phronimos*) by seeking for those general standards that comprise 'sympathy.' The Smithian world is individualistic (because conscience rescues a man from the bonds of conformity) but not egoistic. There is, in the phrase coined by him, 'the Great Society.' Economics, as an aspect of it, is inextricably normative and moral." Bell (1981: 55–56).

[8]Mill was astute in combining efficiency and justice concerns in his writings. He was greatly concerned with the income or wealth distribution of his day, where the produce of labor was apportioned: "...almost in inverse ratio to the labour — the largest portions to those who have never worked at all, the next largest to those whose work is almost nominal, and so in descending scale, the remuneration dwindling as the work grows harder and more disagreeable, until the most fatiguing and exhausting bodily labour cannot count with certainty on being able to earn even the necessaries of life..." At the same time, Mill did not neglect what later came to be known as "allocational efficiency." One good example of how he could reconcile the two things is his treatment of taxation, advocating from an efficiency viewpoint proportional taxes on income above the subsistence level to maintain incentives while at the same time arguing for heavy transfer taxes to correct a highly unjust distribution of wealth, believing that wealth taxes would affect incentives much less than would income taxes (Mill, 1926: 208).

[9]The others include Devas, Smart, Hobson, Ashley, Price, Nicholson, Money, Sidgwick, and Cunningham (Maloney, 1985, Chap. 9). This list does not include such critics as Carlyle and Ruskin, who would have argued that all economics should be completely subservient to ethics. Sidgwick could perhaps be counted as an exception, depending upon the view one takes of his pronouncements in the category of the "art" of economics. It perhaps goes without saying that economists who were not afraid to get involved in "ethical" arguments in this era were also not afraid to invoke utility judgments, working from their own introspection and/or some principal agent notion. See the discussion of utilitarianism in economics below.

[10]Maloney (1985: 193–194).

"normative," and "value judgment" were not much used by economists in Marshall's day.[11]

The Marginalist Revolution

In the early 1870s, three economists, William Stanley Jevons, Carl Menger, and Leon Walras, working more or less independently, showed the value to economic theory of working with variables "at the margin," both on the demand side ("diminishing marginal utility") and the supply side ("marginal cost" and "marginal revenue").[12] This introduced great new analytical possibilities into the discipline while, at the same time, tending to reduce the interest of economists in areas where such rigorous methods could not be applied. Maloney describes the process quite well:

> Inevitably, the scientific flavor of marginal analysis advertized and dignified the limited objectives to which it could be put. By comparison, policy pronouncements which involved matters of long-term growth or distribution seemed amateurish, ideologically loaded, perched on an economic base which had somehow shrivelled. This was particularly true of distributive justice, for whereas classical and Marxian theory gave a context for discussing whether current evils were permanent or even increasing, the statics of marginal productivity theory could not frame answers as to the justice of distributive trends...Theoretical advance, then, fatally broadened the gap between the precision of the tools and the indecision of the craftsman.[13]

What made the marginalist paradigm so alluring to economists was its potential for rigorous mathematical modelling involving, in particular, the methods of the differential calculus. But the flip side of the coin is

[11]Maloney (1985: 186). As used by economists in the twentieth century, "positive" meant consistent with logic and empirical fact only, without ethical content. "Normative" denoted the taking of an ethical value position, or any position which implies one outcome is better than another.

[12]As Bell put it, "What the marginalists did was to make *relative* price and *relative* scarcity the fulcrums of economic analysis." Bell (1981: 50).

[13]Maloney (1985: 40).

that the paradigm could only be made to work when individuals could be assumed to maximize their own selfish material gain, a stipulation which mostly limited the subject matter to market-tradable goods and the motivation to narrow self-interest. The discipline was even given a new name, "economics," the science which "treats of the laws which govern the relations of exchangeable commodities."[14] (Before this, the discipline had been known as "political economy," a term which at least suggested the broader concerns of Aristotle). This area had always been considered by economists as their own turf, but with the introduction of mathematical techniques it was possible to build ever higher walls around this turf since only trained economists had access to the technical sophistication required to deal with it.[15]

For professional economists, the new "economics" provided a marvelous domain in which to work, even though somewhat narrower in breadth than many had viewed economic concerns theretofore.[16] Given the obvious advantages of limiting their domain to market-tradable goods, economists quickly developed a set of reasons why holding to such a limitation could be justified. Social scientists ought to engage in specialization and division of labor. Here is the domain for economists; other goods can and should be left to other disciplines. Economists should only deal with scientific endeavors which are "value-free;" other concerns, such as those involving collective goods, are often directly related to moral questions which

[14]The first use of the term "economics" in this manner apparently was that of MacLeod in the journal *Contemporary Review* in 1875, from which this quotation is taken (McLeod 1875: 893). Lionel Robbins ventures to give credit to a specific publication for the origination of the narrower view of economic science as opposed to political economy: the publication of Alfred and Mary Marshall's *Economics of Industry* in 1879 (Robbins, 1984: xxvii).

[15]Thus, one of the issues which was of considerable concern to Alfred Marshall was an attempt to "professionalize" the discipline (see Maloney, 1985, Chap. 2). It can be said also that in this quest, Marshall was quite successful. By the latter part of the twentiethth century, it has become clear that part of the legacy of mathematical expertise has become a curse rather than a blessing, with mathematical form taking precedence over economic substance (see Blaug, 1998a, 1998b; McCloskey, 1994, Chap. 10).

[16]As Bell (1981: 69–70) explains, the world dealt with by economists became much less realistic, where "...an economic *system* is not an economy; it is an analytical abstraction, an ideal, closed world where resources flow freely in response to price, where comparative advantage dictates a shift of resource utilization, where labor is not people but units of skill (or lacks thereof), where there are no political boundaries, and where machinery, capital, and commodities distribute themselves to the maximum benefit of mankind."

objective scientists must avoid at all costs. And collective goods, the major area excluded from the neo-classical paradigm, are often difficult to measure and define; it is difficult to ascertain consumer demands for them as well. And so stands the state of economic methodology to this day. There are two domains, one inside the pale, the other outside.

The Role of Utilitarianism

Before discussing the place that economists' use of the utilitarianism idea had in these developments, a short digresssion for some definitions is necessary. The following are five benchmarks of ways in which utilitarianism has been used over the years in welfare aggregation. It may be that all approaches to welfare aggregation in social science can be described by a combination of these benchmark cases. The first four involve degrees of utilitarianism: *cardinal utilitarianism, principal-agent utilitarianism, shared-value principal-agent utilitarianism,* and *no utilitarianism (ordinalism).* The fifth, *two-dimensional welfarism,* is a variant in which proxy variables are used to represent welfare.

1. *Cardinal utilitarianism.* Suppose we could find a machine which would objectively measure the positive or negative utility a person experiences at any time, and that the machine had well-defined units and origin and that all this was fully comparable (in some scientifically justifiable way) across all persons. This would be full cardinal utilitarianism. Upon implementation of any social policy, aggregate utility is found simply by noting the utility readings for each person and adding them all together.[17]

2. *Principal-agent utilitarianism.* In this approach, we would assume that individuals, or at least some individuals, can make useful interpersonal utility calculations. "Useful" is here defined so that a sympathetic observer can compare alternative social states and make accurate (or what many consider to be accurate) estimates of both total utility gains and total utility losses resulting from a given policy. In addition,

[17]Many writers (for example, Gordon and Riley) would not accept simple addition as necessarily yielding the final moral answers. The correctness of simple addition is not being argued here; merely the point that it would somehow be possible (Gordon, 1980: 30 ff.; Riley, 1988: 44 ff).

the observer can roughly estimate amounts of utility gains and losses by individuals, such that he or she can spot individual utility losses from any policy which are "unacceptably large" and point out the compensation required to deal fairly with these.

3. *Shared-value principal-agent utilitarianism.* In this kind of utilitarianism, it is posited that there exist the kind of agents described in (2). In addition, each agent's assessments are considered to be consistent with notions widely shared in the population at large in the sense of "shared values" as discussed in Chapter 2.
4. *Ordinalism (no utilitarianism).* In this kind of utilitarianism, all persons agree that it is without exception *always* impossible to make interpersonal welfare comparisons of any kind. All that is possible is for individuals to be able to rank alternative social states, but no comparisons of these rankings is in any way possible.

In addition to the four basic approaches to welfare aggregation just described, there is a fifth, somewhat less pure, approach which has been used a great deal in contemporary welfare economics and particularly in the area of taxation, where it goes back about 150 years. This is:

5. *Two-dimensional welfarism (two-dimensional Paretianism).*[18] Under this approach, economists have used two variables for representing all welfare. The first is the maximization of efficiency with respect to market-tradable goods and material wealth, while the second is a proxy variable meant to stand for all other welfare dimensions. The most widely used candidate for this second variable has been distribution of income, where it is assumed that welfare is inversely related to some overall measure of income disparity. In taxation analysis, the second variable has been some measure of equal sacrifice. This approach is flawed in that one variable cannot be made to represent a large number of other variables when those variables are not highly correlated with each other.[19]

---

[18]This is my own label (see the discussion in Kiesling, 1992: 8, 24–25, 71).

[19]In addition, we might mention, as a possibility at least, single-dimension welfarism, where welfare is totalled up for market-tradable goods alone. This does not fulfill the basic welfare economic requirement of relating the market sector to the rest of the world, however, and so this alternative was omitted from the list of possibilities.

Utilitarianism before the marginalist revolution

It is probably correct to say that the nineteenth century was the golden age of utilitarianism, although this does not mean that very many economists of the period believed in the possiblity of full cardinal utilitarianism. The most noteworthy exception may have been Edgeworth, who entertained hopes that one day a scientific utility measuring machine, or *hedometer*, would be developed. On the other hand, the nineteenth century was replete with writers who were optimistic believers in the possibility that utilitarian thinking could lead to viable real-world policy choices. For example, the taxation literature was full of serious speculation concerning the nature of "realistic" estimates of the functional form taken by the income-to-utility relationship.[20] Most of this optimism was undoubtedly supported by strong beliefs in some combination of principal-agent and shared-value principal-agent utilitarianism, together with a fairly pervasive belief in the idea of social harmony. As Myrdal points out, the social harmony assumption[21] allowed utilitarians to avoid the need to find empirical estimations of individual utilities. This is tantamount to placing utilitarianism on a foundation consisting of widely shared values.[22] But the important point for our purposes here is that nineteenth century economists had available such optimism about the usefulness of utilitarianism that they could confidently indulge in broad policy analysis which involved political and ethical value judgments. With some noteworthy exceptions, this is exactly what they did. During the nineteenth century, the ethical tradition was alive and well, but it was not fated to last very far into the century that follows.

Effect of the marginalist revolution on utilitarianism: the "ordinal revolution"

The emphasis on rigorous mathematical methods introduced into economic science by the marginalist revolution, in addition to changing the nature of economic analysis, had another important effect. It affected profoundly the nature of utilitarianism. Economists increasingly became disinclined

[20]See Kiesling (1992: 33, 60).

[21]Myrdal terms it the "communistic fiction" (Myrdal, 1955: 54).

[22]With respect to the idea of harmonious order, see also Gordon (1991, Chap. 10).

to accept inexact and non-rigorous procedures, such as the principal-agent varieties of utilitarianism. The only mathematically acceptable approach would have been full cardinal utilitarianism, and it seemed obvious that achieving *that* would not be possible. This had undoubtedly become obvious to most of the major economists even before Lionel Robbins published his monumental 1932 essay, *The Nature and Significance of Economic Science.*[23] Any doubters who remained were surely convinced by Robbins' logic and eloquence.

This was a monumental development. Henceforth, economists were led to believe that *no welfare comparisons of any kind would be possible,* at least in *their* science. The profession had then achieved the fourth benchmark case enunciated above, the *no utilitarianism* case. From that time on, economists posited that ordinal rankings were the most that would ever be possible,[24] and all subsequent efforts use these as the basis for welfare economic policy comparisons. While some writers, such as Samuelson presumably, might disagree, the consensus of almost all economists with expertise in the social choice area is that these efforts have failed, as further discussed below.[25]

Can the Discipline of Economics be Reduced to Market-Tradable Goods?

According to the specialization in the social sciences approach as it seems to have developed, economists would concentrate only on material gain and market-tradable goods in a world of egoistic motivation. Could such an approach be made to work, even in principle?

In order for the approach to work, economists would have to give up all professional concern with any human activity besides selfishly motivated transactions involving market-tradable goods, which seems a terrible price to pay. Most analysis of what is normally considered social policy would have to be forsaken, including all the broader ethical concerns of human existence. Economists, who tend to be perceptive and interested observers of the major social issues of their day, would likely find this

[23]Robbins (1984).

[24]Except for market-tradable goods.

[25]See, for example, Mueller (1989: Chap. 19).

quite frustrating, although it is true that economists in their role as *citizens* could still participate. (Many would surely chafe at not being able to make pronouncements as *economists*.)

One benefit of the approach, from one point of view at least, would be that economists could give up on what has proven to be a difficult quest to find a viable welfare economics (the sub-discipline of economics meant to deal with decisions involving broad questions of social policy.) That there exists a sub-discipline of welfare economics at all would suggest that economists have not been willing to take this step. If efforts on the part of economists to produce a viable welfare economics had been successful, the very problem of failing to deal with collective goods would have been solved. No problems would remain. It is unlikely that economists would abandon what many consider one of the more important sub-disciplines. Indeed, many economists seem to still believe that extant welfare economic techniques are viable for making policy judgments, a position which requires further examination in this chapter.

Boundaries of Economics and the Principle of Scarcity

Another awkwardness of the narrower approach is its clash with one definition considered proper by many highly respected economists over the years: that the subject of economic science ought to be *scarcity*. The idea that scarcity problems range more widely than to material concerns alone goes far back. The first specific suggestion of the possiblility may have been due to Hume,[26] although it is also suggested by Adam Smith's broad-ranging interests in his *economics* treatise and in Aristotle's sentiment that wealth is to be considered only as a means for attaining "more basic goals." Other economists who adopted the broader definition before this century include Menger,[27] Seligman,[28] and

[26]Robbins (1984: xiii).

[27]In the *Grundsaetze*, as cited by Robbins (1984: xiii).

[28]Seligman wrote the definition of economic science included in the *Encyclopedia of the Social Sciences* (1942: 344) before the current 1968 edition, where he stated that economics had sometimes been defined as featuring material needs only, which was an unsatisfactory definition: "Economics sometimes has been defined as the science of wealth and as the science of welfare; it has been spoken of as centering about the business enterprise and including the entire range of economic behavior."

Sidgwick.[29] More recently, many of the major textbooks have adopted the broader approach too.[30]

Perhaps the most important logical challenge to the material conceptualization of economics based upon the implications of the scarcity concept is that stated by Lionel Robbins in his memorable 1932 *Essay on the Nature and Significance of Economic Science*. It has since been brought up to date in his 1982 Ely lecture delivered to the American Economic Association. Since Robbins also specifically argues for the inclusion of collective goods in the concerns of economic science, his treatment is worth quoting at some length. Neither in the original essay nor in the lecture 50 years later does Robbins mince many words, stating in a direct and rather elegant manner the only logical conclusion possible: the scarcity problem is at the heart of all economic investigation.

> From the point of view of the economist, the conditions of human existence exhibit four fundamental characteristics. The ends are various. The time and the means for achieving these ends are limited and capable of alternative application. At the same time, the ends have different importance. Here we are, sentient creatures with bundles of desires and aspirations, with masses of instinctive tendencies all urging us in different ways to action. But the time in which these tendencies can be expressed is limited.[31]

And, therefore, the central importance of scarcity to economic science:

> ...Scarcity of means to satisfying ends of varying importance is an almost ubiquitous condition of human behaviors.[32]

and

---

[29]While Sidgwick died in 1901, remarkably enough his definition of economic science is still being carried in the current edition of *Palgrave's Dictionary of Economics* (Vol. 2, 1987: 58), which was published in 1987! The following is his complete definition: "'economy' in modern languages has come to denote generally the principle of seeking to attain, or the method of attaining, a desired end with the least possible expenditure of means."

[30]Alchian and Allen (1967: 2); Lipsey and Courant (1996: 4); Samuelson and Nordhaus (1985: 30); Baumol and Blinder (1985: 35).

[31]Robbins [1984 (1932): 12–13].

[32]Robbins [1984 (1932): 15].

> "Economics is the science which studies human behavior as a relationship between ends and scarce means which have alternative uses."[33]

Furthermore, if it is necessary to remove any doubt as to exactly what is being claimed, the fundamental and defining characteristic of economic science is that it

> ...focuses attention on a particular *aspect* of behavior, the form imposed by the influence of scarcity. It follows from this, therefore, that in so far as it presents this aspect, *any* kind of human behavior falls within the scope of economic generalizations...There are no limitations to the subject of economics save this.[34]

Robbins argues that the idea that economics should be limited to the study of scarcity only with respect to material welfare cannot be correct because it attempts to use a *"classificatory* approach," in which the attempt is made to mark off "certain kinds of human behaviour...as the subject matter of economics." This is contrary to the more basic *analytical* defining characteristic of economics for economic science: the presence of scarcity. Also misguided, in Robbins' eyes, is the idea that economic science needs to be restricted to discussions of the scarcity of market-tradable goods, the view that behavior which is "not specifically social...is not the subject matter of economics:"[35]

> But it is one thing to contend that economic analysis has *most interest and utility* in an exchange economy. It is another to contend that its subject matter is *limited* to such phenomena. The unjustifiability of this latter contention may be shown conclusively by two considerations. In the first place, it is clear that behavior outside the exchange economy is conditioned by the same limitation of means in relation to ends as behavior within the economy, and is capable of being subsumed under the same fundamental categories...The exchange relationship is a *technical* incident...subsidiary to the main fact of scarcity.

---

[33]Robbins [1984 (1932): 16].
[34]Robbins [1984 (1932): 17]. Emphasis in the second quoted sentence has been added.
[35]Robbins, [1984 (1932): 17].

> In the second place, it is clear that the phenomena of the exchange economy itself can only be explained by *going behind* such relationships and invoking the operation of those laws of choice which are best seen when contemplating the behavior of the isolated individual...[36]

Given these statements of Robbins, little more needs be said to buttress a case for including collective goods in economic science. Robbins considers incorrect the view that "specifically social behavior" is not part of the subject matter of economics, stating that scarcity is to be conceived of as "the relationship between objectives *either personal or collective*, and the means of satisfying them."[37] (emphasis added). Given Robbins' apparent stature in the economics profession (his Ely lecture received a lengthy standing ovation, and being asked to give it in the first place is, of course, a sign of stature), one can hope that these sentiments are taken seriously, although the evidence suggests that aside from a small (but growing) group of critics, they are given more lip service than actual loyalty.[38]

The Problem of Interactions

If economists were determined upon a narrow view of their discipline merely as a matter of *definition*, there is no reason they could not be successful if only they wished to do so badly enough. Rather than adopt the scarcity approach suggested by Robbins and others, they could agree to adopt the alternative classificatory approach. Then they could resolve not to deal with ethical concerns at all, hence leaving them strictly to others. However, there is a more technical and inescapable reason why the strict narrow approach must fail. Complete separation of what economists have come to call "allocative efficiency" (efficiency of the

[36]Robbins [1984 (1932): 19–20].

[37]Robbins [1984; xiii].

[38]In their more expansive moments, such as in presidential addresses to the American Economics Association, even prestigious economists sometimes admit that economics should deal with social aspects of the human experience. See, for example, Robert Solow's 1979 presidential address in which he concluded that the "economic man...is in a social category" [Quoted in Bell [1981: 78)].

production and consumption of market-tradable goods, often just termed as "economic efficiency") and concerns of justice and liberty will not work because it is technically impossible to accomplish. There are inescapable interactions between "economic" and justice variables. Such interactions are especially important in areas such as public economics where most policies have strong distributive justice ramifications, but there is no area of economic science where interactions do not assume at least some significance. The type of tax system adopted will have substantial effects upon the distribution of income and wealth, for example.[39] This is also true in labor economics, the economics of poverty, and in the field of welfare economics itself.

The nature of the problem has been captured well in a comment made in a graduate level textbook on public economics written by Richard Tresch:

> ...Because an economic system is a closed system in which all systems are ultimately interrelated, any public policy decision made with respect to the distribution question will affect *all* public policy decisions relating to allocational issues as well. Thus, the government cannot simply make a particular redistributional decision, for better or worse, and be done with it.
>
> Public sector economics has never totally come to grips with this problem. Economists have all too often assumed away distributional problems in order to analyze more comfortable allocational issues, knowing full well that dichotomizing allocational and distributional policies is often not legitimate, and may produce normative policy prescriptions quite wide of the mark.[40]

The possibility of separating efficiency and justice concerns has long been an appealing idea to economists. Above we saw an early but important implicit step in this direction in the taxation suggestions of John Stuart Mill (footnote 8). We have also seen how economists increasingly retreated

[39]See Kiesling (1992: 309 ff).

[40]Tresch (1981: 9). Also see the statement of Rosen in the chapter epigraph. Rosen is a highly respected mainstream economist.

into their cocoon of marginalism with respect to market-tradable goods beginning with Marshall and Jevons. The very webbing of this cocoon is the assumption that a separation is feasible.[41] The figure who has most been associated with the idea since the middle of the twentieth century has been Richard Musgrave, who has long advocated studying the economics of the public sector by dividing all government concerns into three completely separate areas, labeled by him as the "allocation, distribution, and stabilization branches of government."[42] In fairness, it should be added that Musgrave considered this division as a convenient analytical tool and did not deny the problem of interactions between the three branches, although he did feel that it would be feasible for "each manager…to plan his job on the assumption that the other two branches will perform their respective functions properly."[43] Nor would many economists deny the frequent necessity of dealing with one kind of problem at a time and there is an extent to which Musgrave's efforts to make public finance problems manageable is to be applauded, although the question arises as to how far the approach can properly be carried out. As Tresch's comment suggests, this sometimes may not be very far.[44]

---

[41]Methodologically, attempts to separate off parts of a social science from the rest of the world in this manner is likely to be one ramification of attempts by economists to employ procedures similar to those in the natural sciences, where such walling off, or "insulation", is possible. There is further discussion of this in Chapter 4.

[42]Musgrave (1959: 5ff).

[43]Musgrave (1959: 5).

[44]Perhaps the definitive, as well as classic, response to Musgrave's approach is Samuelson's comment at a 1966 conference of public economics held in Biarritz, France "…Musgrave's paper…commenting on Lindahl and Johansen does seem to perceive the essential theorem, recognising tacitly that the proper reallocation of income is not *prior* to public good determination, but must be done *simultaneously* with it. (This is also the case in a Good Society involving only private goods and optimal income distribution.) But in the following paragraphs, Musgrave is too easy on the Pseudo-Demand mechanism; in his desire to be 'parochial', attributable perhaps to an underlying desire to be 'practical,' he overlooks the *necessarily* pseudo character of the [solution of the general equilibrium problem for public goods.]…Moreover, he lapses into the cardinal sin of the narrow 'new welfare' economists: 'If you can't get (or even define!) the maximum of a social welfare function, settle for Pareto optimality', as if *that* were second best or even 99th best" (Samuelson, 1969; Musgrave, 1969).

Is There a Viable Welfare Economics Which Solves the Problem of the Neglect of Collective Goods?[45]

As was suggested above, if economists were able to construct a viable welfare economics, they would be able to include all important human welfare goals in their policy analysis and the central problem discussed in this book would no longer exist. Economists differ in their opinions as to whether a usable welfare economics exists, although I believe most would agree that in terms of analysis *generated strictly inside of economic science*, the exercise fails.

Utilitarians in the nineteenth century had a way, in principle at least, of comparing the relative social welfare of moving closer to all human goals, social or individual. With the ordinal revolution, this ability disappeared, except *perhaps* for market-tradable goods.[46] The destruction of all possibility of interpersonal welfare comparison left a gaping hole in the economics of policy analysis, or *welfare economics*, as this had come to be called. The very *raison d'etre* of social science is to advance human welfare, and this is a process which cannot even be begun if the analyst does not possess a definition of welfare itself, something quite impossible if all comparability is denied.

Above, we discussed the demise of the idea that utilitarianism could form a viable basis for welfare judgments which occurred in the first two or three decades in this century, the *coup de grace* perhaps being Robbins' monumental essay published in 1932. It was only a few years later that a brilliant young man began his career in economics at the University of Chicago and at Harvard University: Paul Samuelson, who later was to become the first single winner of the Nobel Prize for economics. Some forty years later, Samuelson described the intellectual climate that

[45]Readers who have little interest in the fortunes of this sub-discipline of economics may wish to skip this section and proceed to the discussion of methodology.

[46]For an excellent discussion of the problems involved in making empirical estimates of demands for economic commodities, see Clarkson (1963), especially Chapters 6 to 8. Clarkson suggests that testable models of demand will require testable models of individual decision-making behavior and that, while these seem possible, they are as yet little developed even for individual goods. Such models will require sophisticated models of individual decision-making, for which the ideas of the goal model suggested in this book seemingly would qualify, and so such models surely could be developed for collective goods too.

existed in the mid-1930s when he was a beginning graduate student at Harvard University:

> I have recorded somewhere in print how in the year 1935 as a puzzled student I could not get satisfactory answers anywhere in the Harvard Yard or the University of Chicago quadrangle to the simple question: Exactly why is it *right* for price to equal marginal cost? ...When Robbins sang out that the emperor had no clothes — that you could not prove or test by any empirical observations of objective science the normative validity of comparisons between different persons' utilities — suddenly all his generation of economists felt themselves to be naked in a cold world. Most of them had come into economics seeking the good. To learn in midlife that theirs was only the craft of a plumber, dentist, or cost accountant was a sad shock.[47]

Samuelson went on to state that the only approach economists had in those years was one that was heuristic and "muddled," in which economists simply had faith that given the law of large numbers taken over long periods of time, policies that increase marketplace efficiency would in the end add positively to human welfare. This was, he implies, both non-rigorous and unsatisfactory.

The Bergson social welfare function

The answer to this dilemma, as viewed by Samuelson and others, came with the publication in 1938 of Abram Bergson's landmark paper, *A Reformulation of Certain Aspects of Welfare Economics*.[48] In that paper, Bergson nicely stated the problem facing welfare economics and then suggested a solution which would mostly require individual *ordinal* rankings of alternative social states. The ordinal rankings themselves would be enough in situations involving unanimous agreement (which would be very few, however). Otherwise, "social welfare functions" could be constituted with the help of outside arbiters who would provide the

[47]Samuelson (1981: 226).

[48]Bergson [(Burke), 1938].

necessary ethical interpersonal comparisons. The implication for this "social welfare function" approach which seems to have been left by Bergson and seconded by Samuelson in his 1947 book, *Foundations of Economic Analysis*, was that the ordinal ranking provided by each individual would be enough data to make the approach viable. Subsequently, there has been a large debate in the social choice literature as to whether this was true, with the result that most social choice specialists have concluded that it is not — that Bergson's approach would not work without cardinal interpersonal comparisons of some kind, presumably supplied by an ethical arbiter.[49] This carries Bergson squarely back into the classical utilitarian tradition, requiring either full cardinal comparisons or, at the very least, one of the principal-agent approaches.

The current state of welfare economics

The following is a further statement beyond Samuelson's characterization quote above that welfare economics in the 1930s was heuristic and muddled. He points out that economists of the period held to the following

> *Heuristic theorem.* Most technical changes of policy choices directly help some people and hurt others. For some changes, it is possible for the winners to buy off the losers so that everyone could conceivably end up better off than in the prior status quo. Suppose that no such compensatory bribes or side payments are made, but assume that we are dealing with numerous inventions and policy decisions that are quasi-independent. Even if for each single change it is hard to know in advance who will be helped and who will be hurt, in the absence of known "bias" in the whole sequence of changes, there is some vague presumption that a hazy version of the law of large numbers will obtain: so as the number of quasi-independent events becomes larger and larger, the chances improve that any random person will be on balance benefited by a social compact that lets events take place that push out society's utility possibility frontier, even

[49]A good overview of this discussion is presented in Mueller (1989, Chap. 19).

> though any one of the events may push some people along the new frontier in a direction less favorable than the status quo.[50]

This is, I believe, an excellent statement of how economists have viewed the subject of welfare aggregation in *contemporary* times. Samuelson, however, seems to believe that this thinking only took place in the mid-1930s, that the situation was improved and the problem solved with the advent of Bergson's contribution. Unfortunately, here Samuelson seems to be in error. I believe that most contemporary students in the area of social choice would agree that, instead of making an excellent statement of how things were viewed in the 1930s, it is in fact a true statement of the situation *now*. The state of welfare economics is in complete disarray.[51] Economists tend to concentrate upon the maximization of economic welfare in the market sector only, and then to cross their fingers and hope that the law of averages and large numbers will make the outcome come round right in the end. But this simply will not wash. In all of the sizable literature on the relationship between economic justice and marketplace efficiency, there is little support for the notion that "any random person" will be benefited from marketplace efficiency in the long run because of the law of large numbers. The income and wealth distributions generated from market solutions, efficient or not, are highly unequal. While it may be possible to justify these differences within the same generation using desert and efficiency arguments, with the passage of generations this becomes far less true and, therefore, the institution of inheritance needs to be brought directly into the analysis, a step conspicuous by its absence in all twentieth century economic science.

To conclude, then, about welfare economics in contemporary economic analysis, the only way that welfare variables can be obtained from outside the domain of market-tradable goods would be for judgments to be supplied from outside the discipline, from non-economists, whether by politicians, clergy, or whomever. This maintains the strict separation between economics as the study of material goods with market-tradable goods and

[50]Samuelson (1981: 227).

[51]James Buchanan has been stating this for many years. See, for example, Buchanan (1960, Chap. 5).

everything else. Thus, welfare economics, *as a discipline internal to economic science*, fails. From the standpoint of the workings of economic science itself, collective goods are neglected.[52]

Methodological Aspects

It would be surprising if the arguments used by economists to justify the exclusion of collective goals from their professional concerns were not somehow related to the broader discussion dealing with the methodology of social science. In the introductory chapter, I reviewed, in capsule form, two traditions in social science: "objectivism" and "subjectivism." Patrick O'Sullivan, in his 1987 book on economic methodology, terms the two approaches "objectivist-behaviorist" and "subjectivist-interpretive", respectively. In the former, the human subject of social science is viewed primarily as an *object*, or a *thing*, and the role of social science is to explain actions by showing how such "objects" are acted upon by outside forces. These forces are to be examined empirically using methods similar to those in the natural sciences, that is, through "objective" observation with the use of the five senses, by third parties. (See the summary of views of those in the objectivist tradition in the Introduction.) The objectivist-behaviorist approach in economics is, in large part, due to "scientism" on the part of economists, that is, their attempts to adopt the methodology of the natural scientists.[53]

---

[52]In the last decade or two, economists have become increasingly sophisticated with respect to the influences which institutional arrangements, such as property rights and contract enforcement mechanisms, have upon economic efficiency. In this, they are at least getting close to treating superior institutional arrangements as a collective goal explicitly. See, for example, Clague (1997).

[53]Scientistic tendencies on the part of economists were reinforced in the twentiethth century by an interesting group of social scientists centered in Vienna, Austria, in the 1920s and 1930s and known as the "Vienna Circle." These writers expounded a brand of extreme behaviorism and empiricism which came to be known as "logical positivism." Their views included, besides behaviorism and empiricism, the idea that science should be able to predict, the idea that useful theories should be simple as opposed to complex, the idea of the unity of all science (methodological monism), the idea that it is possible to establish scientific 'Truth' with a capital T, and the idea that good scientific results should be generalizable beyond the limitations of culture and history. See also Chapter 4, note 2, and the discussion of scientism.

The "subjectivist-interpretive" approach, on the other hand, reserves an important place in the social science model for teleological explanations — explanations which center on the fact that persons have goals and make choices — where empirical investigations can proceed with respect to human mental states. It is a humanist approach to social science, which has a small but devoted (and, I believe, growing) following in all of the human sciences, as further discussed in Chapter 4.

O'Sullivan argues convincingly that by precept economists have been rather convinced objectivists while, in practice, they have added significant amounts of subjectivism to their procedures. But whether by precept (lip service) or practice, they seem to have been quite successful in omitting collective goals from their analytical models.

According to O'Sullivan, the objectivism of professional economists has taken three different forms each of which he considers mistaken. First, there is the "instrumental" approach. Proponents of instrumental objectivism, while not denying that "man is a self-conscious, purposive and freely-acting being," propose to establish the objective forms of hypotheses they wish by resorting to "behaviorist fictions," which seem to describe the phenomenon at hand even though the investigator realizes that the fiction itself is just that. The example familiar to economists is Milton Friedman's argument in his *Methodology of Positive Economics*.[54] O'Sullivan dismisses this approach on the grounds that the instrumentalist "has in effect abjured the quest for truth in science," since he admits that all theories are mere fictions.[55] Secondly, there is the "reductionist" approach, in which social scientists merely deny that man is anything more than a highly complex organism without much self-consciousness and freedom to make choices. This pessimistic view of mankind, which seems to deny the possibility of culture and morality, has obvious problems, although O'Sullivan goes on to assert that "whenever a positivist-inclined thinker resolves to distrust all assertions with regard to subjective states,

[54]Friedman (1953). In this essay, Friedman argues that the assumptions on economic theory may depart from reality so long as a theory predicts well.

[55]O'Sullivan (1987: 34). He goes on: (since) "instrumentalist fictions do not offer genuine explanations, a serious question mark must hang over their usefulness for policy purposes", a point particularly relevant to the discussion in this book. O'Sullivan also mentions an awkwardness that the instrumentalist will not be able to make a distinction between science and sorcery.

the eventual espousal of some such materialist reduction is inevitable (given the illegitimacy of the instrumentalist version of objectivism)."[56]

The third variant of objectivism O'Sullivan discusses is termed "superficial monism." Writers taking this approach do not deny the subjectivist nature of individuals, but do stress the very great difficulties encountered when applying natural science methods to dealing with man as a subject, difficulties due in large part to the widespread belief among social scientists that interviewing and polling techniques are "unscientific." (See the O'Sullivan quotation in the chapter epigraph.) Thus, while accepting humans as subjective, they insist on treating them in the manner of the natural sciences anyhow, as if they were objects. O'Sullivan argues that this ploy is tantamount to falling back on the instrumentalist version of objectivism.

Turning to the subjectivist approach, which economists seemingly would prefer to avoid, it turns out that, in practice, they use it — up to a point at least. In this, they follow the lead of a group of Austrian economists (not to be confused with the members of the Vienna Circle discussed in note 53) who, in fact, did take the subjective seriously. However, many of them deal with it in a way which is not far from the methods used by many other (objectivist) economists, that is they depend on their powers of empathy to allow them to make *assumptions* about human subjective goals.[57] In particular, the assumption is that humans have important goals whereby they selfishly seek material gain. This is certainly close to what most mainstream economists typically assume and, therefore, many of them are close to the Austrians in this sense. (It is also fortunate for economists that the selfishness assumption, in fact, seems to be reasonably accurate for that portion of the human experience which economists have chosen to study.)

There is another way in which economists emulate the hard sciences which leads to the neglect of collective goals. We should recall that a key aspect of the highly successful methods used in the natural sciences is the building and testing of models which are used to predict outcomes.

---

[56]O'Sullivan (1987: 55).

[57]It should be noted that the same approach existed in economics before the Austrian economists were active, beginning in the 1930s. The Austrians gave it somewhat more specific justification.

Of key importance in this process is the ability to "wall off" one part of a discipline in order to conduct controlled experiments. This assumption that parts of science can be "walled off," or "insulated" from the rest of the science, as well as from the rest of the world, is important in how it relates to the human sciences, an importance which has been widely overlooked. Social sciences, including economics, are not amenable to being "walled off." Terwee makes this point quite well stating arguments based on the work of Thomas Kuhn.

> Kuhn considers puzzle-solving to be an essential ingredient of normal [natural] science and he maintains that such puzzle-solving is only possible in a state of relative insulation. Scientists try to solve the puzzles considered to be most significant by their paradigm community, not by the general public. Now consider the difference between this and the situation in the social sciences. The problems encountered by these disciplines are often called relevant, and rightly so. Attempts at insulation are usually distrusted, and rightly so: insulation of a field and its language would form a threat for the relevance of the solutions offered. But this means [according to Kuhn] that "the really pressing problems, for example, a cure for cancer or a design for lasting peace, are often not puzzles at all, largely because they may not have any solution...[58]
>
> I think the notion of insulation helps to provide a good explanation for the problem why the social sciences are so different from the natural sciences. A [social scientist] might put the question like this: "Why does my field fail to move ahead in a way that, say, physics does? What changes in technique or method or ideology would enable it to do so? The answer is that psychologists work to help and understand an audience of non-professionals: clients, patients, the general public, schoolteachers, or judges in court. They have to speak two languages and be able to translate their professional concepts into everyday discourse. Insulation is an impossible ideal for most sub-disciplines of psychology...

[58]Kuhn (1970: 37).

While Terwee's remarks were oriented towards psychology, the same can be said for most sub-disciplines in all the other social sciences. The tax analysis problems alluded to above form a perfect example of this "insulation" problem: economists wish to consider tax analysis in terms of narrow marketplace efficiency only, walling it off from the rest of the world, an impossible exercise because of all the interactions between efficiency and justice goals.

In summary, modern mainstream economists seem to neglect collective goals in three ways. First, they admit the importance of goals but limit them to egoistic material goals.[59] Second, they hold that consideration of subjective states must be avoided altogether. Third, they avoid collective goals in order to achieve scientific "insulation." The first way is the Austrian position; the second is superficial monism. The third stems from the requirements of scientific experiment — despite the fact that controlled experiments are not possible in the human sciences. All three positions are consistent with the strongly held view on the part of most economists that subjective states, with regard to collective goods, must be avoided because of the special problems associated with such goods, free riding in particular.[60] But, in fact, economists do very little with subjective states at all since even the assumption of material goals in the realm of market-tradable goods is seldom tested empirically, and the consideration of subjective goals which are collective in nature is omitted entirely. In practice, most mainstream economists fall somewhere between superficial monism and that group of Austrians who assume, without much further proof, that most economic analysis, including policy analysis, needs only the motivation provided by material goals as its single driving force.

To conclude the methodology discussion, the discipline of economics has, in practice, been very successful because, first, it has used teleology and human goals and, secondly, because it has found it possible, *up to a point*, to use a subjective-interpretive approach. Unfortunately, however, the approach has only been used part way. One important segment of all human goals has been omitted from consideration and the subjective

[59]If utilitarianism is used, it is denominated in terms of material goals, profit and wealth.

[60]The more general version is what the philosophers call the "other-minds problem," the inability to be absolutely sure that a person will not respond to a question (as in an interview) untruthfully.

has been admitted into economic investigations only superficially. It would seem that some way should be found for re-incorporating the omitted goals and expanding their inquiries into the subjective domain, including the employment of interviewing techniques or, at the very least, economists should find a way to do this in conjunction with practitioners in other social science disciplines.

Chapter 2

Rationality and Motivation

Rational choice is instrumental: it is guided by the outcome of action. Actions are valued and chosen not for themselves, but as more or less efficient means to a further end...Rational choice is concerned with finding the *best* means to given ends. It is a way of adapting optimally to the circumstances.

Jon Elster
Nuts and Bolts For the Social Sciences, 1989

Since social scientists take as their purpose the understanding of social organization that is derivative from actions of individuals, and since understanding an individual's action ordinarily means seeing the reasons behind the action, then the theoretical aim of social science must be to conceive of that action in a way that makes it rational from the point of view of the actor. Or put another way, much of what is ordinarily described as non-rational or irrational is merely so because the observers have not discovered the point of view of the actor, from which the action *is* rational.

James Coleman
Foundations of Social Theory, 1990

...(I)t is a common (even common-sensical) view that...things are valuable only because (they are) seen from a personal point of view, only because somebody takes them up as a goal — call them "personal values."...But it is doubtful that there are any such things as "personal values." For me to see something of value, from any angle at all, requires my being able to see it against a backdrop of general human aims; my own personal aims are not enough.

James Griffin
Against the Taste Model, 1991

I will argue that rational beliefs rise out of informed judgements that have been submitted to the community of competent individuals for evaluation and criticism.

Harold Brown
Rationality, 1988

When the intellectual history of contempory social science comes to be written, one of its major themes will be the relation of social science to value. It will be a story of mutual isolation, affecting theory and practice alike, with losses to both the social sciences and the philosophy of value.

Abraham Edel
Social Science and Value, 1964

Rationality — the subject area dealing with the use of human reasoning abilities — is important in the social sciences, as well as to our theory of knowledge. Dictionaries have two basic definitions for "rationality." The first, which is the more general, is "having the faculty to reason," or "the state of being agreeable to or in accord with reason,"[1] while the second is meant to imply the proper, or sensible, use of reason: "exercising (or able to exercise) one's reason in a proper manner; having sound judgement, sensible, sane."[2] While these definitions are related, the second is more relevant to the discussion in this chapter where the focus is on the uses of rationality in social science and policy analysis,

[1]*Random House Dictionary of the English Language,* College Edition (1969); *Oxford English Dictionary* (1971).
[2]*Oxford English Dictionary* (1971).

in particular "the exercise of reason in a 'proper' manner." The key relevance of rationality in social science comes through its role in the establishment of *motivation*, the principal causal agent of human action. In building their explanatory models, social scientists need to establish motivation which is "proper" in the sense that it is *predictable*. We saw in the previous chapter how economists have tended to do this by assuming that persons have selfish material goals (the rationality of choosing ends) and that they work to achieve these in certain intelligent ways, for example, through profit maximization (the rationality of choosing means).

In this chapter, I wish to examine the rationality concept carefully with an eye toward showing that the methodology just described is incorrect, leading, amongst other things, to an undue neglect of collective goals. I also wish to investigate what can and cannot be done for obtaining a human motivation concept for social science and policy analysis. To do this, I propose to begin by taking a look, from the ground up, at the rationality problem facing social scientists.

For Complete Policy Analysis, What Would a Proper Rationality Construct Look Like?

We might begin the task of looking for a rationality construct for social policy analysis by reviewing the role of social science, especially as it relates to policy analysis. Suppose the government or the group executive is considering a new policy. They are, of course, interested in predicting what would happen if the policy were introduced and for this, they seek help from relevant social scientists. The role for the latter is then to predict what changes would take place in the *actions* of group members from the proposed public policy. To do this, they need an understanding of the motives of group members in the relevant policy area, or put another way, what group members consider as *rational*.

The rationality of group members in turn works with respect to two issues: first, what they think about the importance of various social goals relative to their own selfish goals; and second, what they think about which implementation methods are best for achieving social goals. (The *rationality of ends* and the *rationality of means*, respectively.)

It should be noted that the approach is consistent with the one mentioned in the Introduction and Chapter 1 as the "subjective-interpretive" approach, which I suggest in this book is necessary for correct social science. (I do not argue that objectivist approaches should be discarded completely: objectivist analysis has a definite role to play.) The approach I consider proper is similar to the one which has become traditional in microeconomic analysis, except that other personal goals besides the selfish and material are admitted to the analysis.

Given the importance of human motivation in models of policy analysis, it may be useful to devote a bit of attention to the exact nature of motivation and to what it would take to use a full teleological approach to social science. For this reason, the following section is devoted to some discussion of human purpose and intention. Some readers may want to skip down to the next section dealing with a framework for viewing rationality.

A Note on Purpose and Intention[3]

Motivation in social science arises from the presumption that human actions (those of any interest to social scientists) are taken for a *purpose* and, furthermore, the actions are not taken for a random purpose: they are taken for that purpose, or combination of purposes, considered by the decision-maker at that moment to be *best*.

Perhaps a better term for indicating the kind of purpose necessary to motivation is *intention*. Purposive behavior implies the presence of causation, but causation originating from human intention.[4] There are terms introduced by philosophers which are useful in understanding intentional behavior. "Registration" is a representational state which includes belief, perception, and plans, and which implies mentality or cognition, such that a person "registers" or apprehends that certain things will happen. "Singular reference" is the ability to attribute purposive behavior to specific individuals.[5] Thus, the intentionality which provides

---

[3]I wish to thank Scott Gordon and Julie Pedroni for useful comments on this section.

[4]Causation itself can, of course, also be purely mechanical or biological. While it is possible to put any causal law into the language of intention (my heart has the "goal" of making the blood circulate through my body), the teleological behavior of interest to social science and moral philosophy involves intention.

[5]Bennett (1976: 46); de Sousa (1987: 89).

the motivations required in social science includes: the apprehension of a goal, as goal, *and* its desirability; and the apprehension of means for achieving the goal and their function *as* means. The role of goals is central, as is the fact that, almost always, goals exist because of perceived needs.

The problem of subconscious behavior

If purpose must be present in establishing rationality, sooner or later we must ask how subconscious behavior affects the rationality concept. It is at least possible that the source of some motivation for purposive action is so deep in the subconscious mind that it is no longer subject to the human will and, thus, lacks full mental intentionality. This is a difficult area, even for persons with appropriate training. A useful treatment is provided by de Sousa who discusses mental intentionality in the emotions. He points out that if behavior cannot be directly attributed to conscious direction, there are three possibilities:

> ...When a putative "registration," although apparently teleological in function, is due to phylogenetic programming, there is no call for introducing the language of mentality. But when (1) it has been at least partly conditioned ontogenetically, and (2) it involves a level of relatively irreducible representations, and (3) it involves a capacity for singular reference as well as a general capacity for differential response, then it makes sense to speak of unconscious mentality.[6]

Thus, if purpose stems from a person's subconscious, it is still purposive behavior in the sense relevant to individual rationality if the subconscious events producing it are unique to that individual. At a minimum, unconscious mentality must be active, representational in nature, and not innate. These conditions are, of course, easier to establish theoretically than empirically. On the other hand, it would be just as difficult to establish, empirically, that the intentional nature of such behavior is *not*

[6]de Sousa (1987: 101).

true. For subconscious behavior, we can only conclude that individuals often act *as if* there are goals and reasons for their actions, of which they seem unaware, even though it is difficult to verify whether they actually do, in fact, have such reasons. Finally, however, it is worth observing that for most issues of interest in social science, we deal with *conscious* purposiveness, where empirical testing is meaningful.

A Framework for Viewing Rationality

We can now turn to the task of searching for a rationality construct proper for multi-dimensional policy analysis. We are interested mainly in providing a model of rationality which will allow us to investigate whether useful motivation statements can be made for collective goals, and to what extent such statements (as hypotheses) can be grounded empirically. We can apply rationality concepts either to individuals or groups, and then either with respect to the identity of the decision-maker or the nature of the goal. This gives rise to four possibilities, as follows (the first word indicates the identity of the thinker, the second the type goal):

1. *Individual-individual.* John Green's thinking on how best to take a trip by himself to Chicago.
2. *Individual-social.* John Green's thinking on the correct size of the US Central Intelligence Agency.
3. *Social-individual.* Ideas held in common by most group members on the best way for John Green to get to Chicago.
4. *Social-social.* Ideas held in common by most members of a church congregation on how best to enlarge their religious education building.

Needed are rationality statements about motivations (and, therefore, goals) for these four types of situation. These might be obtained through logical reasoning or empirically; and if the latter, inexpensively (from readily available data) or at considerable expense (from expensive polling or interview techniques). The derivation of moral principles only through logical reasoning in the manner suggested by Immanual Kant (see below) is an example of rationality obtained via reasoning alone. An example of an inexpensively obtained empirical result would be noting, through introspection and casual observation, that most persons are strongly motivated by money, while an example of expensive empirical investigation would be determining, through polling or interviewing techniques, the weights people place on alternative social goals.

Many social scientists have limited rationality concerns to what is known as the "instrumental approach," the central tenet of which is that rationality requires determining "correct" means to achieve given ends.[7] This implies that it is possible to ascertain what are "correct" means. The overall conclusion using the approach here is different: it is not possible to find "correct" means for achieving ends either for individuals or for groups. The key reason is that as social scientists we must proceed using the methods of science, and science — social science in particular — can never be completely free from error. Perfectionistic rationality judgments or infallible motivation predictions are impossible to obtain.

For those not already convinced, there are two reasons science cannot be free of errors. The first is financial. Except for highly trivial problems, empirical verification is expensive, and good empirical verification is still more expensive. If verification is prohibitively expensive, social scientists are likely to try to make do without it by, say, using "reasonable" assumptions. Sometimes, the financial motive is buttressed by ideological motives. For example, many economists feel it is correct, for reasons of methodological ideology, to assume tastes as given, while others who would greatly prefer to shed this assumption find it difficult to do so because of the very great expense of doing empirical studies on the development of consumer tastes from birth into adulthood.

The second reason for error is more theoretical: it is simply impossible to pin down perfect empirical proofs in social science, or in all of science for that matter. The fundamental reason is the induction problem, which lies behind the inability (for example) to "prove" that the sun will rise tomorrow from the fact that it has always done so in the past. This is often a fairly trivial and perfectionist problem which does not deter us from practical analysis, but sometimes the problem runs parallel with that

[7]See, *inter alia*, Elster (1989) and the quotation in the epigraph, Etzioni (1988); O'Sullivan (1987, Chap. 4) and Simon (1987).

of cost. The great example of this in economic science (also relevant to the rationality discussion) is the virtual impossibility of empirically verifying the consistency of individual choices. An apparent instance of irrational behavior, such as intransitive preferences, for example, may have, in fact, been due to a change in attitude that took place in a person's mind between the time he or she was asked about an attitude and the time he or she actually made the choice.[8] While the degree of difficulty introduced by such problems can vary, most of them can be dealt with in practical empirical analysis if some amount of predictive error is considered acceptable.

Individual rationality

There is more that can be said concerning perfectionism in rationality for cases involving individuals and groups. Beginning with the individual, there is no alternative but to accept the fact that a person's choice behavior is strictly his or her own doing, determined by his conceptualizion of his own good *and from nothing else.* As Professor Simon states:

> One point should be set immediately outside dispute. Everyone agrees that people have reasons for what they do. They have motivations, and they use reason (well or badly) to respond to these motivations and reach their goals. Even much or most of the behavior that is called abnormal involves the exercise of thought and reason. Freud was most insistent that there was method in madness, that neuroses and psychoses were patients' solutions — not very satisfactory solutions in the long run — for the problems that troubled them.[9]

Given that actions are taken for reasons the actor considers best, it must follow that from the perspective of the individual deciding upon an action

[8]For a good statement of the dangers of introspection and casual empiricism, see Churchman (1966: 250 ff).

[9]Simon (1987: 25).

to take at a particular moment of time, *it is not possible for the action to be considered irrational.*[10] This is because it is not possible to provide empirical proof to the contrary. The statement of James Coleman in the epigraph above to the effect that what is often considered irrational is only because we have not discovered the point of view of the actor is relevant here.[11]

Collective rationality

It seems dubious that canons of absolute correctness can be established for rationality with respect to groups, although there are those who would argue otherwise.[12] There are two ways in which ideal empirical verification of group rationality might be attempted. The first requires finding some mechanical way to go from individual to group preferences. This is impossible for well-known reasons: it runs afoul of the Arrow-type impossibility theorems or of the impossibility of making cardinal

[10]The concept that no action can be considered irrational from the actor's point of view has been termed by de Sousa (1987: 159–60) the principle of *minimal rationality,* the idea that "any intentional state amenable to rational criticism must fit some true description that represents the state as rational": "This is most easily explained by reference to actions. No event is an action unless it has teleological structure. Actions are determined by wants and beliefs. The wants determine the goal of the act (even if the act is done 'for its own sake'). The beliefs pertain to the circumstances and to ways of attaining the goal. And if the description of the act is sufficiently circumscribed, no distinction can be made between the act's teleological structure and its rationality¼This applies to the craziest act, providing it is still an act." The only possible exception to this statement would be in situations of extreme mental or physical illness, where the person is incapacitated to the point of incoherence.

[11]Coleman (1990: 18). For an additional, more technical reason for this, given the assumption of high standards of proof, see note 16 below. However, the principal reason irrationality cannot be established is that the investigator must accept the actor's reason for why he acted. A minor exception to this might be in the area of practical scientific knowledge, such as the fact that an open pan of gasoline will catch fire if a lighted match is thrown into it, or that engineers can construct an automobile that will move at 100 miles per hour. Persons denying these "facts" could be certified, presumably, as "irrational."

[12]As Scott Gordon reminds me, the very idea of "collective rationality" is an oxymoron, since human groups, as such, do not have minds.

interpersonal comparisons.[13] Social choice theorists are in virtual agreement that mechanical aggregation methods simply will not work.

The second way to provide a social rationality with ideal levels of empirical proof would be to use logical reasoning processes to derive a morality which is "correct." A group of philosophers or clergy might derive a set of first principles so persuasive that all will agree they serve as a fail-safe guide to the principles needed for a judgment-oriented rationality. If such an approach were possible, social scientists would have a non-scientific basis for rationality. There are those who argue for moral truths built up solely from logical reasoning — moral philosophers who believe in the "naturalistic fallacy." Given the potential damage to scientific rationality statements that could be caused by the naturalistic fallacy argument, we need to give it careful examination. This may seem a detour in our story here, but it is an absolutely crucial one.

Before proceeding to the naturalistic fallacy discussion, a comment concerning definitions would be useful. Arguments about the possibility of the naturalistic fallacy center on whether ethical propositions can or cannot be established using the methods of science. Thus, it seems crucial to define with precision exactly what this means; otherwise, the disagreement could be due only to semantic misunderstanding.

When a person holds an ethical belief, it is, of course, highly personal to him or her, but this does not mean that it is universally correct in some absolute sense, or that some scientific procedure can be found to establish it as such. A person may believe strongly that when there is (what she deems to be) a serious chance of great harm to one's educational future, an abortion is justified. There is no way of establishing this as being scientifically correct. If this is what is mean by those who claim the existence of a naturalistic fallacy, they are correct.

However, there is a second way the issue can be viewed. Many would agree that in social situations relevant to policy-making, it is of interest

[13]Arrow showed that it will always be possible to find "logical" ways to prove it impossible to aggregate preferences from individuals to groups. The logical requirement that is most often violated is that of "transitivity," which means that if one thing is preferred to a second, and the second preferred to a third, then the first must be preferred to the third (Arrow, 1963; Mueller, 1989, Chaps. 19 and 20). Cardinal measures are those which have a common origin and unit of measure, like inches on a yardstick.

to know whether a person holds a certain ethical belief or if a large majority of members of a group hold a certain belief. For example, policy-makers would find of interest the percentage of a population that holds the belief about abortion outlined above. This can be established empirically and is central to our understanding of motivation, which also can be established empirically. If this is what is being denied by proponents of a naturalistic fallacy, then I believe they are wrong. It may be questioned, perhaps, that this is the position being taken, but I suspect that it is. This is because so many social scientists and moral philosophers have held precisely that scientists *qua* scientists — natural or social — must *always* avoid *any* discussion of concepts in the ethical domain. In addition, many moral philosophers have argued, along with Kant, that correct ethical positions can be arrived at through the process of pure reason. It is this history which requires a discussion of the naturalistic fallacy here.

The Naturalistic Fallacy

A great many moral philosophers have held to the belief that there was something about moral philosophy that was "special;" that it could not be dealt with satisfactorily using the methods of science, but that some other approach — involving pure reason, perhaps — would be necessary. It is almost a mystical view. As one student of moral philosophy stated, "in our tradition [that of mainstream academic moral philosophy], the majority position has been that a scientific approach in values is not fully adequate; some even maintain that scientific inquiry is basically irrelevant to values."[14] Historically, the most important writer to attack ethical naturalism was the great philosopher Immanuel Kant.[15]

[14]Handy (1969: 13). The date of Handy's book should be noted. Given the increased criticism of the naturalistic fallacy argument by moral philosphers in recent years, his comment is somewhat less true now [see, for example, Simpson (1987)].

[15]Also important in this century was G.E. Moore, whose criticism of ethical naturalism was convincing to moral philosophers over many decades. However, Moore's arguments in recent times have increasingly been considered erroneous by moral philosophers (see Simpson, 1987, Chap. 1) and the references he cites. In the first half of the eighteenth century, David Hume noted how, in studying systems of morality, he found that persons

It is a great irony that Kant's view that moral philosophy was beyond scientific investigation was due, in part, to the great admiration he had for science itself. Kant was genuinely impressed with the possibilities of science, although this view was accompanied by a narrow view of its boundaries. He thought of "science" as being entirely composed of what we now call "physical science." He also thought all things that are knowable, that is, all "facts," to be those things which are generated by science (as he defined it). But this definition is just as important for what it leaves out as for what it includes. Kant's "science" provides no understanding of what is "noble" in human existence. In Kant's view, questions of good, or the "noble," are not generated by science and, hence, are not facts that can be known as facts. Instead, they reside in the domain of the will, which is outside of the "factual" world (the realm of "science").

The lack of knowledge about the human will could be viewed as a real weakness in Kant's epistemology, but instead Kant made something of a virtue out of it: he saw this factual ignorance as evidence of the existence in humans of a self-moving, spontaneous, and self-legislating free will. Thus, the "is" is not related to the "ought;" the "ought" floats free.[16] This lack of having an anchor also has its dangers, since it would seem difficult to build a coherent moral structure out of such "free-floating" conditions, but in Kant's hands this situation turns into a magnificent opportunity for humans to use their minds and to engage in fruitful thought processes. Morality, as such, is believed to derive from pure thought; facts, as such, are not required. And finally, when humans employ their thought processes in a manner which properly harnesses their own selfish desires, they cannot help but conclude that the only right actions are those which can be universalized, by which process they will arrive at the idea of the categorical imperative, and where humans

begin speaking of propositions with respect to human affairs using the verb *is*, but then after a while they subtly change to using the verb *ought*. Moral philosophers often cite this as the first reference to the "naturalistic fallacy." I believe it possible to find non-mystical reasons underlying Hume's statement. Persons doing this may implicitly be invoking a form of principal-agent utilitarianism, or they feel their own judgments superior to those of others, or they are taking categorical positions as a rhetorical device (Hume [1978 (1739)]; quoted in Beauchamp, 1982: 350).

[16]Subject, of course, to logical constraints.

can be treated only as ends, not means.[17] Kant is nothing if not consistent in his approach in that he insists that the categorical imperative and the generalization result come not from cognitive processes, but from volitional ones. The realm of morality is outside the factual world and, instead, is inside the world of pure reason.

As we know, Kant's moral theories have had great influence. His separation of facts from values has been a key ingredient of the "naturalistic fallacy" arguments put forward over the course of the century. Just as was true with Kant, I believe that the basis for naturalistic fallacy arguments is the tendency on the part of many moral philosophers to view science narrowly, as consisting of physical science only. If this is done, the domain of the will and questions of the satisfaction of desires cannot help but fall outside of science and, thus, outside of the world of "facts," or of "nature," and, hence, the existence of a naturalistic fallacy follows.

The obvious criticism of naturalistic fallacy arguments then, and also of Kant's more general argument that the will is not a part of the factual world, is that the approach incorporates a faulty definition of science and "nature."[18] While it is true that much in the social sciences dealing with human goals is not amenable to the controlled experiment, it would be difficult to deny that the social sciences, including psychology, are amenable to scientific methodology. Psychologists would take considerable umbrage at the suggestion that their discipline is not a science. There is no reason human attitude development cannot be examined scientifically; attitudes and beliefs are stable enough to generate testable predictive models for the choices that persons make, including choices with respect to collective goods.[19] On the other hand, if the skeptics are correct in saying that human motivation cannot be studied objectively, including

---

[17]Just as Rawls (1971) had no right to dictate what outcome would obtain from the deliberations of persons in the initial condition, neither did Kant have the right to dictate the nature of the conclusions people would reach in whatever "initial condition" he envisaged.

[18]By "nature" is meant the physical world, the world of "things" (see Simpson, 1987: 113 ff).

[19]In this respect, it is interesting to note, however, that the strongest criticism that can be made by the philosophers of social science is that economics (and so, presumably, psychology too) does not deserve the status of "science," because of the inability to make demand predictions of this kind, for *any* goods, individual or collective. A good statement of this criticism has been made by Bruce Caldwell, who questions the ability of economists

the empirical test, then the existence of a "naturalistic fallacy" is more likely. My argument in this book is that human motivation *can* be studied with the methods of science (in the definitional sense outlined above), and that these critics are simply wrong.

Shared Values

With no naturalistic fallacy, there are no moral values or rationality propositions which are absolutes, a conclusion which places causation in social science on an insecure, relativistic foundation. To this dark conclusion, there is one hopeful possibility for useful social science, particularly in policy analysis, at least sometimes, and that is the likely existence in many instances of widely shared values among the members of groups.

The shared value idea has been rather neglected in recent times, which is remarkable since classical writers such as Hobbes, Hume, and Adam Smith stated the idea quite explicitly and considered it of fundamental importance. These writers believed that humans could arrive at shared values through introspection, as indicated in the following remark of Hobbes:

> ...whosoever looketh into himself, and considereth what he doth, when he does *think, opine, reason, hope, fear,* etc., and upon what grounds; he shall thereby read and know what are the thoughts and passions of all other men upon the like occasions.[20]

It should not be difficult to find widely shared values from our observation of others, introspection, and our sense of empathy, as well as empirical

to predict choices on the basis that there must always be a period of elapsed time between when we ask someone what he would choose (and why) and when he or she makes the actual choice, during which period the person may have changed his or her mind (Caldwell, 1982: 158). This point is well taken, but I believe overly perfectionistic. Just because a person could have changed his mind does not mean that he changed it in fact, and this is a process subject to empirical test. *No science of any kind makes claims of being able to make predictions without the possibility of error.*

[20]Hobbes (1960: 6), quoted in Ostrom (1986: 231). As Ostrom points out, David Hume and Adam Smith enunciated similar sentiments (see note 31 in Chapter 3).

investigation. Broad agreement among group members, where it exists, can provide empirical foundations for hypotheses concerning motivation as well as for highly accepted ways to reach group goals, that is, for operational notions of rationality and even moral judgments.

Linguistic demands for shared values

Interestingly enough, the best place to begin to look for insights for understanding the existence of shared values and their importance is in the area of linguistics. Donald Davidson argues persuasively that viable human communication could not take place without a significant area of common ground of agreement as to what is being discussed.[21] It would not be possible to understand what others are saying to us unless we share many of their ideas, especially beliefs, but also preferences and desires. Such beliefs, preferences, and desires are inferred from choice behavior and from ideas held in common as to what the choice behavior means. A similar process takes place with respect to interpersonal welfare comparisons, which are only possible if persons have a basis on which to make them. If person A is to make a welfare comparison of person B with person C, three sets of values come into play, those of B and C, and those of the evaluator A. The welfare comparison itself will not be intelligible unless there is a considerable area of common understanding and shared fundamental values between A, B, and C.[22]

Davidson also shows how the needs of the communication process itself create pressures toward commonly shared values in both beliefs and preferences. For belief, the pressure is toward transitivity of preferences, a point of obvious relevance to our present topic. Pressures also arise in the communication process with respect to preference agreement. Because humans must communicate efficiently with each other, there are large areas of agreement, "essential determinants of the content of the beliefs, desires, and preferences that we attribute to each other."[23] As

[21]Davidson (1980, 1986).
[22]Davidson (1986: 196–198).
[23]Scanlon (1991: 36).

Scanlon states, "If Davidson is correct, then there is no such thing as understanding the strength of other people's preferences without supposing that they assign the same values as we do to many alternatives:"[24]

> ...In justifying our actions and our requests to one another, we normally make our case by explaining why it is that we want a certain thing rather than merely by citing the fact that we do prefer it and indicating the strength of that preference. In a situation in which there is real disagreement over what is to be done, (refusing to do this)...amounts to deliberate incommunicativeness,...a refusal to lay out the reasons for one's preference so that others can understand them and can judge whether these are reasons that they are prepared to recognize generally as having a claim on them.[25]

An important factor in judging what is "rational" involves being able to explain one's reasons in a convincing fashion.

"Normal" reaction to sociality and social goals

Due to commonalities in our early emotional and educational training, there are many conceptions shared by most persons in any society as to what is, in general, valuable in life.[26] This is especially true with those parts of our lives which involve social interactions. As Griffin states,

> ...(I)t is a common (even common-sensical) view that...things are valuable only because (they are) seen from a personal point of view, only because somebody takes them up as a goal — call them "personal values."...But it is doubtful that there are any such things as "personal values." For me to see something of value, from any angle at all, requires my being able to see it against a backdrop of general human aims; my own personal

[24]*Ibid*.

[25]Scanlon (1991: 38).

[26]See de Sousa (1987, Chap. 7), Frank (1988, Chap. 8) and Kagan (1984, Chaps. 4 and 5).

> aims are not enough...To see anything as valuable, we have got to see it as an instance of something generally intelligible as valuable and, furthermore, as valuable for any (normal) human.[27]

Origin of shared values

While discussing shared values, it will be useful to consider how they originate, a topic which will assume importance in the empirical investigation of how values and motivations develop. Why do groups have the shared values that they have? To answer this, we must first inquire into why persons have beliefs and opinions in the first place, in particular about social issues considered important. As was discussed in the Introduction, such reasons stem from the reaction of persons to the *perceived needs* of their society. Groups have needs, as do individuals. All groups, as groups, face problems; problems which are perceived by their members. The fundamental force driving the beliefs and opinions of group members, with respect to the problems facing the group, is their understanding of what must be done to overcome them. In Griffin's words, "For one to see something of value, from any angle at all, requires him or her to be able to see it against a background of general human aims."[28]

An important contribution to our understanding of the origin of shared values comes from recent work concerning the learning process for emotions in the child development literature. Jerome Kagan has cited considerable empirical evidence that all persons seem to go through a number of similar stages in childhood, in which they naturally learn to take the social viewpoint. This learning does not depend completely upon direct instruction by parents and teachers. Emotions which develop naturally and perform this function include empathy, a sense of responsibility not to harm others, anxiety about social disapproval, and self-esteem (see Chapter 3). Kagan also points out that these developmental steps seem to be quite similar across cultures and, if true, this provides a common source for *universally* shared values.[29]

---

[27]Griffin (1991: 50–51).

[28]Griffin (1991: 50–51).

[29]Kagan (1984, especially Chaps. 4 and 5).

Many other writers in a variety of contexts have touched on the derivation and importance of the shared value idea. The early twentieth century American economist, B.M. Anderson, spoke of the existence of a "mind of society."[30] Bellah and his associates, in their interview study of American values, speak of shared concepts with respect to ideas of individualism and conclude that "in spite of their (Americans') differences, they all to some degree share a common moral vocabulary, which we propose to call the 'first language' of American individualism..."[31] In their study summary, they conclude that

> ...we have never been, and still are not, a collection of private individuals who, except for a conscious contract to create a minimal government, have nothing in common. Our lives make sense in a thousand ways, most of which we are unaware of, because of traditions that are centuries, if not millennia, old. It is these traditions that help us to know that it does make a difference who we are and how we treat one another.[32]

Writers such as Gauthier and Habermas suggest that important shared values have a contractarian basis, that rational persons make implicit contracts in view of perceived returns to long-term cooperation.[33] Ortuno and Roemer present an interesting theory concerning how ideas about cooperation could spread through a society from a mechanism involving the spread of "local expertise."[34] Other writers such as Koford and Miller, Harsanyi, Sugden, and Ullman-Margalit implicitly or explicitly discuss the origin of shared values as part of the process of the development of norms and conventions.[35] And finally, the shared value concept is important in the arts and literature, in that artistic creation (in particular, fiction

[30]Anderson (1911: 84).

[31]Bellah *et. al.* (1985: 20).

[32]Bellah *et. al.* (1985: 282).

[33]Gauthier (1986, Chap. 5 and *passim)*. Habermas' contribution is discussed in de Jasay (1989: 97).

[34]Ortuno-Ortin and Roemer (1991).

[35]Koford and Miller (1991), Harsanyi (1982), Sugden (1986) and Ullman-Margalit (1977). Also consult the other papers in the Koford-Miller volume.

and drama) will only be effective (believable) if legitimated by widely shared values.[36]

Rationality and Emotion: Summing Up

Contemporary economic methodology has become an awkward combination of the empiricism of the objectivists and the teleology of the subjectivists. While economists have tried to adhere to the path of treating humans as objects, they have, in practice, followed the lead of the Austrians and others and taken the subjective seriously although eschewing actual empirical examination of motivation in favor of the belief — based on simple observation and introspection — that humans pursue goals involved with selfishly seeking material gain. This characterization of motivation, which has come to be called "cognitive rationality," has been the driving force behind most twentieth century economic theory.

Besides the emphasis on selfish material goals, the rationality approach used by most modern economists deals with means, but not ends: the "instrumental" approach to rationality. Economists have rather stubbornly clung to the idea that ends are given and are outside the scope of their analytical concern; their attention is given to the methods by which goals are achieved, methods involving straightforward utility maximization (translate as *wealth* or *profit* maximization) as viewed in certain intelligent ways. Following Benn and Montimore (and similar to numerous others), O'Sullivan describes instrumental rationality — which he terms "practical" rationality — in the following terms:

> An action is said to be practically rational if it meets and follows three conditions: [a] the action must be directed to some goal;

---

[36]In his article "The History of Aesthetics" in the *Encyclopedia of Philosophy*, Monroe Beardsley (1967: 28) quotes Immanuel Kant as arguing, with respect to validation in the arts, that "this can only be done¼if it can be shown that the conditions presupposed in such a judgment are not confined to the individual who makes it, but may reasonably be ascribed to all rational beings¼Since the general possibility of sharing knowledge with each other, which may be taken for granted, presupposes that in each of us there *is* a cooperation of imagination and understanding, it follows that every rational being has the *capacity* to feel, under appropriate perceptual conditions, the harmony of the cognitive powers."

[b] the goal aimed at must be consistent with other goals pursued by the agent; and [c] the action must be geared to achieve the maximum level of the attainment of the goal subject to the constraints of the agent's situation and in light of the information available to the agent.

O'Sullivan also discusses how Benn and Montimore posit another, stronger, concept: "epistemic rationality." "We say that a proposition is epistemically rational if we have absolutely conclusive proof of it."[37] This stronger concept, as most writers realize, is simply impossible to realize for reasons discussed above. Such an assertion would require a group rationality to which no exception could be taken. But the concept which many persons consider more practical — instrumental rationality — reasonable as it seems to be, is just as impossible. It requires a collective rationality and again, as shown above, collective rationality positions are impossible to attain. To see the problem with instrumental rationality requires that we deal with the question of *who is to decide* which method of pursuing a given goal is the correct one, or which goals are consistent with the other goals pursued by the agent, or which method will achieve "the maximum level of the goal subject to the constraints of the agent's situation." For that matter, we can reasonably ask who, in fact, had the power to decide that rationality was to deal with means and not ends in the first place.

Martin Hollis, in his essay "Rational Preferences," also comments on the problems presented by the "rational man" model from standard microeconomics, according to which a person's preferences are "given, current, homogeneous, and determining." The "given" preferences, he claims, are usually taken to mean short-run preferences, and he asks why this should be.[38] (Indeed, how does one decide on a proper time horizon?) Also, the assumption of given ends raises questions about human identity. One must consider ends as well as means if the rational agent is "no longer just a throughput. The man of honor prices the manner of actions, whereas the textbook agent prices only their consequences."[39] The homogenous assumption denies that there may be desires of differing

[37]O'Sullivan (1987: 222), citing Benn and Montimore (1976).
[38]Hollis (1996: 50).
[39]Hollis (1996: 54).

strength,[40] and the determining condition is contrary to the existence of such things as the "paradoxes of collective action."[41]

Thus, no "proper" rationality is possible. There is no way to aggregate group preferences empirically; logical constructs such as that of Immanuel Kant do not hold water either. Nor is it possible to second-guess the rationality of individuals — either with respect to means or ends — because we must assume that any individual decision-maker correctly followed his own conceptualization of his own good. There are no "Answers" with a capital A, with the possible exception concerning straightforward science statements alluded to earlier. The only definite answers we can find with respect to human motivation are those we can obtain empirically. Subjectivists are optimistic in this regard; objectivists pessimistic. The fact that widely shared values exist in most societies should make the task somewhat easier. And some valuable social science may not require empirical estimates for motivation, beyond establishing which goals are generally considered important.

The conclusion that human motivation, and hence human values, can only be found empirically places values held in society, shared or otherwise, upon a foundation of relativity, as observed earlier. It is worth noting, however, that there are three features about the origin of values, often shared values, which can introduce considerable stability into the values held, even if absolutes remain illusive. First, and foremost, are the goals themselves, which are based on social problems and have a fixed quality. The existence and nature of major social problems can be objectively noted and are subject to broad agreement. Second, the process of noting important social problems is itself subject to consensus-building via social communication as described above.[42] This also extends to discussions of what ought to be done, although, again, there will be much less consensus about solutions to problems than about the existence of the

[40]Hollis (1996: 55).

[41]Hollis (1996: 57).

[42]It is interesting to notice the process by which shared values taken as accepted in "more advanced," or "civilized," societies spread to more backward and repressive societies and eventually take root. Efforts in recent times by highly respected members of the Chinese intelligentsia to petition the Chinese leadership to end political repression is one example (see Tyler, *New York Times, 1995*). Also of interest in this respect is the model of the spread of shared values presented in Ortuno-Ortin and Roemer (1991).

problems themselves. And third, stability is introduced because of the similarities among individuals in the process of emotional development.[43]

What can be said about the age-old debate concerning the separation of science from ethics? In the scenario the objectivists have in mind, the methods of science are applied in the natural sciences and in that part of social science which can be deduced from human behavior. Aspects of the human experience highly related to inner motivation, feelings, moral values, and so forth stay outside: emotion, religion, art, and whatnot. The approach suggested here, on the other hand, is that all human goals are to be treated in the same way and all are equally rational. (More on this in the next chapter.) Furthermore, analysis with respect to *all of them* can be pursued empirically by finding out which goals are important to individuals. There is no separation of science from ethics in this sense. The sense in which there is separation is the one mentioned above — the ethical views of individuals cannot be allowed to influence scientific analysis. But scientific analysis itself can and will include descriptive material on how persons, and groups of persons, value non-material (what used to be called "ethical") goals and how this may relate to policy analysis.

In the Introduction, I outlined the features of good policy analysis. The most useful and important is that in which social scientists merely provide information concerning the trade-offs that must be made to achieve the more important social goals. If this is true, the empirical work of greatest interest for policy analysis purposes, it seems to me, is determining which social goals are important to sizable subsets of any group.

---

[43]Steven Lukes (1982: 262) argues that this constitutes the only truly viable argument against relativism: "I start from the position...that in the very identification of beliefs and *a fortiori* of belief systems, we must presuppose commonly shared standards of truth and inference, and that we must further presuppose a commonly shared core of beliefs whose content or meaning is fixed by application of the standards. Neither the evidence of cross-cultural variation in schemes of classification, nor that of radically divergent theoretical schemes or styles of reasoning, nor arguments for the possible applicability of alternative logics undermine this position, which must, indeed, be accepted before the problem of relativism can be set up in the first place." Barnes and Bloor (1982: 36) comment that Lukes and others have not made serious attempts to define this common core, or to mark its boundaries. Presumably, some of the common emotional responses pointed to by Kagan might qualify as core components (also see Hollis, 1982; Lukes, 1973).

Chapter 3

Emotion

The title of this book strikes many people as a joke: it is commonly assumed that emotions are substantive and irrational, or at best arational...

Ronald de Sousa
The Rationality of Emotion, 1987

By reconceptualizing accounts of passion — including the role of the passions in constituting human beings as moral and political actors — feminists have often related differently to the passions than have other thinkers, adopting a unique, dual strategy for thinking about them. The first move is to demonstrate the feminine capacity for nurturance, love, empathy, and care for others; the second is to rescue the capacity of the self so reconstructed in terms of moral and political agency — that which has been denied to emotional beings in general, or women in particular.

Cynthia Burack
The Problem of the Passions, 1994

The fact that evaluative language is selectively applied to thoughts and acts that can provoke anxiety, shame, guilt, or pride implies the existence of a special class of ideas. I shall call this class a *standard*,...

Jerome Kagan
The Nature of the Child, 1984

There is a widespread convention according to which emotional concerns are not as important as cognitive concerns. It is a convention more subscribed to by males than by females, and its importance varies widely by culture. For the most part, the more male-dominated the culture, the more important the convention. Likely, it is correlated with the rationality conventions of mainstream economists discussed in the preceding chapter, although it is hard to know what the causation patterns between the two conventions have been. It is likely a strong factor in the sizable "gender gap" that existed in the American general election campaigns in 1996. It involves the belief that emotions are not quite rational — "sissy stuff" — and, therefore, of less importance than cognitive (and especially selfish material) concerns.

I believe this convention is one of the more egregious examples of the damage caused to social policy-making by the neglect of collective goods, if, as I hope to show, conventions based on the emotions are collective goods, for which the demands are as rational as the demands for any other goods. Also discussed in this chapter is an area closely related to the emotions — involving collective goods important to any society (and often neglected in policy forums) — the arts.

Most persons find the emotional domain quite fascinating, even when they denigrate its importance. The importance of emotions seems to have waned somewhat in modern times. Classical writers such as Thomas Hobbes, David Hume, and Adam Smith considered emotions, which they termed "passions," rather important.[1] In modern economics, in particular, the emotions seem to be overlooked. In Chapter 1, we saw how moral concerns (which closely involve emotion) were important to economists before, but not after, the marginalist revolution. Given this timing, the developments in economics since the marginalist revolution may be somewhat implicated in the low esteem in which emotions have been held in modern times.

In investigating the role of emotions, we are singularly fortunate because of the recent publication by Ronald de Sousa of his *tour de force*, *The Rationality of Emotion*,[2] which has been an important source of material used in this chapter. de Sousa is himself quite succinct in his reaction to the widespread convention of denigrating the importance of emotion:

---

[1]See note 31.

[2]de Sousa (1987).

> The title of this book strikes many people as a joke: it is commonly assumed that emotions are substantive and irrational, or at best arational...By and large, common sense holds that emotions are both subjective and irrational...This belief (that emotions are subjective and irrational) has tended to have either of two equally deplorable effects. Among those who prize knowledge and rationality, it promotes the idea that emotions are essentially unimportant, or important only as distractions from the serious business of life. On the other hand, given the irrationalist premises that pervade much of current culture, it fosters the automatic justification of any behavior on the grounds that one must "go with one's feelings:" since feelings are "purely subjective," no sensible debate or rationalization of them is possible.[3]

In order to show that the neglect of emotion translates into harmful neglect of collective goods, it is necessary to show, first, that important aspects of human emotions can be identified as collective goods; and second, that emotions themselves can be considered rational, since collective goals *are* rational goals. My objective in this chapter is to establish both points, but before doing that, it is necessary to explore the nature of emotions, including how emotion differs from the process of cognitive reasoning.

The Nature of Emotion

While most of us feel that we have a good idea of what an emotion is, the apparent simplicity of the idea is misleading. Disputation among philosophers (and in this century, psychologists) as to its exact nature traces back to Aristotle. A widely used psychology textbook about emotion begins by stating that "as commonly conceived, emotion is bound up with feeling." It then proceeds to give the definition from the *Shorter Oxford English Dictionary* that emotion is "a mental feeling or affection, distinct from cognitions or volitions," and concludes that the concept means a lot of things to a lot of people and "at present emotion defies definition."[4]

[3]de Sousa (1987: 241–242, 142–143).

[4]Strongman (1978: 1–2).

The word "emotion" comes from the latin "movere," meaning "to move," the idea being that to be emotional is to be literally moved, in the bodily sense. Thomas Hobbes spoke of "passions" as "the interior beginnings of voluntary *motions.*"[5] However, there grew a tradition among philosophers whereby emotions were viewed as being more exclusively a mental phenomenon, a tradition which Lyons feels can be traced to the influence of Decartes, who viewed emotions as arising from the soul and, thus, were primarily a mental state, even though they might sometimes trigger physical responses.[6] Psychologists have also tended to accept the mentality of emotion in terms of causation but, consistent with their infatuation in modern times with behaviorism, they have tended to seek explanations for emotion in terms of behavioral consequences. This preoccupation with behavior has led psychologists into considerable frustration since it is easy to demonstrate that emotions are sometimes experienced where there is little or no operant behavior. Grief is a good example, but likely there is no emotion for which it is not possible to find instances where the emotion was experienced in the complete absence of outward behavior ramifications.[7]

In the past decade or two, there seems to be growing in both philosophy and psychology a more cognitive view of emotion, following a tradition tracing its roots to Aristotle but neglected in the twentieth century because of the Decartes and behaviorism influences. As Lyons states, the accepted view for the cognitive theory of emotion "is one that makes some aspect of thought, usually a belief, central to the concept of emotion and, at

[5]Hobbes (1962, Chap. 6; emphasis added).

[6]Lyons (1980: 60).

[7]For this reason, modern psychologists have not been very successful in dealing with the subject of emotions, sometimes giving up in frustration as evidenced in the textbook quotation presented above. As Lyons (1980: 25) notes: "...sections on emotions in textbooks of psychology often give a purely descriptive account of the observed physiological and behavioral aspects of particular emotions without even making any attempt to show why such behavioral or physiological patterns are to be grouped together as emotional, or are to be identified as this or that emotion. So one of the marked influences of...(behaviorism) has been to curtail attempts to give answers to the question 'Why do we say this group of behavioral responses are emotional ones?'...The failure of the behaviorist account of emotions has led, in some quarters, to a total abandonment of the attempt to make sense of emotion." This is, of course, one more example of the counter-productive effects of the scientism that has pervaded modern psychology.

least in some cognitive theories, essential to distinguishing the different emotions from one another."[8] More recently, the concept of "belief" is interpreted in the sense of being an evaluation. The evaluation then becomes important in that it gives rise to motivations leading to real or potential actions. As Arnold puts it, "Emotion seems to include not only the appraisal of how this thing or person will affect me, but also a definite pull toward or away from it," where "appraisal" is meant to be "a direct and immediate evaluative judgment of an object as 'good or bad, pleasurable or dangerous for us,' though this evaluative judgment can be reflective as well."[9]

It should be emphasized that the increased acceptance of the cognitive by students of emotion in recent times does not mean that feelings are unimportant. Here, we can visualize a continuum where all human mental processes are some combination of cognitive and feeling. Points along the continuum would be viewed as an open set, there being no instances of either the pure cognitive or pure feeling. (Although most of us can undoubtedly visualize instances which come close.)[10] Stated in everyday language, an emotion is experienced by a person when something happens to him which he evaluates as affecting him personally in an important way. This triggers both a physical reaction as well as a more or less automatic (or quasi-automatic, where cognitive reasoning is also involved) wish to pursue an appropriate ("correct") objective to deal with the situation brought about by whatever happened to him in the first place. "Physical reaction" here means either a palpable bodily effect, such as increased heartbeat, or an affective feeling, such as love, or both.

---

[8]Lyons (1980: 33).

[9]Arnold (1960, Vol. 1: 172, 175), as quoted in Lyons (1980: 45).

[10]A good discussion of the synthesis between feeling and cognition, along with the problems that still remain in describing and defining emotion, is to be found in William Alston's article on emotion in the *Encyclopaedia of Philosophy* (1967). After concluding that no single characteristic is enough to define what an emotion is with precision, he suggests that the best that can be done is "to construe an emotion as some complex of evaluation, bodily upset, and sensation thereof" (Alston, 1967: 485). That is to say, some combination of cognitive evaluation, physiological effects (which, from the context, is what I consider Alston to mean by "upset"), and feeling. He suggests that *usually* all three factors are present, although sometimes one or two of them may not be, which is what makes the concept so illusive.

Can Emotions Be Considered Rational?

In his book, Ronald de Sousa carefully describes the complete set of circumstances present with the existence of an emotion.[11] The more important of these include the following: there is a *target* to which the emotion relates; there is a motivating *focus of attention* or agent which is causal in nature; the emotion has an *aim* so there is purpose involved; and the motivating agent or agents are *rationally related* to the emotion they cause. For example, suppose a hiker comes across a grizzly bear which appears angry for having been disturbed. The emotion is fear, the motivating agent is an angry bear; the aim is to remove himself from harm's way, and few persons would consider this aim or motivation not to be rationally related to the emotion being felt and the target of the emotion.

Is there anything about emotions which should cause us to think they are inherently less rational than other human volitional activities? de Sousa argues, to my mind convincingly, that there is no difference. In the formulation of normal market demand for widgets, a person first notes a perceived need, next forms a goal of obtaining the item if this is possible and if the perceived benefit per dollar cost justifies it, then proceeds to purchase a widget. The emotion experience described above contains the same set of characteristics. The noting of a perceived need can occur suddenly, as in the example given, or slowly, as when a person gradually becomes angry when she perceives a condition in her office gradually getting worse. The same is true for the demand for market-tradable goods. A person might gradually notice that he is getting hungry, or that his automobile is becoming undependable, or he can experience a sudden event, a pang of hunger or the failure of a starter-motor, which triggers his demand motivation. The perceived need triggers a motivation to do something in both kinds of situation; it causes the person to define a new *goal* he or she wishes to reach. In both cases, the person may or may not take some overt action to move closer to this goal, in the process taking into account the opportunity cost of doing so in terms

[11]de Sousa (1987, Chap. 5).

of moving further away from other goals.[12] The process in both kinds of situation is identical.

Despite the similarity of the process of forming goals from perceived needs in both cognitive rationality and emotion, in light of the emotion's "bad reputation," could it be that there are some special phenomena restricted to the emotion domain where rationality fails? Three areas might qualify: extreme emotional behavior, insanity, and the subconscious.

It is in the area of excessive responses where emotion has earned much of the "bad press" referred to above. A person becomes "frozen with fear" and fails to extricate himself from a dangerous situation when this would have been possible had he remained calm. As the result of an insult, a man in a bar punches another man in the jaw where the second man is larger, meaner-looking, and possibly armed. Such behavior surely can be considered irrational according to the definitions developed in the preceding chapter.[13] There can be no doubt that such behavior can be considered "erroneous," (in the short run at least; see the previous note), but it is possible to argue that equally erroneous behavior sometimes obtains when emotion is not present. A diabetic person, fully knowing better, persists in eating chocolate candy. I doubt if emotion has any special claim on erroneous judgment. It could be argued, perhaps, that emotional error is more difficult to correct, but this is doubtful as well. Hair-trigger tempers can be reformed just as well as can alcohol addiction.

While insanity is sometimes characterized as "emotional disorder," it would appear that it is much more general than that. Students of schizophrenia, for example, tend to think of it strictly as an illness. Studies of schizophrenia show both a strong genetic factor and important family influences (themselves often of genetic origin), but discussions of schizophrenia do not seem to distinguish between logical and emotional dysfunction.[14]

---

[12]A motivation can, of course, take place without an overt action resulting at that time. The individual may simply note to himself that this is an area that needs to be watched for the possibility of taking an action in the future.

[13]As Frank points out, there may be long-term benefits which accrue even to "apparently irrational" emotional behavior of this sort. A smaller man is ill-advised to punch a larger one, but if he (or smaller men in general) obtains a reputation for quick and somewhat "ill-considered" response, it could be that others (even if bigger) will leave him alone to avoid "trouble" (Frank, 1988, Chap. 1 and *passim*).

[14]Smythies (1968, Chap. 1), Wolman (1977: 45) and Corsini (1994: 345).

The role of the subconscious was addressed to some extent in the preceding chapter, where it was concluded that subconscious behavior cannot be considered other than purposive. Since emotion involves purpose as well, again it seems dubious whether the emotional domain can be set aside as a special case, although it is true that purpose conceived in coldly rational terms often seems to have a weaker role in the emotional domain. This is a difficult topic, far beyond this author's competence, but it seems likely that for our purposes in this book that any differences in the operation of the subconscious in cognitive rationality and emotion can be disregarded.[15]

In sum, it is possible to conclude, along with de Sousa and a number of other recent commentators, that there is little justification for the argument that the emotional domain is outside the realm of cognitive rationality. This will become even clearer as we turn to the question of how emotions are formed.

Emotion Formation and Collective Goods

Having established that emotion can be considered part of the rational domain, we can now consider the relationship between the emotions and collective goods. Emotion plays a key role in the process by which humans form their moral beliefs, a role best understood if we have some understanding of the origin of emotions.

Our best guide for understanding the formation process for emotions is, again, de Sousa:

> My hypothesis is this: we are made familiar with the vocabulary of emotion by association with *paradigm scenarios*. These are drawn first from our daily life as small children and later reinforced by the stories, art, and culture to which we are exposed. Later

[15]To be sure, the operation of emotion in the deep subconscious mind sometimes appears to escape rationality. One noteworthy example of this was the experience of a former Miss America, Marilyn Van Derber, who entered into a state of catatonic helplessness suddenly at age 39 when her daughter reached the age when she (the mother) had first been sexually abused by her father. Before that time, she had successfully sublimated the experience, having lived an apparently happy life (see Zaloudek, 1996; *Denver Post*, 1995).

> still, in literate cultures, they are supplemented and refined by literature. Paradigm scenarios involve two aspects: first, a situation type providing the characteristic *objects* of the specific emotion type...; and second, a set of characteristic or "normal" *responses* to the situation, where normality is first a biological matter and very quickly becomes a cultural one. It is in large part in virtue of the response component of the scenarios that emotions are commonly held to *motivate*...An essential part of education consists in identifying these responses, giving the child a name for them in the context of the scenario, and then teaching it that it is experiencing a particular emotion. This is, in part, what is involved in learning to feel the right emotions which, as Aristotle knew, is a central part of moral education.[16]

We are taught emotional reactions according to the type of situation for which they are relevant, and then the expected "normal" response which is appropriate. These are reactions in terms of feelings, but they go along hand in glove with cognitive responses. The emotional component is important in that it gives the child the ability to react quickly to situations *by type*. Emotional training imparts to a child (and later the adult) the ability to make mental short cuts through a complex world in a way that would not be possible if we had to make a separate cognitive diagnosis of each situation we may find ourselves in, since any two situations are seldom exactly the same. (The extreme complexity that would obtain in a world without these short cuts is known as the "philosophers frame problem.")[17] This is how a culture "pre-programs" its members to respond to situations, although one must be careful not to carry this analogy too far since, with few exceptions, each individual maintains ultimate control over the nature of his or her own reactions.

While a person's education, with respect to emotion, begins with earliest childhood — the most important time — emotional education continues throughout a person's lifetime, although the older we get the more difficult it becomes to modify our fundamental emotional patterns or to increase our emotional repertoire. We do so "with increasing

[16]de Sousa (1987: 182–183).
[17]de Sousa (1987: 192–194).

resistance," as de Sousa puts it.[18] The degree to which this process takes place depends in part upon intelligence and sensitivity, and some emotions are more thought-dependent than others:

> If the paradigm scenario cannot be apprehended without complex language skills,...we shall not expect to find in someone who lacks these skills an emotion specifically tuned to that scenario. That is why, as Iris Murdoch has put it, "the most essential and fundamental aspect of culture is the study of literature, since this is an education in how to picture and understand human situations." [On the other hand,] pre-linguistic responses such as flight or attack can subsist to define so-called primitive emotions of fear and rage.[19]

It appears from the human development literature that we learn the greater part of our emotional responses at a very young age in two ways. First, we learn from authority figures, parents, teachers, and so forth; and secondly, through a natural process which Kagan views as a kind of inner direction where we "figure things out" on our own. Thus, there are four ways in which humans receive moral instruction: combinations of direct and indirect instruction on the one hand, and of inner- and outer-directed instruction on the other. By "indirect instruction" is meant instruction coming through emotion from the construction of "paradigm scenarios" meant to place social choice situations into categories which allow mental short cuts, as described above. "Direct instruction" is that which proceeds one lesson at a time (typically administered by parents or teachers), a mechanical accumulation in the mind of experienced events. "Inner-directed instruction" is self-instruction, "outer-directed instruction" is instruction by others. Such are the capabilities of the human mind that very little of this instruction, no matter what the type, is long separated from emotional categories. Hence emotion is important to all moral attitudes and beliefs.

Under the influence of behaviorism, psychologists over much of this century tended to stress the importance of direct outer-directed moral instruction. In recent decades, this has changed with more emphasis on

---

[18]de Sousa (1987: 184).

[19]*Ibid.* The Murdoch reference is Murdoch (1970: 34.)

the role of emotions, both outer-directed through the paradigm scenario device, and through inner-directed emotional instruction obtained naturally as a result of the emotional stages we pass through during the first years of our lives. Some of the most important work which has been done in espousing the latter approach is that of a student of child development, Jerome Kagan, most particularly in his 1984 book, *The Nature of the Child*. According to Kagan, the process of emotional maturation involves a partial changeover from outer direction to inner direction:

> I do not suggest that exposure to adults who praise the proper and punish the improper is irrelevant, but I do believe that all children have a capacity to generate ideas about good and bad states, actions, and outcomes.[20]

Emotions as collective goods

Despite their poor reputation, upon reflection most persons would surely agree that emotions are socially useful. This may be true in any number of ways, but at least three immediately come to mind. First, emotional training allows us to respond quickly to situations and dig our way through considerable complexity, dealing with the "philosophers' frame problem." Secondly, it is through the emotions that persons derive a sense of altruism toward their fellows. And thirdly (an extension of the second way), emotions are important to the process by which persons learn morality and ethics. The first of these — the quick mental sorting ability — is of great social importance, and civilization as we know it would hardly function did we not have this capacity. But since the collective goods of interest to us here are those subject to some degree of social control, further discussion is problematic since these abilities seem to obtain quite naturally in the early training of everyone.[21]

The other two uses, which perhaps can be considered together as one, are more amenable to social intervention. As mentioned, instruction in

[20]Kagan (1984: 130–131).

[21]If this assessment is in error, then presumably a society could affect this capacity and might wish to do so, improving it where necessary, if this could be done expeditiously.

altruism and morals obtains in two ways: outer-directed learning of emotional responses and moral standards from authority figures by way of rational and emotional instruction; and from the development of inner-directed moral standards. Kagan explains the latter process:

> The fact that evaluative language is selectively applied to thoughts and acts that can provoke anxiety, shame, guilt, or pride implies the existence of a special class of ideas. I shall call this class a *standard*...Admission of the idea of standard into the working vocabulary or psychology is based on the fact that some ideas and actions are classed as good or bad, and each evaluation is related to feeling states.[22]

In the development of standards, the changeover from outer-directed to inner-directed emotional instruction begins at a very young age and is a very important part of the process of maturation. Kagan supports his contentions with extensive references to the empirical child development literature, including a number of his own studies. Children first become aware of standards some time after the middle of their second year when they begin to be aware that something is wrong with such things as broken objects, torn clothing, and the like.

The evidence suggests that a child's concern about such matters is caused by an ability he or she has acquired to create representations of how things "should appear in their ideal state as a function of how they normally appear."[23] Also, at about the age of two, a child seems to acquire the ability to project his own painful experiences, such as getting hurt and being spanked, into the feelings of another child, that is, the child begins to develop a capacity for empathy. Somewhat later, a child learns how to be frustrated that he or she cannot attain goals through his or her own efforts. Having developed the ability to conceptualize goals, this leads to the conceptualization of standards as: "success is accompanied by a pleasant state and failure by an unpleasant one."[24]

At the age of three or four, the child first begins to evaluate an act as bad with regard to the self, thus demonstrating increasing self-awareness

---

[22]Kagan (1984: 112).

[23]Kagan (1984: 126).

[24]Kagan (1984: 128).

and the ability to think of the self objectively. By this time, the unpleasant association connected with being bad then begins to create inhibitions in the child with respect to the violation of standards.[25] The ability of the child to think of an act extended to the self develops into the ability to conceptualize the self as an object, which in turn allows the child to gain a "conscious awareness of intentions, feelings, standards, and the ability to attain a goal," and then somewhat later, to make "comparative evaluations of self in relation to others, especially other children."[26] Finally, this evolves into the ability to identify with others, one of two mechanisms Kagan identifies as being important to the child's moral development somewhat later on, the other being the development of a "need for cognitive consistency among beliefs, actions, and the perceived demands of reality."[27] The identification characteristic is important because of the tendency for children to adopt and identify with models, such as a beloved parent, for example, and then to project into the self the model's desirable characteristics and adopt the model's standards.

An important result of all these developments for emotional motivation is the development in each person of a sense of self-esteem. Standards are important to the child (as well as to the adolescent and the adult) as a source of motivation because the child "wants to reassure the self of its moral goodness,...to validate a morally positive evaluation of self."[28] Involved here is also the tendency of persons to seek moral self-validation through the finding of moral flaws in others. This then becomes important in explaining the motivations of persons who engage in other-regarding behavior. One important source of human motivation stems from this quest by persons for the affirmation of their own self-worth. There can be no doubt that the achievement of such affirmations is pleasurable, that is, it gives "utility."

---

[25]Evidence from diverse cultures suggests that children are aware of standards on prohibited behavior by age three and are expected to regulate their behavior accordingly by age seven. Thus appears the "fundamental human capacity, which various nineteenth century observers called *moral sense,* (without which) the child could not be socialized" (Kagan, 1984: 129, 131).

[26]Kagan (1984: 138).

[27]Kagan (1984: 134).

[28]Kagan (1984: 143).

Finally, there is an interesting and important ramification to this increased emphasis on the natural process of inner-directed emotional discovery suggested by the empirical findings. Since it seems reasonable to expect the fundamental process of emotional discovery to be reasonably similar in most cultures (although empirical verification of this will be required), we have grounds to expect the existence of fundamental moral values which are universally shared. Again, Kagan:

> (Can there be universal standards? Probably not.) I believe, however, that beneath the extraordinary variety in surface behavior and consciously articulated ideals, there is a set of emotional states that form the bases for a limited number of moral categories that transcend time and locality.[29]

Kagan posits a set of five fundamental unpleasant emotions as common across all cultures: anxiety from physical harm, social disapproval, or task failure; empathy; responsibility to not harm others; fatigue or ennui from repeated gratifications of desire; and uncertainty from encountering phenomena which are not understood.[30] These interact to provide the feelings of guilt and shame which are the fundamental motivations in our moral education.[31]

---

[29]Kagan (1984: 118–119).

[30]Kagan (1984: 119–120).

[31]Many of the points made above, as well as those in the previous chapter on "shared values," were closely approximated by the insights of David Hume and Adam Smith 250 years ago. Hume and Smith (and to a lesser extent, Thomas Hobbes) pointed to a process of the development of norms based largely on a person's "feeling," as well as the feelings of sympathy, which resulted in a system of commonly shared moral values. As Ostrom (1986: 235) states: "The capacity to conceptualize and distinguish ways of ordering human relationships with one another, Hume sees as being grounded in the emotional quality in which human beings experience a sentiment of sympathy or fellow feeling in relation to the emotional feeling of others...(Hume believed that) human cognition of moral distinctions...is grounded in feelings where virtue is initially associated with a feeling of pleasure and attraction, and vice is associated with feelings of pain, aversion, and uneasiness." To quote from Hume (1948: 220) directly, "... the intercourse of sentiments...in society and in conversation, makes us form some general unalterable standard by which we may approve or disapprove of characters and manners." Ostrom (1986: 236) also points out that Adam Smith had somewhat similar views: "Smith conceives sympathy to be 'our fellow feeling with any passion whatsoever' as expressed in situations which

Social Intervention in Emotional Development

We might begin discussing the possibilities for intervening usefully into the process of emotional development by asking ourselves the question: "Are emotions important collective goods?" This question in turn suggests two questions: "Are emotions important?"; and "Are emotions collective goods?" Their importance should by now be obvious from the discussion above. Emotions are of crucial importance in allowing us to deal with the complexity of the world, the so-called "philosophers' frame problem," and they are important as a source of human moral beliefs. As Kagan states:

> When the community's emotional reaction to violation of a standard is weakened, the rational argument against it also becomes fragile, and the standard can slip into conventionality...(Parents fear that) the child who witnesses too much aggression, dishonesty, sexuality, and destruction will stop experiencing the emotions of fear, anxiety, and repugnance that sustain the standards for such acts.
> ...Because humans prefer...a reason for holding a standard, they invent the arguments that rationalists regard as essential... (However,) without the original emotional reaction, the standard may never have gained persuasive power.[32]

According to Kagan, we emulate emotions we have been taught (have observed) much more readily than we would exhibit them because of purely logical or cognitive instruction. Children raised in homes filled with love or cruelty tend to be loving or cruel parents, respectively, but neither type of behavior as parents would be forthcoming nearly so much if they had been raised in a strictly neutral environment and given verbal instruction in love or cruelty. In sum, it would appear that, just as some of the greatest of classical writers saw things 250 years ago (see the

---

excite particular passions¼Sympathy and the capacity to take the perspective of others enables human beings to function as spectators capable of forming judgments of approval and disapproval about the way that people act and order their relationships with one another with reference to general standards of propriety (that is, right and wrong)."

[32]Kagan (1984: 121–122).

previous note), emotion seems to be a more important grounding for morals than is reason. In any event, it would be difficult to deny that in the process of moral instruction, emotions are *important.*

Turning to the second question, as we have defined "collective goods," emotions as collective goods implies the ability on the part of humans to affect them in purposeful fashion. As suggested above, not much is known about our ability to affect how our emotions deal with the "philosophers' frame problem." Hence we tentatively conclude that in this respect, emotions may not be collective goods. But when it comes to emotions as the foundation of morality, the story is different. To reiterate, there are two ways in which that process operates, "outer-directed" and "inner-directed." Outer-directed emotional instruction comes about through the direct teachings by authority figures, including, in particular, the use of rewards and punishments. For society to intervene in this would require efforts to upgrade the parenting skills of parents and other authority figures. In particular, presumably, this kind of objective would be applied to families often termed as "dysfunctional." Efforts along these lines are visible in many societies and are of particular relevance in the US, where there is a high incidence of childbirth by girls in their teens and, sometimes, in their early teens: "babies having babies." Teaching parenting skills to these, as well as to many other parents and authority figures, is a social need that has been much discussed in recent times.

The second way in which emotions build morality is through more natural processes of investigation exhibited by young children, in which they develop their own consciences in spontaneous fashion, in part at least. This suggests a somewhat different type of social intervention. Now, the center of social attention is the danger that the benefits of such inner instruction become *undone* by virtue of dysfunctional family situations. There is considerable casual empirical evidence that this is exactly what often happens. In the school district where I reside, tutors and counselors noticed substantial differences in the receptivity to outside tutoring and counseling by six- and seven-year-olds as opposed to twelve- and fourteen-year-olds. Even in the worst of family situations, the six-year-olds have not had their natural tendencies toward empathy and compassion and self-esteem driven away, but by the age of fourteen, after several years of failure and problems, such as poverty and parental abuse, all, or almost all, empathy and compassion is lost. This fact may provide an insight for what may be the most efficient of all social interventions. If such early tutoring could lower the drop-out rates in American schools by 10 or 20 percent, or more, it is difficult to conceive of a more important *collective good*. This is merely one example of an instance where emotions are important social goods.

Finally, we might mention as social goods instances where current harmful practices are removed. If de Sousa is correct in his statement that the belief that emotions are subjective and irrational has resulted both in their being considered merely as distractions from the serious business of life, and as the justification of erratic behavior on the basis that one should "go with one's feelings," then the removal of such beliefs would in itself constitute an important social good.[33]

Emotions and the Arts

It would be possible to discuss issues of collective goods and the arts separately and at length, but since the arts are closely related to the emotions, it seems appropriate to deal with that subject in this chapter. As we saw above, the novelist Iris Murdoch has observed that "the most essential and fundamental aspect of culture is the study of literature, since this is an education in how to picture and understand human situations."[34] If Murdoch is correct, there is an important role for the arts, in this instance, literature in the human understanding of interpersonal relationships. Modes of artistic expression can often be considered collective goods, dealing largely with the emotions, and important to the development of the moral fiber of the society. Literature and drama are most directly implicated in this, but all kinds of aesthetic appreciation are probably of importance. And it can be argued that the role of the arts in our social existence has been neglected in the social sciences in much the same manner as has the role of emotion.

The several forms of art accomplish two things for humankind: the giving of pleasure and the imparting of instruction. Learning itself can be pleasurable, of course, whether cognitive or cognitive-emotional,

[33]Mancur Olson (1989: 117) has suggested that, in any given society, morality can be viewed as a scarce resource, and that societies must structure their incentives accordingly.
[34]Murdoch (1970: 34).

although the latter is more so given the relative difficulty humans have in learning about the inner emotional life of others. In addition to this, most of us simply enjoy an interesting story. The great advantage of art, literary art especially, is that one is *transported* into a situation as if he or she is experiencing it directly. This gives us much more inner understanding of the human experience, much more than learning about it through mere description from reading newspapers, history books, social science accounts, and so forth. As Beardsley states, closely following John Dewey:

> When experience rounds itself off into more or less complete and coherent strands of doing and undergoing, we have..."*an* experience;" and such an experience is aesthetic to the degree in which attention is fixed on pervasive quality. Art is expression, in the sense that in expressive objects there is a "fusion" of "meaning" in the present quality; ends and means, separated for practical purposes, are reunited to produce not only experience enjoyable in itself but, at its best, a celebration and commemoration of qualities ideal to the culture or society in which the art plays its part.[35]

To be sure, our "transportation" into other situations through fiction is not quite the same as if we had been there in person, but it can, if the artistic form is interesting and absorbing enough, come very close.[36] We become educated about human situations in their full complexity, both *cognitive and emotional.*[37] As Zeraffa states:

> Most great novelists are theorists of their art because their work poses the most insoluble of all problems of interpretation: what meaning and, therefore, what form, should we give to the

[35]Beardsley (1967: 31), referring to Dewey (1925, Chap. 9).

[36]Indeed, a perceptive person may take more away from reading an absorbing play or novel than would a somewhat unperceptive person (as we all are sometimes) by being physically present.

[37]Recall how one function of emotions is dealing expeditiously with complex situations. An art form which educates us regarding the full complexity of the human experience is of obvious value for the education of emotions. As was mentioned above, the novelist Iris Murdoch has pointed this out quite explicitly.

> unceasing flow of human life?...The novel thus assumes the guise of oracle, since more directly than other arts it confronts us openly with the issue of the meaning and value of our ineluctable historical and social condition.[38]

It is difficult to overstate the significance of this process because it is of key importance to our moral and emotional education through ART. John Hospers describes the workings of such moral instruction quite well:

> But how then does art achieve a moral effect, if no moral is specifically stated? It does so by presenting us with characters in situations (usually of conflict and crisis) that generally have a greater complexity than our own everyday experiences. By deliberating on the problems and conflicts of these characters, we can enrich our own moral perspectives; we can learn from them without having to undergo in our personal lives these same conflicts or having to make the same decisions, for in art we can view their situations with a detachment that we can seldom achieve in daily life, when we are immersed in the stream of action. Literature is often a potent stimulus to moral reflection, for it presents the moral situation in its total context, with nothing relevant omitted — and nothing less than this is required in making one's own moral decisions.[39]

There is another important aspect to the "education" that we receive from novelists and other artists, which have to do with the role of the imagination. Again, quoting Hospers:

> ...The chief moral effect of literature doubtless lies in its unique power to stimulate the imagination. Shelley's defense of this position in his essay "A Defense of Poetry" stands virtually unchallenged to this day. "The imagination," wrote Shelley, "is the great instrument of moral good, and poetry administers to the effect by acting upon the causes." Through great literature, we are carried beyond the confines of our daily life into the

[38]Zeraffa (1972: 38–39).

[39]Hospers (1967: 50).

> world of thought and feeling more profound and varied than our own, and in which we can enter directly the experiences, thoughts, and feelings of people far removed from us in space and time. Through the exercise of the sympathetic imagination, art, more than preachment or moralizing, tends to reveal the common human nature that exists in all men behind the facade of divisive doctrines, and thus to unite mankind more effectively than the doctrines themselves could ever do.[40]

As Hospers is pointing out, the great use of moral and emotional imagination to mankind is in the fact that it is a vehicle of *compassion*, and I would argue that the workings of human compassion are under-utilitzed and under-implicated in many instances involving the collective goods being discussed in this book. Art is instrumental in our moral and emotional education and, therefore, important in the process by which we move toward many of our collective goals.

Emotion, Moral Values, and Norms

One of the many suggestions in recent times for improving the mainstream rational egoist model used in economics has been to take moral values and norms directly into consideration. One writer in this group has been Robert Frank, who suggests that other-regarding behavior is so much a part of the mainstream of human behavior that economists dare not disregard it.[41] There is also the group of writers who contributed to a volume edited by Koford and Miller about *Social Norms and Economic Institutions*,[42] who discuss the possibilities for including habits, customs, and norms in economics, including a thoughtful two-part paper by Griffith and Goldfarb entitled "Amending the Economist's 'Rational Egoist' Model to Include Moral Values and Norms."[43] All this is a good step in the right direction, but in the development of moral values and norms one aspect that has been so far neglected is the role played by our emotional

[40]Hospers (1967: 50–51).

[41]Frank (1988).

[42]Koford and Miller (1991).

[43]Griffith and Goldfarb (1991); Goldfarb and Griffith (1991).

growth (including the role of the arts therein)[44] as discussed above. Not only should moral values and norms be included in economics, but so should the emotions and their development. The simple way to do this would be to expand the list of goals included in economic models (and those in all of social science) to embrace collective goals.[45]

[44]The social scientist can, in fact, learn a great deal about all this from the arts themselves. As merely one example of the legion that could be cited, in the play, *Honour,* by Joanna Murray-Smith (1977), a heretofore happily married middle-aged writer wishes to end his marriage because of infatuation with a much younger writer, in the process ignoring all other obligations and commitments. In the end, the younger writer herself becomes wiser and confronts him with the question of why "the heart should take precedence...over kindness. Over loyalty. Over history. Whatever. Let's say: Justice —" While the dilemma in the plot turns out poorly, as seems realistic, the audience becomes educated to the importance of the broader human goals of kindness, of conforming to tradition, of loyalty, and of justice, relative to the pandering to selfish infatuation. Murray-Smith has instructed the audience as to the importance of "mainstream" social goals and, it seems to me, probably without knowing it, she has pointed out the major weakness in the "rational-egoist" model used by professional economists.

[45]Griffith and Goldfarb include in their paper (Part 2) an interesting discussion of arguments for treating moral values as constraints as opposed to preferences. The goal model approach I suggest in this book would suggest preferences as determined from goals, although goals, if considered important enough, could be the basis of constraints as well.

Chapter 4

The "Other" Social Sciences

Unless our laboratory results are to give us artificialities, mere scientific curiosities, they must be subjected to interpretation by gradual reapproximation to conditions of life...The laboratory...affords no final refuge that enables us to avoid the ordinary scientific difficulties of forming hypotheses, interpreting results, etc.

John Dewey
Presidential Address to the American Psychological Association, 1899

The concept of the public interest plays a central role in discussions of public policy, political action, social value, and individual interest; and yet there is at present no agreement as to what we mean when we use the term.

Virginia Held
The Public Interest and the Individual Interest, 1970

The dominant approach in sociology today, that of functionalism,... views society as a set of institutions serving its functional needs, ignores historical perspective, and sees change and conflict as deviations rather than inherent social processes. The dominant concern of functionalism is with order in society — an order based on man's conformity to shared values, and one in which joy, freedom, self-fulfillment, and other aspects of man stressed by the humanistic psychologist usually don't appear...Although it is acknowledged that

> social order is a function of shared values, the values themselves are seldom considered and are thought of not so much as man-*made*, man-*transmitted*, or man-received.
>
> John Glass
> *The Humanistic Challenge to Sociology*, 1972

In the introductory chapter, we saw how social goals (or collective goods) have been excluded from the models used in modern mainstream economic analysis. But economics is not the only social science. Could it be that other disciplines have taken up the slack left by the economists? This is the question addressed in this chapter. Causation in social science requires motivation: how humans can get closer to their various goals, both as individuals and as members of groups. A thorough policy analysis of major issues requires looking at all relevant goals. In the Introduction I cited, from my earlier book, some basic human concerns which relate to major tax provisions. I also suggested that it is possible to identify the concerns (human goals) most relevant to any individual policy problem. These can be established empirically, through polls and interviews of representative citizens or decision-makers, or they can be identified from written materials produced by interested parties, such as congressional hearings.

It is also true, however, that useful social science need not deal with *all* social goals. Much is possible by tracing the relationships between just some of them, even though biases remain when policy analysis is attempted and other researchers will be needed to add the missing elements. In economics, for example, there has been highly useful analysis of the workings of the market sector when motivations are selfish and materialistic (as they often are.) The approach falters when it is extended to justice considerations.

The workings of the other social sciences relative to the approach being suggested here is a complex topic to discuss, even for persons trained in the respective disciplines; it is still more troublesome for one whose training lies elsewhere. Nor does space allow for a thorough treatment. Nevertheless, given the importance of the topic, I forge ahead, although not without extending sincere caveats to the reader. The disciplines discussed are so vast and complex that no generalization I make here will be free of virtually certain exceptions. When I think the exceptions are significant, I do my best to point them out. The discussion to follow is organized under three topics, all dealing with a methodological aspect of the approach I am suggesting. The first deals with the degree to which the disciplines use only the methodology of the natural sciences (scientism). The second deals with the degree to which the disciplines depart from procedures where they use human subjective motivation based on all relevant goals (a comprehensive goal rational choice model). And, finally, the third deals with the extent to which they use good-quality empirical investigation of subjective motivation. But before proceeding further into these topics, it might be useful to state my main conclusions upfront —an exercise not without its dangers. The following is my attempt to do this for the four main disciplines (psychology, political science, sociology, and anthropology), a sub-discipline which crosses discipline boundaries (public choice), and, for comparison purposes, a review of economics. In this capsule summary, I simply and briefly list the strengths and weaknesses of each discipline as viewed from the perspective of the approach I am suggesting.

Economics

Strengths

Does very well in providing highly sophisticated analysis of the market sector. Has a very fine model of causation based on the most important single human motivation: that of selfish (and near-selfish) material gain. Economists have developed mathematical and econometric tools which are highly sophisticated and powerful.

Weaknesses

Does a poor job of dealing with human goals other than selfish material gain, both in attributing human motivation and, more generally, in analysis. Does not do well in making empirical studies of human motivation for both material and non-material goals. With an excessive emphasis on mathematical sophistication, it often tends to sacrifice economic substance to mathematical form. Economists tend to have a strong sense of "turf," which causes useful contributions from other disciplines to be overlooked.

Psychology

Strengths

Has provided a wealth of insights concerning human psychological functioning, especially those based on personal relationships. Has provided strong insights in areas of psychoanalysis, personality development, and increasingly, humanistic psychology. Has provided important knowledge in areas of social psychology which can be explored with large-scale "quantitative"-type public opinion polls.

Weaknesses

There has been an overemphasis on the empiricist tradition and underemphasis on humanistic or hermeneutic aspects of human psychology. In laboratory exercises and elsewhere, social influences on the human psyche have been unacknowledged. There has been substantial neglect of qualitative forms of empirical investigations.

Political Science

Strengths

Has done a very fine job of providing informative analysis of all aspects of human functioning which involve power relations, and especially formal power relationships. Has provided important knowledge of public views on political and social issues, where such topics can be explored with large-scale "quantitative"-type public opinion polls. Along with practitioners in other disciplines, has provided highly sophisticated mathematical analysis of the theory of social choice.

Weaknesses

An overemphasis on the empiricist tradition which has resulted in a view of politics as a contest for power and adjustment of private interests among political actors, and an underemphasis on politics as a means to secure the common good and address collective goals. Partly in the name of "turf," political scientists have avoided the rationality approach of economists, even to use it with emendations, which has resulted in the use *of ad hoc* criteria for goodness. Because of overemphasis on the empiricist tradition, forms of public opinion polling, which include qualitative elements, have been largely avoided.

Sociology

Strengths

Has provided a wealth of valuable descriptive and analytical work on a great number of human social concerns. Sociology's macro-social emphasis approach to human affairs has provided considerable useful insights. A number of interesting techniques have been used to interpret human social relationships, resulting in varying insights into social functioning.

Weaknesses

There has been a general tendency in sociology to overemphasize the empiricist approach and, with exceptions, to underemphasize subjective approaches. There is a tendency to overemphasize macro-social influences without explaining the role of individual human motivations in how they came to be that way. Sociologists tend to avoid the rationality approach of economists, even to use it with emendations (with a few noteworthy recent exceptions.) There is a strong sense of "turf" which causes sociologists to pass up opportunities to use material from other disciplines.

Anthropology

Strengths

Anthropologists deal broadly with all aspects of human culture and do not set limits either on subject matter or on types of inquiries used to get information. Thus, they have avoided empiricism. Their analyses are firmly grounded in micro analysis ("fieldwork"), but they move readily from micro to macro concerns and vice versa. They are quite sophisticated with respect to interviewing techniques. Anthropologists have a good understanding of methodological questions.

Weaknesses

Anthropologists have failed to use insights they could have obtained from microeconomic theory and analysis.

Public Choice

Strengths

Public choice social scientists include persons with primary training in economics, political science, and sociology. They have adopted the motivational approach used in economics to provide a large number of important new insights into the workings of human institutions outside the market sector in ways that manage to go beyond traditional discipline boundaries using causation provided by individual motivation.

Weaknesses

In adopting and using the strengths of the economists' motivational causative model, the public choice writers have tended to import many of the economists' weaknesses as well. There is an overemphasis on selfish human motivation and underemphasis on collective goals and non-selfish motivation. Motivations are assumed, without reference to empirical support, nor is there much (if any) empirical work delving into human subjective motivation.

In sum, except for anthropology, there is a consistent strain of influences throughout the social sciences which cause them to underemphasize subjective motivations and collective goods. (Anthropologists ignore some collective goods which might have been inferred from microeconomic theory and analysis.) Except for anthropology, the empiricist tradition, along with strong scientistic influences, is strong throughout. The result has been a substantial underemphasis on the subjective in social science, and an underemphasis on qualitative forms of empirical investigation of the subjective. The answer to the question posed above — whether other social sciences take up the slack in the treatment of collective goods left by the economists — will have to be "no."

With this summary in hand, we can now turn to how the three major social sciences being discussed fare according to each of of our three topics. (Anthropology is discussed separately, without regard to the topics, which are less relevant for that discipline.)

First Topic: Scientism in the Social Sciences

The very success of the natural scientists over the modern period suggests that they have used methods which are correct, or at least very close to being so. Facts are gathered objectively using some combination of the five senses; hypotheses are formed and tested using those facts. With the confirmation of hypotheses, models are built which correctly predict outcomes. The hypotheses typically deal with tiny portions of the whole science and are tested using procedures which insulate the area under discussion from the rest of the science, thus allowing for controlled experiments. Other hypotheses are found and tested which deal with how the separate areas interconnect.

Social scientists have been so impressed by the success of these procedures that many of them have tried to import them into their own disciplines. While the controlled experiment has seldom been available, "natural" experiments with large numbers of observations have been, with sophisticated statistical procedures, substituted for control and for the insulation required ("holding other things equal"). "Objectivity" in fact-gathering has been the rule, which has meant that any facts found using approaches different from those of the hard sciences are discounted. The one source of data uniquely available to the social sciences, that coming from human experience, has largely gone untapped. This has resulted in the neglect of human goals and, in particular, human collective goals.

The purpose of this section is to examine the extent to which this improper emulation of the hard sciences, "scientism," has invaded the social sciences being discussed.[1] My investigations show that it has invaded all of them to significant, but varying, degrees (except, apparently, for anthropology), and it is difficult to pinpoint the exact nature of these differences.[2]

Scientism in psychology

It could be argued that scientism has been more important over the century in psychology than in any other social science. There have been changes in this situation over the past few decades, although fairly marginal in nature. A strong scientistic influence has obtained despite the clear advice given psychologists by John Dewey, then the president of their national association, in 1899, as quoted in the chapter epigraph: "...our laboratory results...must be subjected to interpretation by gradual reapproximation to conditions of life."[3] Any number of highly respected psychologists have pointed this out over the years. Most recently, the point has been made well by Terwee (1990) and Wertz (1998). Terwee lists the methodological principles thought proper for psychology, reproduced from a recent Dutch book in which, according to Terwee,

[1]According to Desmond King (1998: 442), one reason for scientism in the social sciences has been the influence of the National Science Foundation in the US and the Social Science Research Council in Great Britain.

[2]There has been a similar scientistic presence in economics. According to Patrick O'Sullivan (1987: 147–148), "Mainstream economics, being a largely Anglo-American science, has come under the strong influence of broadly positivist ideas. [This has happened] in two ways: (a) directly, since positivism regards the natural sciences as the paradigm of all valid cognition and, hence, *a fortiori* a valid method for the human sciences; and (b) indirectly, because economists, whose grasp of philosophical issues is at best superficial, have turned to the works of leading philosophers of natural science for methodological inspiration." (See also Chapter 1, note 54)

[3]Wertz (1998: 49) points out that the essential differences between the subject matter of human science and natural science were discussed by Dilthey in 1894.

the author "introduced American research principles into Dutch psychology:"[4]

1. Research is to be conducted according to an "empirical cycle." Tentative solutions to problems are formulated in the form of testable hypotheses. These lead to predictions. Predictions are tested in experiments or through systematic observation. (One only has knowledge when one is able to predict.)
2. Results of empirical tests are evaluated statistically. If the null hypothesis (which one does not believe to be true, and which is not predicted) may be discarded, the hypothesis is regarded as confirmed: the probability of truth is increased.
3. The correctness of predictions may be verified; the truth of basic statements may be assessed objectively and with certainty.[5]

These tenets reproduce the natural science methodology outlined above almost exactly. According to Terwee, these assumptions "are still prevalent in present-day psychology."[6] Wertz also points to the dominance of empiricism-behaviorism in mainstream psychology, in part by making a survey of history of psychology textbooks where he found that the humanistic approach, the subjective alternative to behaviorist methodology, was discussed sympathetically in only a few.[7] Wertz points to the failure of the behaviorist, or "cognitive," approach to "faithfully capture the meanings of individuals' experiences."[8]

> ...This failure stems most fundamentally from the discipline's scientistic approach, that is, proceeding as if reality can be truthfully known only by a hypothetico-deductive approach. Cognitive psychologists hold the conviction, carried over from behaviorism without any revolutionary rethought, that only behavior can be observed, and mental life must be

[4]Terwee (1990: 20).

[5]Terwee (1990: 20–21), quoting from de Groot (1961: 92,96,106; Dutch edition).

[6]Terwee (1990: 21).

[7]Wertz (1998: 47).

[8]Wertz (1998: 53).

> inferred...Where spontaneous personal expression is admitted, in the form of self-reflection and verbal reports, it is subordinated to generating or verifying these abstract explanatory concepts and carries little methodological status, ultimately rejected as not satisfying the demands of scientific rigor imported from the physical sciences. The experimental method, which is considered the privileged way of assessing human psychological processes, is itself borrowed from the natural sciences, and its *modus operandi* in principle falls short of the meaningful structure of human life, which is necessary for an authentic psychology.[9]

Another psychologist who has pointed to the scientism of contemporary psychology is Seymour Sarason, who speaks of psychology's divorce from philosophy and how overemphasis on the individual has been due to psychology's "embrace of the scientific ethos and methodology." The approach of academic psychologists, Sarason continues, has been to take the attitude that

> If psychology were to be scientific, it needed a subject matter amenable to scientific study, preferably in a laboratory. And if psychology were to be true to scientific tradition, experimentation had to be possible and that meant that one sought to isolate psychological phenomena from extraneous, contaminating influences. And, in practice, that meant isolating not only the individual from his or her social historical context, but also parts of the person from other parts of himself or herself.[10]

Sarason also points out that one aspect of scientistic thinking may be a misguided notion that the psychology of studying real-life applications is much less important than "sophisticated" psychological theory:

> To recast the theory-practice dichotomy requires changing one's values about theory and practice and giving up mindless devotion to familiar methodologies and modes of analysis, as well as changing the sites and conditions of one's work. *What is involved*

[9]Wertz (1998: 53–54).

[10]Sarason (1981: 94). See the discussion of "insulation" in the discussion of methodology in Chapter 1.

is no less than ceasing to ape the so-called hard sciences. The question is not where and how one conducts one's research, (as if in the abstract one can prescribe a methodology) but whether the conditions approximate the naturally occuring context from which the problem arose and to which an answer is sought.[11]

Scientism in political science

The scientistic influence has been surprisingly strong in political science in the twentieth century, although there seems to be considerable diversity of methodological approach, especially in recent times. An important figure in advancing the importance of behaviorism in political science (and in social science more generally) was Arthur Bentley. In his 1908 book, *The Process of Government,* he argued for restating social theory in mathematical terms and that "sociological frames of reference comparable to those used by physicists could be established for dealing with social facts,"[12] a statement highly reminiscent of Durkheim. As Odegard explains, "It was a period in which the social sciences were moving, as Comte had urged them to do, from a methodology based on introspection and imagination to one based on observation and analysis."[13] In his book, Bentley "attacked Feelings and Faculties, Ideas and Ideals as primary causes of behavior."[14] After being at first overlooked, Bentley's ideas grew in importance until gaining wide influence beginning in the 1950s and 1960s. Bessette points out that Bentley was the inspiration of the "group theory," or pluralist interpretation, of American politics that came into prominence at that time and has been important since. One key characteristic of such group theory, it should be noted, is that groups bargain with each other on the basis of their selfish (to the group) concerns. More general collective interests, or what Bessette calls "deliberation," are ignored.[15]

[11]Sarason (1981: 142; emphasis added). Also, with respect to scientism, see Wertsch (1991: 1), Cole (n.d.: 2), and the statement of John Dewey in the chapter epigraph.
[12]Bentley (1908), as quoted in Odegard (1967: xii).
[13]Odegard (1967: xiv).
[14]Odegard (1967: xv).
[15]Bessette (1994: 57). This was also pointed out to me by Professor Ron Oakerson in correspondence.

While this methodology, based on scientistic origins, is still important in political science, modern political scientists have not been loath to go off in their own ways, and there doesn't seem to be a dominating mainstream such as that in psychology. Mainstream journals are likely to publish articles based on interviews, or close reading of politicians' statements, or on memos and communications of supreme court justices, and so forth. Still, as Bessette persuasively maintains, much contempory analysis in political science does not "acknowledge the importance of deliberation about common goals to the functioning of American institutions or to the fashioning of public policy."[16]

Scientism in sociology

As in psychology, the dominant approach in the twentieth century has been that of naturalistic or positivistic sociology, where the attempt is made to consider sociology a science just as the natural sciences are a science.[17] There has been a strong strain of empiricism. In the hands of sociologists, this has fostered a science dominated by macro-level perspectives — where explanations are sought in variables at the social level — Durkheim's "social facts." These variables include social characteristics viewed at the aggregate level, such as religion characteristics, population age characteristics, marital status, and economic conditions. All of these variables can be objectively — and, with application, fairly rigorously — measured.

While it is fair to say that macro-level variables are still central to sociological explanation, there are many cross-currents in the discipline which are, to varying degrees, critical of behaviorist macro-level analysis. As Glass, a humanistic sociologist, states:

> The dominant approach in sociology today, that of functionalism,...is being attacked from many sides. Basically, the functionalist views society as a set of institutions serving its functional needs, ignores historical perspective, and sees change

[16]Bessette (1994: xii).
[17]Paloma (1979: 2).

> and conflict as deviations rather than inherent social processes. The dominant concern of functionalism is with order in society — an order based on man's conformity to shared values, and one in which joy, freedom, self-fulfillment, and other aspects of man stressed by the humanistic psychologist usually don't appear... Although it is acknowledged that social order is a function of shared values, the values themselves are seldom considered and are thought of not so much as man-*made*, man-*transmitted*, or man-received.[18]

As in political science, while scientistic influences are still of central importance in sociology, there are noteworthy exceptions to scientism in sociology. There is a fairly vigorous humanist group, another group that considers the interaction between individuals in sociological phenomena, a linguistic group, and others. The humanist movement is particularly noteworthy. Whenever sociologists conduct micro-level investigations into the fortunes of individuals or small groups, as they often do, they are edging toward humanism. Humanism grew as a reaction against functionalism and other forms of behaviorism, in part because of the natural inclination to look at the world from the standpoint of individuals, their needs, their aspirations, their values, and so forth. For humanists, the key subject matter is the human condition.[19]

The difference between the psychological and sociological humanists is that, for the most part, the latter do not explore the human individual psyche in-depth, but concentrate more on the interaction of individuals with society and on how, in the interaction with each other, they develop social awareness. In doing so, they sometimes explicitly or implicitly deal with human goals, although for the most part I believe individual goals are not given central billing (except for writers employing a rational choice perspective). But humanists, in contrast to the structuralists and others who take purely macro approaches, believe in the individual *qua* individual as an important participant in social activities and, in particular, as being able to exercise choices. As one humanistic sociologist put it, it is time for the sociologists to realize that humans are social, but not

[18]Glass (1972: 2).

[19]See Glass and Staude (1972, Part 1).

entirely *socialized.*[20] An individual person has both a body and a mind, which means that he or she can strike out in directions not completely determined by the social ambience.

Finally, a sub-discipline of sociology, which overlaps with a similar group in psychology, should be mentioned: social psychology.[21] Social psychologists are responsible for a wealth of interesting information about human relationships, much of it approaching a humanistic point of view. This includes inquiries such as how persons become socialized, forms of social interaction, attitudes, the role played by self-identities, the characteristics of close personal relationships, and similar concerns. Social psychologists also studying collective action, but only in the highly restricted sense of actions toward specific goals involving social change, such as movements to protect forests from clear-cutting and the like. While social psychology involves individuals, it does so in a descriptive manner, not in a way which follows up on the working of individual objectives. For example, studies of love and affection tend to record individuals' varying attitudes toward others, having to do with respect, admiration, and confidence on the one hand (a scale of liking), and need, caring, trust, and confidence on the other (loving scale.)[22] These answers are used to make descriptive statements about how persons like and love others. It does not involve careful investigation of personal needs and desires.[23] The approach to social psychology in the hands of the sociologists — and this represents practice in sociology as a whole — is to view these human relationships from on high rather than from within.

Topic Two: Rational Choice Motivation from a Comprehensive Goal Perspective

To reiterate, the policy analysis (and social science) being suggested in this book assumes that individuals take actions based on their goals, a direct adoption of the methodology used by economists, except that the

[20]Wrong (1972: 69; emphasis added).

[21]It would appear that sociology provides the major share of practitioners in social psychology.

[22]Rubin (1979).

[23]This is more likely done by the psychologists of course, although the amount of it in the literature seems to be minimal.

approach gets extended to all important social goals, not just the selfish and material. The motivational procedure of the economists is often termed the "rational choice" approach to social science. In a recent paper discussing the approach for the purposes of sociologists, John Goldthorpe suggests denoting it (but using broader goal sets than the economists do) as "rational action theory."[24] This is the second perspective from which I propose to appraise the three major "other" social sciences: how well do they employ the rational action approach and how well do they consider all sources of human social action (various social goals) in an unbiased fashion?

Rational choice motivation from a comprehensive goal perspective in psychology

In the discussion above, we showed a dominant positivist or behaviorist methodology in psychology due to the strong infatuation with the methods of the natural sciences. The emphasis is on observed behavior and experimental methods, which tends to discount the importance of motivation due to individual goals. In the behaviorist tradition, motivation is largely inferred, not directly investigated. In addition, taking the observational-experimental approach apparently makes it very difficult to deal with human social goals at all. This means that there has been a great neglect of collective goods in modern psychology. As Sarason states:

> The social-historical context — the ground out of which the individual *and* the psychologist emerge,...has, for all practical purposes, held no interest for psychology...(I)n its separation and then divorce from philosophy, and in its embrace of the scientific ethos and methodology, psychology ended up with the nature and structure of individual behavior (overt and covert) as the object of interest and study.[25]

James Wertsch concludes in similar fashion:

> What I...wish to argue...is that much contemporary research in psychology does not in fact have the practical implications so

[24]Goldthorpe (1998: 167).
[25]Sarason (1981: 94).

> often claimed for it. In my view, a major reason is the tendency for psychological research, especially in the United States, to examine human mental functioning as if it exists in a cultural, institutional, and historical vacuum. Research is often based on the assumption that it is possible, even desirable, to study the individual, or specific areas of mental functioning in the individual, in isolation.[26]

In summary, even selfish individual motivation has only been inferred from the outside, not studied from the inside, and the motivation based on any collective good goals a person might have is neglected entirely. This has given rise to a very one-sided psychology, similar in many respects to the one-sided quality of economics.

There are a number of exceptions to this conclusion; they are, however, minor, relative to the mainstream. The first is developmental psychology, which deals with the development of human personality and often uses interview techniques. Developmental psychologists do, however, tend to neglect social influences, as I point out in my discussion of Gilligan's work in Chapter 6. The second exception is, of course, the area of clinical psychology. Clinical psychology restricts itself largely to individual relationships with patients by not venturing further into policy issues.

A third exception is provided by a small group of psychologists who would place a central emphasis on human action and decision-making. Their work is well represented in two volumes of papers, Frese and Sabini (1985) and Pervin (1989). These writers concentrate on human goals and intentions and the cycle involved in the interaction between actions, as affected by the environment, and plans. Their emphasis is definitely social, although their concentration seems to be on objective decision-making rather than subjective aspects. So far, their work seems to have been more theoretical than empirical.

Finally, possibly the most significant exception to mainstream psychology is the area of humanistic psychology. An excellent discussion is to be found in Wertz (1998). This is the area of psychology closest in spirit to the approach to social science being suggested in this book. Humanistic psychologists view humans as having goals and intentions, and making

[26]Wertsch (1991: 2).

choices. They are willing to use both objective and subjective sources of data (including interviews), and to include social influences on human mental states in their analyses.[27] However, according to Wertz, the field is having problems *vis-a-vis* the institutional power of mainstream psychology. While the humanists have four journals, and the mainline journals have been accepting the occasional article by humanistic psychologists, all of the graduate programs, with one exception,[28] are firmly under the control of the traditional behaviorists. Wertz feels that the American Psychological Association "appears to be gaining power as a gatekeeper inhospitable to humanists."[29]

Rational choice motivation from a comprehensive goal perspective in political science

Political scientists typically reject rational choice approaches similar to that used by economists. I believe an important reason for this is their view that it smacks too much of utilitarian concepts which they find unpalatable, in part because the "utilitarianism" of economists often does not include that accruing to the consumption of collective goods. While this criticism of utilitarianism in the hands of the economists has been correct, to use this error as an excuse for discarding the rational action goal approach entirely is throwing the baby out with the bath water.[30]

---

[27]The five basic postulates of humanistic psychology, as stated in the masthead of the *Journal of Humanistic Psychology,* are as follows:

1. Human beings, as human, supersede the sum of their parts. They cannot be reduced to components.
2. Human beings have their existence in a uniquely human context, as well as in a cosmic ecology.
3. Human beings are aware and aware of being aware, that is, they are conscious. Human consciousness always includes an awareness of oneself in the context of other people.
4. Human beings have some choice, and with that, responsibility.
5. Human beings are intentional, aim at goals, are aware that they cause future events, and seek meaning, value, and creativity.

[28]Marquette University.

[29]Wertz (1998: 62).

[30]In fact, despite lip service, economists do not actually use utility directly in their analysis (except sometimes for purposes of simulations.) The goals they use are material gain, such as money, wealth, and profits.

The alternative approach used by the political scientists is to target concepts of the "public interest," although this has not worked out in practice because its users can't agree on what "public interest" is. One prominent student of the public interest idea, Virginia Weld, states the situation as follows:

> [One way to attempt to arrive at concepts of the public interest is with] preponderance theories, [seen most clearly in] utilitarian and aggregationist conceptions which hold that the public interest, if the term has any meaning at all, cannot be in conflict with a *preponderance* or *sum* of individual interests...[But with these, we are faced with the] familiar ethical problem of deriving a normative judgment from a set of empirical statements. Without recounting this well-known argument, I will simply assume the strength of the position that, as the critics of naturalism observe, if we ever wish to consider "X is in the public interest" to be a moral judgment, or a normative claim, it cannot be derived from any set of empirical statements about the capacity of the interests of some individuals (or groups) to outnumber, outweigh, or overpower those of some other individual or individuals."[31]

In justifying her rejection of what she terms "preponderance theories," Held depends on the naturalistic fallacy, the "well-known argument," another example of the mischief that has been caused by that argument (see Chapter 2). Held makes the above statement in her book, in which she seeks to discuss concepts of the "public interest," seen by some political scientists as a way to view human welfare. Held persists in summarily dismissing the economists' approach, despite admitting that political scientists have not been able to find a viable definition of "the public interest."[32]

The result is that political science is left with no set of human goals to use for defining goodness criteria for unbiased policy analysis, or social science analysis more generally. Whether or not this leads to bias will depend on the claims made by the researcher. If he or she claims to

[31]Held (1970: 43, 83–84).

[32]Held (1970: 5).

be using important goals — but it is likely that there are others which have been left out — he has taken an honest approach and, as indicated above, his analysis can still be valuable social science, though flawed. If, on the other hand, he appears to be claiming that the criteria used in his analysis are the *only* criteria of any importance, his analysis is biased and still more flawed, especially for the unperceptive reader.

If Joseph Bessette is correct in his excellent study, *The Mild Voice of Reason*, there has been neglect of collective goals in political science, which is somewhat similar to that existing in economics. The following is taken from his preface:

> ...At the time I completed my dissertation in 1978 on *Deliberation in Congress*, the concept of deliberation, which I defined simply as "reasoning on the merits of public policy," had fallen out of use within the political science discipline. Even the literature on the American Congress, an institution designed to be pre-eminently deliberative, had virtually nothing to say about deliberation. As I wrote then, "One searches in vain among the hundreds of studies to find one of deliberation in Congress. Indeed, the word 'deliberation' or synonyms rarely appear in the congressional literature.
>
> During the intervening decade and a half, the concept of deliberation has enjoyed a resurgence befitting its importance...[but] it must be acknowledged that even as deliberation has attracted renewed attention in recent years, scholars of American government and politics seem increasingly drawn to an analytical framework that sees lawmaking and policy-making as the aggregation of individual interests and preferences — the rational actor, or self-interest model — and not the result of argument, reasoning, and persuasion about common ends or goals...(T)he proponents of such theories do not, as a rule, acknowledge the importance of deliberation about common goals to the functioning of American institutions or the fashioning of public policy.[33]

[33]Bessette (1994: xi–xii).

Common ends or goals: they are precisely the central feature of the comprehensive goal model being suggested in this book. Bessette is suggesting that the political scientists have been ignoring them. Some of his remarks, but not all of them, no doubt refer to the emergence of the public choice school of thought in the past three decades, which I discuss farther along. As already discussed, much of the pluralist writing in the tradition of Bentley dealt with the struggle between competing narrow group interests without reference to ideas of the common good (or common goals).

Having mentioned the public choice writers, it should be noted that political scientists in the public choice school, of which there are a number, specifically use a rational choice approach identical to that used by economists and possessing the same flaws, that is, the failure to include collective goals in their motivational construct.

Rational choice motivation from a comprehensive goal perspective in sociology

As in political science, there is a group of sociologists who believe in following a rational action approach similar to that used in economics, many of them overlapping as writers in the public choice tradition. The most important figure in this development is James Coleman, whose exhaustive treatment of the approach is contained in his impressive work, *Foundations of Social Theory* (1990). Coleman advocates using an approach similar to that used by economists, with a foundation of methodological individualism and individual goals. In Coleman's hands, the approach is broadened somewhat beyond that used by the economists: while material selfish gain is important, he extends the motivation somewhat to include issues such as the emergence of social norms, non-economic social exchanges, and social capital (such as decisions to obtain education).[34] As far as I can tell, the motivations Coleman includes remain selfish, however; he does not seem to include motivations arising from purely social goals.[35] In this, the sociology rational choice movement retains the key defect the concept poses in the hands of the economists.

[34]Baron and Hannan (1994); Frank (1992).

[35]See Frank (1992: 150).

While Coleman has an avid band of followers, I think it fair to say that most other sociologists have been critical of the approach, at least if used without emendation. In any event, there was a fairly pronounced hostile reaction to Coleman's book by mainstream sociologists.[36] As an example of arguments advanced by two of the most noteworthy commentators, Neil Smelser complained that the use of individual motivations will frustrate the ability to make generalizations and that, anyhow, individual motivations are determined by group factors.[37] Meanwhile, Harrison White complained that the rational choice approach cannot handle the evil and capricious, and also that tastes are generally not stable enough to allow its use.[38] While these objections are not without some merit, surely they do not overcome the rational choice approach entirely. Individual motivations can be aggregated into social ones, and there is no reason an empirically verified social science cannot be built on human goals (evil or otherwise) no matter what their origins. Human belief systems are, generally speaking, fairly well fixed; they do not change capriciously.

Given the hostility between the disciplines of economics and sociology for reasons of turf and differences in approach, it seems likely also that sociologists reject the rational choice approach simply because it is used by economists, and because it uses misguided ideas about utility, in a way similar to that discussed above as true for political science. As Robert Frank put it, when sociology went about establishing itself as a discipline, the rational choice approach "was the undisputed territory of economists, and sociology wanted no part of it."[39]

As I noted earlier, sociologists traditionally have, in large part, tended to form their arguments with respect to social phenomena operating at the aggregate or macro level, and to the extent that macro-level variables are central to sociological explanation, it seems clear that sociologists would not consider it necessary to have a rational choice procedure for dealing with individual motivations. The social variables control: M. Rouget's vote is determined by his religion, age, and factory worker status.

[36]Baron and Hannan (1994: 1115).

[37]Smelser (1990: 780, 781).

[38]White (1990: 783, 788).

[39]Frank (1992: 148), Gordon (1991: 300).

This is all very well, and sociologists over the years have arrived at numerous highly informative insights into human social existence using the approach, but it has flaws which make it difficult to extend our understanding of social phenomena very far beyond the superficial. It, too, seldom has anything to say about *why* social variables are as they are, or why they change. It fails to explain phenomena which may take place due to the actions of group minorities, or which do not work as predicted. In my earlier example, the explanatory model for M. Rouget's vote was at a loss to explain what had happened if Rouget failed to vote communist. This problem could be overcome were individual motivations brought into the picture, as humanistic sociologists are doing increasingly (see the discussion above).[40]

Finally, I would take note of an interesting recent paper in the *British Journal of Sociology*, which I hope will come to assume some importance among sociologists. The author is John Goldthorpe and his theme is to suggest that the rational choice approach (he terms it "rational action theory") could be broadened to include goals coming from all human social activity.[41] He claims that a number of other writers in recent years have been edging toward similar suggestions.[42] This, of course, is an almost identical suggestion to that of the goal model I advocate in this book.[43]

Topic Three: Subjective Empirical Investigation

We have seen that, in economics, subjective motivation is important, but it is *assumed*, and not based on the results of empirical study directly.

[40]Some understanding of how the approach by sociologists of the human goals they will study is biased is gained from the following statement of Glass: (1972: 3) "Social science today focuses on man's adjustment to society, on conformity and adaptation, on man as a controlled product of society and culture, rather than as a determiner of his own fate. Sociology's view of man is reflected in the sub-field known as 'deviant behavior,' which deals exclusively with pathological deviations: poverty, crime, delinquency, mental illness, alcoholism, etc. What about deviance in the other (healthy) direction? There are almost no studies of creativity, joy, self-fulfillment, or of social institutions and organizations that facilitate these!"

[41]Goldthorpe (1998).

[42]Lindenberg (1990); Hedstrom (1996).

[43]Further comments on Goldthorpe's ideas appear in the concluding chapter.

The latter would require obtaining information from persons concerning their individual views of what is desirable. Such information could be obtained, in part, from observing their actions, no doubt, but it would also require asking them questions directly, using either survey polling methods or interviewing them face-to-face. The use of direct questions would be especially indicated to elicit individual views on the value of collective goods. This brings up the third way I wish to discuss the "other" social sciences: to what extent do they use direct questions to investigate how individuals view collective goals, and what is the quality of their investigations?

While an adequate discussion of this issue would require a book of its own, I will briefly note here some of the conclusions discussed later (in Chapter 7). The comments here relate to all three disciplines.

There are two parts to the question: to what extent do the social sciences use interviewing techniques involving large-scale survey polls; and to what extent do they use longer interview techniques? Related to the first question is the issue of how good the quality of the large-scale surveys are, since this can vary.

To begin, I note that the amount of subjective interviewing in the social sciences is substantial and has increased in recent years. A study by Presser of journal articles using survey polling techniques showed an increase from three percent to 35 percent from 1950 to 1980 in political science, and an increase over the same period in sociology from 24 percent to 56 percent. Even economics shows a sizable increase over the period: from six percent to 29 percent. Surveys are also used in social psychology and humanistic psychology (these overlap: the percentages for 1950 and 1980 in social psychology were 22 percent and 21 percent, respectively).

The quality of these surveys is difficult to discuss in a few sentences; many of them yield straightforward, factual material which is directly useful and are largely above criticism. On the other hand, as discussed in Chapter 7, there has been an increasing volume of criticism of large-scale survey techniques in the last decade or two, and it would seem that all is not well in the area. One writer who has argued persuasively about errors existing in large-scale polling methods is Elliot Mishler, but there is a considerable literature. The point is that many of the techniques widely (and it seems, often imperfectly) used are so-called "objective" procedures undertaken because of positivist influences.

Of more relevance is the degree to which more qualitative in-depth interview techniques are being used as a supporting tool in quantitative methods. As also discussed below, quantitative methods have "been discredited in recent years, having come under attack by proponents of "quality" research.[44] Presumably, the proponents of "quality" research are mostly sympathetic to the subjective-interpretive approach.

In looking through the journal literature, I note that studies employing face-to-face interviewing techniques, where the interviews are longer than a minute or two per item, are few, but they do exist, largely in humanistic psychology and sociology.[45]

Anthropology

The discussion of the last social science discipline, anthropology, can be brief, in part because the procedures used by the anthropologists do not leave a great deal to criticize. The central subject matter of anthropology is human culture, although anthropologists tend to take responsibility for viewing humans in the most comprehensive possible way. As Nash states:

> ...Anthropologists [unlike what is done in the other social sciences] have tried to look at all aspects of human beings at all times in all places. What do humans have in common? In what ways are they different? Why are they the way they are?[46]

As a rule, anthropologists do not set limits on the type of inquiries they use in getting their information. Much of anthropology builds from micro to macro. "Micro" consists of "fieldwork," where there is a heavy dependence on direct observation, often of primitive cultures, and the investigator participates directly in the activities of the group being studied. Anthropologists resort much less to information taken from written

[44]Donsbach (1997: 25).

[45]Professor Michael McGinnis, in personal correspondence, reminds me of a growing trend in political science, and presumably in other disciplines as well, to utilize focus group methods which can yield results similar to those forthcoming from in-depth interviews.

[46]Nash (1993: 2).

historical accounts, as would be done by historians, historical sociologists, and economic historians. (unless the material is by other anthropologists). Otherwise, anthropologists tend to study humans and their cultures in any way they can, from what they say about each other, their conversations, together with their actions, interviews, behavior, or whatever. But while they begin at the micro level, anthropologists ambitiously attempt to generalize and take increasingly broad perspectives, to whole societies, civilizations, and even world events.[47] Anthropologists, given adequate empirical grounding, are not afraid to start small, to work up from "extremely small matters," as Geertz puts it.[48] They seem to go between the micro and macro levels of culture quite effortlessly. Anthropologists have managed to become quite sophisticated with respect to interviewing techniques.

Relative to the discussion above of humanistic approaches, anthropologists do not avoid making investigations into the mental-state motivations of their subjects. As Geertz puts it, the key method of anthropology deals with "interpretation," or "thick description:" rather than resting content with describing how members of a social group wink at each other in a certain way, they endeavor to find out in the greatest depth possible the meaning (and cultural significance) of the winks to those individuals doing the winking.

Anthropologists tend to concern themselves with methodological questions much more than mainstream practitioners in the other social sciences, and their discussions seem perceptive and intelligent. A good example is Geertz's well-known and highly respected essay dealing with "thick description," in which he discusses topics such as how anthropologists achieve verification or appraisal of each others' works, aggregation problems, and theoretical development.[49] Much discussed among anthropologists is whether to appraise cultures from the "inside" or "outside," that is, whether to use criteria of those native to a culture as opposed to the criteria of outside investigators. My own impression is that the latter discussion has yielded beneficial results overall, since there is something to be gained from both approaches.

---

[47]Geertz (1973: 21).

[48]*Ibid.*

[49]Geertz (1973).

With their comprehensive approach, anthropologists are typically quite astute in divining the nature of the collective goals possessed by the cultures they study; the other social sciences could learn from the anthropologists in this respect. Strangely enough, one social goal area neglected by anthropologists seems to be that dealing with marketplace-like activities. According to Kenneth Boulding,

> ...Some anthropologists have failed to understand certain aspects of primitive societies because they have not seen that exchange was a universal phenomenon which might be overlaid with all sorts of custom, ritual, and conventional behavior, but which nevertheless always involved some "terms of trade" or exchange ratios, which were relevant to the participants and their continued behavior in the role of exchangers.[50]

On the other hand, it appears that anthropologists are able to deal with methods of production in reasonably perceptive, even though descriptive, ways.

All in all, it would appear that there is much that the other social sciences could learn from anthropology.

Writers in the 'Public Choice' School

Finally, a few comments need to be added concerning an interdisciplinary group of writers (most of them economists and political scientists by training)[51] who have adopted the approach used by the professional economists for dealing with *collective goods*, that is, they have adapted the economists' "rational egoist" model for market-tradable goods to the study of political phenomena. This has its virtues but it also results in the same mistake made in mainstream economics: the neglect of collective goods, a particularly egregious sin when it comes to dealing with political phenomena.

---

[50]Boulding (1972: 272–273).

[51]There are a relatively small number of public choice sociologists, such as Coleman, but, especially since Coleman has already been discussed, I focus here on the economists and political scientists.

The public choice writers have introduced a new and useful perspective to social and political choice[52] by bringing to bear a more rigorous methodology outside the market-tradable goods sector, an area previously ignored. In particular, they have brought many new insights into the workings of institutions, an area which had been avoided by economists. They have published many important empirical and descriptive papers. They have also introduced mathematical formulation into these matters in highly useful ways. But, unfortunately, the public choice writers have been all too faithful in following the economists in their overly narrow scheme of motivation, that is, rational egoism with its overemphasis on selfish and material goals. In addition, many of the more influential members of the Public Choice Society are committed to the political and ethical values held by the political right, and have used the public choice approach to further a political agenda.[53] This would be acceptable, up to a point, but it appears that often the political agenda drives their analysis, instead of vice versa.[54]

Presumably, Bessette had these writers in mind when he complained that proponents of "rational actor theories" fail to acknowledge the role of "deliberation" about common goals.[55]

The best critical analysis of the public choice writers is provided by a political scientist in the London School of Economics: Patrick Dunleavy.[56] Among other things, Dunleavy points out a number of ways in which these writers overemphasize the material and selfish at the expense of other objectives. In their study of interest groups, there is an overemphasis on tangible and selfish benefits of group activity as opposed to collective

---

[52]"Social choice" is the academic area concerned with problems having to do with the aggregation of individual preferences into social preferences. "Public choice" is concerned with much the same thing but at a more practical level, such as the operations of constitutional rules and committees in legislatures.

[53]I have been a member of the public choice society almost from its beginning, and have found much of the work in the area interesting and stimulating. I am not a typical member from the standpoint of political agenda. For useful discussions of the public choice contribution, see Buchanan (1986, Chap. 3) and the September issue of *Public Choice* (Rowley, *et al.*, 1993).

[54]See Dunleavy (1991: 5); Paldam (1993: 182).

[55]Bessette (1994: xi and note 11).

[56]Dunleavy (1992, Chap. 1 and *passim*).

benefits, material or otherwise. The same holds true for their views on bureaucracy. Bureaucrats are seen as highly selfish, inherent maximizers, who feather their own nests by expanding the budgets of their agencies. With respect to public decision-making itself, the public choice writers place heavy emphasis on the allegation that interest groups form (unholy) alliances by trading votes in order to get their way at the expense of the rest of the general public, with the result that government expenditures are too large.[57] Finally, public choice writers explain many social programs on the basis of selfishly motivated "rent seeking," in which persons scramble to get larger shares of an existing pie, rather than trying to enlarge the pie itself, or engaging in actions meant to move closer to collective goals.

I want to emphasize that not all writers identifying with the public choice tradition take strong right political stances. Neither do they agree that analysis should be limited to the use of rational choice motivation. It is remarkable, in fact, that a majority of the writers invited to contribute to a recent anniversary volume celebrating the 75th volume of the journal, *Public Choice*, took positions criticizing the exclusive use of rational choice motivation similar to that used by economists.[58] Still, it is true that much of the work of writers in the public choice school have contributed greatly to the neglect of collective goods I point to throughout Part 1 of this volume.

[57]In this, the public choice people studiously ignore the fact that it is equally possible for interest groups to engage in logrolling that results in governments which are too small.
[58]*Public Choice*, **77** (September 1993): Rowley, Schneider, and Tollison, 5; Tullock, 10; Bernholz, 33; Breton, 60; Frey, 99; Kirchgaessner and Pommerehne, 108; Mitchell, 134; Mueller, 148; North, 159; V. Ostrom, 163; Paldam, 178; Poole and Romer, 186; Wagner, 204; and van Winden, 214. The one writer who defends the approach is James Buchanan (70) who claims, without proof, that politicians or bureaucrats in the public sector who try to further the public interest do not survive.

Chapter 5

The Evaluation of Collective Goods Delivery

...There are real opportunities to improve government performance, but availing ourselves of these opportunities will require very different reform strategies than those that have been tried in the past. It is important that this country take a less negative, less destructive approach to government than it has in the past two decades. Governments have essential roles to play in this society...A government that is paralyzed by gratuitous criticism and "reform" attempts cannot give those problems the attention they deserve.

George Downs and Patrick Larkey
The Search for Government Efficiency, 1986

All (of the regulatory reform) proposals rest on theories concerning the behavior of government agencies, private organizations, and elected political officials. Yet the proponents of reform rarely justify their proposals by reference to explicit theories and empirical observations of the interactions among these groups.

...The theory of regulatory behavior is rudimentary and fragmentary, although it is promising and progressing. Empirical work is almost nonexistent on the kinds of issues of interest to policymakers.

Roger Noll
Regulatory Behavior and the Social Sciences, 1985

The first part of this book has been devoted to a discussion of ways in which unjustified neglect of collective goods has been harmful to social science, in particular, in the area of policy analysis. In this final chapter of Part 1, we will consider whether the deficiencies discussed in the previous four chapters may have affected how social scientists and other researchers have *evaluated* activities involving the delivery of collective goods. Since evaluation practices vary by political jurisdiction, the focus of the discussion will be on the US.

Before proceeding to a discussion of evaluation, an important caveat needs to be given. Evaluation is a difficult area to discuss because it can run afoul of the political decision process. If a writer is able to point to areas in which there is poor (or no) evaluation, it could be that this represents the existence of *bona fide* political decisions. Surely, this is a possibility that ought to be kept in mind; on the other hand, there is a true need to evaluate any human activity, not only the delivery of collective goods. Therefore, the student of evaluation has little choice but to proceed with analysis and to arrive at relevant conclusions, leaving decision-makers to interpret these conclusions as they will.

Evaluation of the delivery of collective goods can take place at two levels. The broader level, which I will not be able to pursue here, is where the investigator simply asks about the extent to which any collective good is provided with respect to its relevant social goal. If the goal is that of providing adequate health care to children in the lowest quintile of the income distribution, for example, the investigation would require that we estimate how many poor children are receiving no health care or poor health care (somehow defined) in each of the many health care areas. We might then proceed to learn whether any deficiencies in health care can be attributed to "failures" on the part of one or more of the institutional sectors having responsibilities in the health care area.

The other level of evaluation focuses on the workings of institutions attempting to deliver collective goods. Here, the investigations are more technical in nature and there is a relevant literature. This is the level for which I attempt to provide an overview in this chapter, concentrating on the issue of how competently and thoroughly the evaluations are being performed.

There are four principal methods by which collective goods are delivered: by governments; through professions; by voluntary common-pool resource associations; and through the not-for-profit sector.[1] Of these, the most important are the first two. Delivery by governments is, of course, by far the most important, and indeed governments affect operations of the other three as well. The professions are important and worth considering separately because they often have considerable independent decision-making power. Most of the attention in this chapter will be given to these first two sectors. Of the other two sectors, the first — voluntary common-pool associations — is relatively small and the second — the nonprofit sector — while more important than its size would suggest, does not have a well-developed body of evaluative literature. Comments for the latter two sectors will, therefore, be quite brief.

Features of Evaluations

Evaluations come in two kinds from the standpoint of the agencies responsible for doing them and, again, in two kinds from the standpoint of content, thus giving rise to four possible combinations. With respect to responsible agencies, evaluations can be performed by personnel within the agency itself ("internal" evaluation) or by parties outside the agency ("external" evaluation). With respect to content, following a distinction made initially by Argyris, the types of evaluation are meant to foster "single-loop learning" and "double-loop learning," respectively.[2] An evaluation meant to provide single-loop learning deals with how well a government agency (or other institution) is doing, with respect to its present goals, using methods not too far removed from those currently employed. The interest in single-loop learning is in whether outcomes are consistent with organizational expectations and, if they are not, detecting the reason and correcting it. "Double-loop learning" is more comprehensive. It is evaluation not only aimed at allowing the organization to better carry out its own objectives, but, in addition, it incorporates more wide-ranging questioning of policies, assumptions, traditions, and within limits,

[1]Here, I refer to purposeful collective goods delivery. Collective goods are often delivered as non-purposeful byproducts in the market sector in the form of externalities, positive or negative.

[2]Argyris (1982).

objectives. Double-loop learning requires an opposition of ideas for comparison, where organizations function in a questioning mode with contesting views of operations. Double-loop evaluation can be more painful from an organizational standpoint in that it can involve the candid questioning of the organization's underlying policies and values.[3]

While all four combinations of these features are possible, evaluations involving double-loop learning are usually conducted by external evaluators and those involving single-loop learning by internal evaluators. Internal evaluations are generally conducted in a manner closely observed by an agency's managers, a strength but also a weakness of the approach. Evaluators can deal with issues of direct interest to managers but, on the other hand, there is a distinct sacrifice of objectivity, a result mentioned by most students of evaluation. Internal evaluation, *if done well*, is the centerpiece for Wildavsky's ideal, self-evaluating organization.[4] Students of evaluation differ on how well internal evaluation is typically done, although all agree there are problems. Some seem somewhat optimistic, although sometimes one gets the feeling they are in part discussing ideal types.[5] Others think of internal evaluation as close to worthless.[6] One of the more astute students of evaluation, with respect to government agencies, Sonnichsen, comments as follows:

> ...there is still a serious knowledge gap about the conduct of internal evaluation...Internal evaluation differs from external contracted evaluation by definition since it takes place in an organizational context, yet minimal information is available concerning this endeavor. Equally neglected has been [research concerning] the management of...internal evaluation offices...The literature available on internal evaluation is sparse and, at this time, there appears to be little consensus on successful methodologies for internal evaluations or on successful internal evaluation models.[7]

---

[3] Leeuw *et al.*, (1994: 3–4).

[4] Wildavsky (1979). I have used Sonnichsen's language in this statement.

[5] Examples are Love (1983) and Clifford and Sherman (1983).

[6] See House (1986).

[7] Sonnichsen (1994: 127–128). Sonnichsen gives the following citations with this passage: Love (1983, 1991), Mathison (1991) and St. Pierre (1982, 1983).

Sonnichsen admits that the question of evaluator independence is of key importance to internal evaluation, and that there can be no doubt that the internal evaluation office is affected by the host organization. This is a cause for concern, although he thinks that there is "insufficient evidence" to support House's view that "internal evaluators are incapable of conducting impartial evaluations and become tools of the organization administration."[8]

External evaluation, if done well, can be quite useful to agency managers, but is typically more useful to higher level decision-makers such as members of legislative bodies and higher level executives (as well as academics with relevant interests).[9] Sometimes, the findings from external evaluations can appear threatening to agency managers and often, managers look to such evaluations with less than full enthusiasm for this reason. In the end the usefulness of evaluation, whether internal or external, depends largely on the incentives and constraints that operate within an organization and its higher level organizations, as well as on the ethics and standards of the individuals doing the evaluating.[10]

Evaluation of Government Services

The most important area to discuss, with respect to collective goods delivery, is that of government. It will be useful to divide the discussion into two parts, dealing with direct delivery and regulation, respectively.

Direct service provision

An excellent overview of the state of the evaluation of direct provision of government services is found in Downs and Larkey's book, *The Search for Government Efficiency.*[11] Their conclusions about the state of analysis of government service delivery in the US are not very encouraging. They give the history of efforts to analyze the efficiency of government service

[8]Sonnichsen (1994: 128).

[9]Good external evaluations are often performed by special commissions. See Chapter 7.

[10]Eugene Steuerle made this point to me in correspondence.

[11]Downs and Larkey (1986).

delivery over the past half century as having conformed to the following pattern. Initial optimism from the New Deal era was gradually replaced after World War II with the belief that there are reasons government service delivery is necessarily inefficient. Much of the adoption of this belief was by *assumption*, due in large part to the belief in the superior efficiency of the private profit-making sector, as well as the failure of government delivery systems to have many of the efficiency-producing properties of private industry. The cynicism fostered by this belief in turn led to attempts, beginning in the 1960s, to provide "big fixes" to the inefficiency problem. Of these, the most noteworthy were the planned program and budgeting system, zero-based budgeting, managing by objective, reorganization, and personnel reform. Downs and Larkey survey the experiences with all of these. While each made some contribution, none worked nearly as well as its proponents had hoped, and the overall outcome, by the 1980s, was further cynicism and a feeling of overall helplessness with respect to the prospects of using analysis as the basis of reforming government delivery. This, in turn, has led to a spate of proposals in the past two decades for meat-cleaver types of solutions involving massive tax and expenditure cuts with some well-known results, both in the painful underfunding of programs[12] and in a burgeoning Federal deficit.

These trends are also reflected in the recent experience with evaluation of Federal programs. Bemelmans-Videc and her associates have described the decline in evaluation activity in the US Federal government in the last two decades:

> The United States, leading in the extensive initial development of the planning and evaluation functions within central government, experienced a setback in the 1980s. The retrenchment coincided with the presidency of Ronald Reagan. Evaluation was thought to be a tool of liberal efforts at social experimentation and change. Thus, in his administration, it was viewed as unnecessary and even as in opposition to his philosophy of

[12]One recent example, as I write, involves the slaying of two Capitol policemen by a man well-known to be mentally ill. The sorry state of the treatment of the mentally ill in the US is due in part to the large cuts in funding that took place in the 1980s.

> government...In 1984, there were approximately 140 government units conducting program evaluations, down from 180 in 1980. Most of the decline occurred in federal departments rather than agencies. The professional evaluation staff in the government non-defense agencies had been reduced from 1,507 in 1980 to 1,179 in 1984.[13]

The above statement pertains to the early 1980s. Eight years later, in 1992, the US General Accounting Office (GAO) did a study of the state of program analysis in Federal administrative agencies (as they also did in 1988) which pointed out that the situation had not changed very much in the succeeding eight years. The GAO stated that they had found a 22 percent decline in the number of professional staff in agency program evaluation units from 1980 to 1984 (as shown above), and that a follow-up study of 15 units showed an additional drop of 12 percent from 1984 to 1988. Funds allocated for evaluation went down by 37 percent in constant dollars from 1980 to 1984. While they did not have late data on funding, the GAO concluded that "discussions with the departments and the Office of Management and Budget offer no indication that the executive branch investment in program evaluation showed any meaningful overall increase from 1988 to 1992."[14]

The GAO report continues:

> Apparently, the effort to rebuild the government's evaluation capacity that we called for in our 1988 transition series report has not been carried out. As in 1988, executive branch agencies have often failed to conduct the program evaluations that would provide officials with knowledge about the effectiveness of their programs. As in 1988, the Congress continues to turn to us and our sister agencies — the Congressional Budget Office, the Office of Technology Assessment, and the Congressional Research Service — to do studies that might more appropriately be

[13]Bemelmans-Videc, Eriksen, and Goldenberg (1994: 154).

[14]US General Accounting Office (1992: 7). The General Accounting Office is the arm of the US Congress charged with the task of seeing whether programs mandated by law are being carried out properly in the executive branch. Its duties normally *do not* include evaluation as it is normally understood.

> conducted by executive branch agencies. It is our mission to provide credible information to the Congress and to help ensure that the reports the Congress receives are not limited to those from special interest groups. However, we should not, and indeed cannot, do it all.[15]

Subsection titles in the 1992 GAO report inform us that: "the effects of many important programs are unknown; some agencies are poorly informed about program targeting and outreach; and agencies sometimes rely on flawed studies and ignore or misuse sound analyses." Finally, they include a section entitled "Some Promising Initiatives Do Exist," where they state: "This year, in contrast to 1988, we identified a number of agency evaluations that were well done or work in progress that seems promising."[16] Apparently, the GAO found *no* promising evaluations in 1988; and the list for 1992 was quite short, having only three entries.

From conversations with GAO personnel,[17] it appears there has been a modest trend toward restoring evaluation activity since 1992. Much of this has resulted from initiatives taken by the Congress, in particular from the Government Performance Results Act of 1993 which mandated that each agency construct a strategic plan that includes a statement of its missions and goals, and that it conducts an annual formal review to evaluate its performance relative to its statement. This has given rise to some new evaluation activity, still modest as I write, but showing some promise.

With a few exceptions, there has been very little systematic evaluation conducted in the state governments. There are stirrings of activity in the 1990s: several states have implemented performance review schemes somewhat similar to that in the 1993 Federal act. The examples include Oregon, Florida, Texas, Minnesota, and perhaps a few more. It is difficult to pinpoint what is happening in the many thousands of local government services. I suspect one could find numerous instances of useful, mostly informal, internal evaluation, although my own experience with local government service evaluation is that it is all too sparse. In addition, there

---

[15]US.General Accounting Office (1992: 7–8).

[16]US General Accounting Office (1992: 23).

[17]Dr. Stephanie Shipman, in particular.

have been good evaluations done of some state and local government services by researchers in the academic community and in think tanks, most of it double-loop in nature. Given the size of the problems, the amount of this research which is of high quality is painfully small.

While all evaluation has declined in recent years, external evaluation, the kind that surely yields the most information, has shown the larger decline. As Bemelmans-Videc noted, in the Federal government it has been the broader, or departmental, evaluation which has declined the most. The scholar who may be the most careful student of evaluation in the Federal government, Richard Sonnichsen, states simply that "evaluation by external evaluation contractors and government oversight agencies has waned in the United States in recent years...," and adds that "this represents a major transformation in evaluation practice."[18]

It appears from comparative discussions of evaluation practices in the US and other nations that the US has something to learn from some of them. Canada, Sweden, and the Netherlands are noteworthy in this respect, and of these Sweden appears to be best, as discussed in some detail in the next chapter.[19]

In reading through the government evaluation literature, it becomes clear that one reason for the relatively poor evaluation record in the US in recent years is the pervasive climate of cynicism and hostility with respect to finding ways to deliver collective goods efficiently. In concluding their discussion of what is known about governmental efficiency, Downs and Larkey observe that "it is important that this country takes a less negative, less destructive approach to government than it has in the past two decades...A government that is paralyzed by gratuitous criticism and 'reform' attempts cannot give those problems the attention they deserve."[20]

---

[18]Sonnichsen cites the following studies in support of this statement: Love (1983), House (1986), Patton (1986), and Comptroller General (1988).

[19]Space does not permit a detailed discussion. See, in particular, in the Leeuw, *et al.* volume, the paper by Furabo (Sweden), Leeuw and Rozendal (The Netherlands), Leitch and Rist (The US), and Bemelmans-Videc, Erikson, and Goldenberg (comparison of ten nations).

[20]Downs and Larkey (1986: 259). It seems likely that the efforts of many of the right-wing public choice writers discussed in the previous chapter have contributed to this climate of hostility. The public choice writers, taken as a group, have been reasonably influential.

As was pointed out above, agency managers can be expected to be suspicious of robust external evaluations, but this is especially true when there is a strident strain of hostility toward government. No government manager in his or her right mind will commission evaluations which may include points critical of current practices if he or she thinks there is the slightest chance that it will be leaked to the press and/or politicians hostile toward government provision of services on ideological grounds.[21]

The effect on overall evaluation results from a hostile climate could be considerable. Downs and Larkey point out the mismatch between analysis and politics:

> There are fundamental incompatibilities between analytical approaches to decision-making and political decision-making: (1) there are incentives to bias analysis; (2) analysis is orderly where politics is messy; and (3) there are weak incentives to do analysis and to follow the dictates of analysis when it is done.
>
> ...Analytical approaches confront a dilemma. If the analyses are done by individuals or agencies with no regular standing in the decision process, the analyses are apt to be "objective" but ignored or discredited by affected agencies who, for whatever reasons, disagree with the analytic conclusions. If, on the other hand, the analyses are done by agencies with regular standing in the decision processes, there are great pressures to manipulate the analyses so that they support predetermined positions.[22]

If Downs and Larkey are correct in this appraisal, it tends to show why internal evaluations will be biased and external evaluations not even sought. The problem is redoubled in a hostile climate.

Downs and Larkey also point out at some length how the source of some of the cynicism and hostility toward government service evaluation stems from misplaced comparisons between the operations of private firms and government agencies. To such comparisons, Downs and Larkey

---

[21]There has also been a decline in trust in government (as well as other non-political institutions) on the part of the American public in recent years. See Steuerle *et al.* (1998: 113), and Nye, Zelikow, and King (1997). It seems likely that this would have been less true if there had been a better overall culture of public sector evaluation.

[22]Downs and Larkey (1986: 135–136).

have some rather strong reactions. First, they dispute the claim that the private sector is uniformly efficient by providing numerous examples. Further, they dispute the ability to adapt private sector analysis to the delivery of government services. Most government agencies have multiple goals, some difficult to measure, especially when broad strategic approaches such as those mentioned above are used. Firms in the private sector have the single objective of profit maximization and often have products subject to cardinal measurement.

Downs and Larkey conclude that governments in the US are much more efficient than is commonly thought and that their efficiency does not compare that unfavorably with private sector bureaucracies. They suggest replacing grandiose ideas of broad strategic reforms with more modest, tactical level reforms: "There appears to be an inverse relationship between the amount of fanfare associated with any given reform and its positive effects on government performance."[23] What they are asking for, in effect, is a viable system of internal and external evaluations similar to the procedures in place in Sweden discussed in Chapter 7.

Finally, we should take note of the fact that a number of evaluations of a double-loop nature (but very few single-loop type) have been undertaken by organizations outside the administrative agencies. This has always been true, but has been even more true over the past two decades when the agencies themselves have curtailed their own activities. We saw reference above to evaluations by the GAO and the Congressional Budget Office, agencies which, strictly speaking, are not meant to do program evaluation *per se*. Also, there are meaningful evaluations by think tanks and academic researchers, although this activity failed to come close to the amount required and, as the GAO pointed out, is sometimes not properly appreciated inside government.

Regulation

The area of regulation, important in the US and going back to the 1880s, has come under fairly intense scrutiny by critics and proponents alike in the past three decades or so, thus giving rise to vigorous debate about

[23]Downs and Larkey (1986: 259).

its benefits in the media, scholarly journals, and elsewhere. Often, the positions taken in these debates are factually based and, while the statistical and econometric techniques sometimes leave something to be desired, these debates have contributed to our understanding of the issues. While regulation has had its share of hostile critics, these have been counterbalanced by equally active proponents, and since regulation is fairly open to outside observation, many of the problems discussed above concerning government agency evaluation seem to have been avoided.

There are two aspects to the literature with respect to regulation, one which seems to be somewhat lacking, the other much less so in recent years. The area that is lacking is that of reform analysis (double-loop learning.) This includes work on the understanding of how regulatory bureaus, the politicians, and the public interact; how regulatory policy is devised and how it then affects justice and efficiency concerns. One of the scholars most knowledgeable in the regulation area, the economist Roger Noll, feels that not nearly enough is known about this aspect of regulatory behavior because the required empirical work is missing. In his 1985 book on regulatory behavior, Noll concludes a section on reform proposals with the statement:

> All (of the) proposals rest on theories concerning the behavior of government agencies, private organizations, and elected political officials. Yet the proponents of reform rarely justify their proposals by reference to explicit theories and empirical observations of the interactions among these groups.[24]
> ...The theory of regulatory behavior is rudimentary and fragmentary, although it is promising and progressing. Empirical work is almost nonexistent on the kinds of issues of interest to policy-makers.
>
> Certainly the most productive scholarly research at this stage would be detailed studies of how regulatory agencies actually work and what factors influence their performance...Many more case studies of agencies and policies must be undertaken to begin sorting out which theoretical models actually work best.[25]

[24]Noll (1985: 14–15).
[25]Noll (1985: 63).

Noll makes very similar comments to this in his 1989 article on regulation in the *Handbook of Industrial Organization.*[26] What Noll complains about here likely are the general problems with the empirical study of bureaucracy discussed above and in Chapter 4.

The second aspect of the evaluation literature in regulation is that dealing with the effects of the regulation itself. This has seen the burgeoning of any number of useful studies over the past 25 years. It would be difficult to even begin to document them all here, but two useful reviews provide a good starting point: Joskow and Rose (1989), and Viscusi, Vernon, and Harrington (1995).[27] The latter book includes, *inter alia,* useful discussions of numerous studies in the areas of cable television, airlines, telecommunications, eyeglasses, state usury laws, crude oil and natural gas, health, safety, the environment, and pharmaceuticals. There is a large and generally very useful regulation literature, most of it full of evaluations attempting to appraise the net benefits accruing from regulatory activity.

There is another, more worrisome aspect of the state of regulation in the US where critics are likely to be closer to being on target. One of the more formidable efficiency problems relating to government to arise in the last half of the twentieth century is the growth of complex rules and regulations, all having the force of statute. Over the past two or three decades, many institutions, both private and public, in the US have come to view themselves, not without some justification, as existing in a cumbersome morass of rules, regulations, and red tape. Much of this rule-making has been promoted with the very best of intentions and often has had salutary effects. But there is a built-in dilemma when governmental and regulatory rules have the force of law. A general rule is promulgated. Then it is noticed that there are types of situations where the original rule is either unfair or contrary to the original wishes of the legislature. The next step is to promulgate a large series of further rules which are meant to cure these problems. But then these cause still further anomalies, and the process continues. One of the more important efforts to discuss this problem was Charles Schultze's 1982 book, *The Public Use of Private Interest.* A more recent effort which has captured

[26]Noll (1989: 1281).

[27]Joskow and Rose (1989); Viscusi, Vernon, and Harrington (1989).

considerable interest is Philip Howard's *The Death of Common Sense.* As one government official stated it, a rule can be compared to

> ...a screw that could only be tightened. With each challenge to a rule by those regulated (and their attorneys), state agencies respond with more rules.[28]

While there seems to be a trend toward ending some of the worst abuses of this system,[29] it still has not gotten very far[30] and one wonders why serious students of government have not been pointing to this problem more forcefully than they have.[31] It should be added, however, that there are indications that in the last decade or so there has been a trend in Federal rule-making, at least toward a less formal and more flexible approach, as described in the informative 1986 book by Magat and others about Federal government rule-making.[32]

It is possible to speculate that there is still another instance where the existence of the problem is due in part to the suspicion and hostility with which government workers have been viewed over the past 25 years or so. People behave as if it would be dangerous to leave too many decisions up to the discretion of individual civil servants, even high-ranking ones. Thus, rules and regulations must be written in detail in an attempt to anticipate all possible contingencies in advance. In the US, this approach has likely been highly counterproductive. Perhaps other nations trust their civil servants more, with better results.[33]

---

[28]Statement by Ben G. Watts, Transportation Secretary of the State of Florida (Booth, 1995).

[29]One example involves recent developments in the State of Florida, where there has been a concerted effort to replace rule books with regulatory guidelines (Booth, 1995).

[30]Mancur Olson has advanced the interesting thesis that as societies grow older, interest groups become more established and, in the process of their lobbying for their own goals, a social "hardening of the arteries" occurs, which has the effect of slowing social and economic progress. An important part of the process is a steady growth of stultifying rules and regulations. Whether or not this process is inevitable, the part about stultifying rules and regulations has certainly been true in recent times (Olson, 1982).

[31]It could be that intervention into the lives of Americans by excessive rules and regulations carrying the force of law is a factor in the apparent recent growth in anti-government sentiment, including that on the part of so-called "militia" groups, and which seems to have been involved in the bombing of the Federal building in Oklahoma City in April 1995.

[32]Magat *et al.* (1986, Chap. 2).

[33]Smith (1984); Stanley (1984).

Professions as Suppliers of Collective Goods

The professions form an important sector which supplies collective goods, a fact often overlooked. When there is market failure due to information failure, the lapse can be made up by government or by nonprofit agencies, as discussed in the following section, or finally, by the professions. Professions have their place where knowledge requirements are highly sophisticated. The knowledge difficulties which require professional solutions are typically beyond the evaluation reach of even the most astute observer, especially without large investments of time, money, and effort. In areas such as law or medicine, there is small possibility that the final consumer of the service can judge its true nature in any detail. The need for highly sophisticated knowledge on the part of the consumer leads to what has become known as "the principal agent problem" where, because of lack of knowledge, the ultimate consumer must hire an agent on his behalf to do his consuming for him (in effect), and where the agent is difficult to supervise because of the substantial knowledge advantage he or she has over anyone else.

There are five salient points in the discussion of professionalism. First, many services highly useful to mankind require great expertise, which can only be acquired through long and costly periods of training. Second, given the great knowledge advantage possessed by those possessing such expertise, and the extreme difficulty for even the most astute outsiders to obtain it, it is possible for those having the expertise to use it to their own selfish advantage. Third, in addition to financial remuneration, an important element of "selfish advantage" in the occupational workplace is the degree of autonomy the worker has, that is, the degree to which he or she is free from the direct supervision by others. Fourth, such autonomy can be used to advance the worker's own material rewards and/or it can be used by the professional to make sure his or her service is of a high quality. Finally, it is easier to avoid the supervision of others and obtain selfish rewards and/or high quality if it is possible to show (or successfully claim) that the worker's own advantage overlaps, to a large extent, with the welfare of his or her clients.

An important aspect of how we evaluate the professional sector are the circumstances with respect to the design of professional "production." Products and services can be produced using different methods, different types of machines, workers with different levels of training, and so forth.

These designs affect the cost and quality of the goods and services delivered. From this point of view, our most important evaluative concern is whether the highly trained and high-priced professionals gain the power to decide upon the production design and then use this power to slant the design heavily in favor of their own highly priced and highly trained types of inputs, when the same service could have been produced less expensively with fewer such inputs.

In evaluating these issues, a key variable in the delivery of professional services (and, therefore, its evaluation) is the degree of altruism and other-regardingness which the individual professional brings to his or her work. A person may trust the professional as being truly other-regarding to the point of denying his or her own selfish interests to some extent, one has one view of how the professions function. If, on the other hand, one believes that professionals take a more lively interest in their own selfish welfare, the evaluation of professional delivery systems changes. We might term the more extreme ends of this continuum of behavior the "idealized" and "cynical" views of professional delivery systems, respectively. In the end, which view one can justify is a matter for factual investigation.

During the earlier decades of this century, there were almost no independent evaluations of professions *made by evaluators who were outside of the respective professions.* Whatever the reasons for this, a strong argument can be made that this was a mistake which was very costly socially. Part of the reason for it was that empirical work done over the first half or so of the century, such as it was, tended to support the more ideal explanations of the role of professions.[34] The general opinion abroad in the land was that professions had the integrity and ethical standards such that no outside supervision was necessary.

Beginning in the 1960s, students of professionalism began to take a much more critical stance, based in large part upon empirical studies which showed ill effects from substantial market power. Many of these empirical studies dealt with the field of medicine, but there were some on law, optometry, and others as well.[35] Some of the more critical earlier

[34]Much of this was in the discipline of sociology. An important figure was Talcott Parsons.
[35]Benham (1972); Benham *et al.* (1968); Evans *et al.* (1973); Fein (1967); Feldstein (1970); Friedman and Kuznets (1945); Johnstone and Hopson (1967); Kessel (1958, 1970); Lees (1966); Newhouse (1970); Zander (1968).

studies were themselves criticized later, but in general there was a growing belief that professional licensing practices led to harmful monopoly rents and other problems, such as doctor shortages (before the 1980s). Much of the more recent work deals with the cost side of the professions, often emphasizing excessive costs. This includes work by sociologists, and has been especially true for the US, where the percentage of the national income captured by the professions is high. These studies, taken as a whole, comprise the "evaluation" we have had of the professions, much of it quite valuable. In the last two or three decades, there have also been a number of studies which take the viewpoint of double-loop learning, particularly in medicine.[36]

Without going into further detail beyond the sources mentioned in the previous two footnotes, it is possible to conclude that in the US there is both excessive cost of (and expenditure on) professional services and overuse of high-priced professionals, although at the same time the overall quality of professional services is quite high. The high prices mean that typically a large percentage of the poorer members of society cannot afford adequate professional services, although the professions, with the support of governments, have often provided assistance to the very poor. Professional services in the US absorb a very large percentage of the GNP, much larger than any other nation.[37] There are large social costs from having many persons without adequate professional services, and considerable opportunity costs from the high percentages of the GNP spent on the professions when some of those resources could have been used elsewhere. On the other side of the coin, the social good has been furthered both from the high service quality itself and the technological

[36]This has been especially true in the 1990s with the rise of the health maintenance organization movement and all the analysis and scrutiny that has resulted.

[37]Health care expenditures consume about 14 percent of the GNP; about one dollar in seven. In no other country is this figure over ten percent, and in only two other nations is the figure above 8 percent. Using purchasing power exchange rates, health care expenditures per capita in the US are about $2,600; the next highest is Canada at $1,800. The US has the highest ratio of lawyers to population of any country in the world, is by far the most litigious society, and has the highest percentage of GNP devoted to legal services. Only three nations spend a larger portion of their GNP on higher education: Canada, the Netherlands, and Finland. (However, the US has the largest percentage of persons attending post-secondary institutions.) (OECD, 1992: 20).

progress it has promoted.[38] There have been both costs and benefits from professionalism, and not nearly enough evaluative attention has been paid to the ratio between the two.

The Nonprofit Sector

The nonprofit organizations sector of the economy is more important than its size would indicate.[39] As the name implies, the nonprofit sector comprises organizations restricted from (directly) paying any surplus they may generate to owners or anyone connected with the organization. Nonprofit organizations are either "proprietary" (mostly organized to further the interests of their own members), or "non-proprietary" (more other-regarding in nature.) The latter are of more interest here, although some "proprietary" organizations also provide some spillover social benefits. Churches provide fundamental moral instruction. Church congregations and service clubs involve themselves in charitable activities. Choral societies and orchestras give free concerts, and even their very existence often affords a community an artistic dimension it would otherwise not have. Sports clubs improve the public health and physical well-being. Churches,

[38]But the search for very high quality itself has side effects which cause problems. For example, there is considerable cost to the extensive due process safeguards built into the legal system. Often, some of the extremely expensive diagnostic tests used in the medical sector are not necessary. (The latter are sometimes ordered because of excessive fear of malpractice litigation, a higher than necessary quality feature of the legal system.) College education would be less expensive if less of it were given by high-priced research professors, or better still, if it were given more selectively. More public school education could be delivered by paraprofessionals, or even volunteers. These are examples of production design bias referred to above.

[39]Although the size of the nonprofit sector worldwide and in the US is growing. In Germany, France, and the US from 1980 to 1990, employment in the nonprofit sector grew at a rate more than double the average growth rate for all employment (Salamon and Anheier, 1996: 28). In the US in 1990, expenditure by the nonprofit sector was $346 billion; 6.3 percent of gross domestic product. Nonprofit sector employment was 6.9 percent of total employment and 15.4 percent of service employment (Salamon and Anheier, 1996: 34–41). The considerable growth of the nonprofit sector is shown with more recent figures presented by Steuerle and Hodgkinson for 1996, when expenditure was $434 billion and employment was 11.7 percent of total employment (Steuerle and Hodgkinson, 1998: 5; Fig. 2).

private clubs, service clubs, and the like make up about half of the total number of nonprofit organizations, although they only account for about ten percent of the total payroll generated in the nonprofit sector.

A more important part of the proprietary group of nonprofit organizations — about 76 percent of the total nonprofit sector expenditures[40] — is made up of hospitals, private universities, and related activities. While proprietary, virtually all of these have a charitable component in that they provide many services below cost to the poor.

Many nonprofit organizations provide an important overall social benefit which Boulding has described as providing "social glue" that holds a society together, an ambience based not on quid-pro-quo trades, but on grants and gifts. Thus, the nonprofit sector is important in the building of social cohesion which Boulding calls the "integrative system," the important basis in any society of "legitimacy and community,"[41] the feelings of identity and benevolence which persons have toward each other. These integrative values are fostered much more by "one-way trades," that is, gift exchanges, than by the standard two-way exchanges in the market.[42] One-way transfers, or gifts, tend to foster feelings of both benevolence and obligation which operate in serial fashion through time to create a culture of reciprocity. It should be noted that much of the workings of such gift exchanges in the nonprofit sector are not gifts of money but labor grants, that is, volunteer efforts. Such efforts seem ubiquitous, especially in American society.[43]

Also important in the nonprofit sector are trust type activities, carried out by those agencies which provide services requiring special amounts of personal trust. As Burton Weisbrod observes:

---

[40]Salamon and Anheier (1996: 51; for 1990).

[41]Boulding (1972, 275).

[42]A similar point was argued by Joseph Schumpeter, who gave it as a key reason he thought the capitalist system would break down.

[43]Percentage of persons aged 14 and above who reported donations of labor in the past 12 months on a 1985 Gallup survey included, by type of organization, 23 religious, 9 health, 13 educational, 4 arts and cultural, 7 social services and welfare, 10 recreational, and 8 civic, social, and fraternal. About half of Americans made volunteer time donations, typically to more than one kind of organization (Weisbrod, 1988; Table A.8).

> Imagine that every commodity is a bundle of attributes. Some attributes — Type 1 — are easy for a buyer to observe and evaluate. Other attributes — Type 2 — are very costly to observe and evaluate. The taste of a chocolate cookie and the location of a nursing home are of Type 1. The extent to which a nursing home actually provides "an atmosphere of love, courtesy, and understanding" and the success of police in preventing crime are Type 2 attributes. Although consumers are poorly informed about the Type 2 attributes, producers are often better informed.[44]

For services where there is a large information imbalance, such as that which obtains with "Type 2" attributes, nonprofit firms are considered more trustworthy than for-profit firms. This is because the non-distribution of profit constraint means less incentive to cheat. Without the profit motive, suppliers have incentives for providing more of a love and understanding ambience, and buyers choose nonprofits for this reason, even at a somewhat higher cost.

While the collective goods delivered by nonprofit agencies are of obvious importance, it is difficult to evaluate nonprofit sector activities, especially since the amount of Type 2 evaluations of nonprofit institutions is almost negligible. Since many activities involving trust have considerable client participation, the fact that they exist in the first place may imply an overall positive evaluation, although there are dangers in taking this approach. There may be factors which force client participation despite their better wishes. Thus, the argument may only hold if the scope of government provision is held constant, which is not a very viable assumption in recent years.[45]

There are a few studies, though not very many. Burton Weisbrod has done some interesting work in which he compares profit-making and not-for-profit organizations in the same sector, such as nursing home care.[46] Using seven criteria, Weisbrod found that consumers placed more trust

[44]Weisbrod (1988: 50). The quoted phrase was taken by Weisbrod from a nursing home advertisement.

[45]James and Rose-Ackerman (1986, Chap. 3).

[46]Weisbrod (1988, Chap. 8).

in the not-for-profit agencies than in their profit-making counterparts.[47] Another study where a similar approach was taken is by Holtman and Idsen, who showed that higher cost for nonprofit nursing homes (as compared with those making profits) can be explained by the higher quality of nurses as measured by wages, years of experience at the same institution, and education level.[48]

Voluntary Associations in Common Pool Resource Situations

Common pool resource problems exist when it is difficult to define and implement a viable system of property rights and pricing, even though it is technically possible to do so. Such problems often exist in the type of situation referred to as the "tragedy of the commons,"[49] as, for example, when a number of farmers have grazing rights in a single large expanse of pasture where overgrazing occurs so that the farmers arriving on the scene first with the most cattle reap the largest selfish benefits. The key is the existence of *free access* to any resource[50] that gives rise to the need for some kind of cooperative effort to share the resource properly. It should be noted that common pool resource problems arise in situations involving *rival* goods, where it is possible and feasible to price them to individuals or to small groups. To an extent, therefore, the common pool problem is not a pure collective goods problem in the sense that we have been discussing in this book. Some aspects of the collective goods problem, such as the free rider difficulty, remain however. It often happens that participants, in the sharing of a common resource, band together to solve the pricing problem with some kind of voluntary arrangement. Instances

[47]The criteria: was there a waiting list; were waiting lists longer; are consumers better informed about periodic reviews; are sedatives used less; are consumers more "satisfied;" are consumers more satisfied in five specific areas; and are consumers more likely to complain? (Weisbrod, 1988: 156).

[48]Holtman and Idsen (1991). The differences in expenditure levels, wages, experience, and education were, however, not very large.

[49]This phrase is usually attributed to Garrett Hardin (see Hardin, 1968: 1244). In point of fact, the idea was anticipated by Scott Gordon (1954) in his classic article on the fisheries.

[50]I owe thanks to Scott Gordon for emphasizing this aspect of the problem to me.

where such efforts have been reasonably successful are numerous.[51] Failure is always possible, however, especially when the resources are widely distributed. Current examples of failure involve the overfishing taking place off Alaska, on the Cape Cod fishing banks, and in the international whale fisheries.

There is no dearth of evaluative studies of common pool resource situations, although this has only been true for the last two decades or so. Important here is Elinor Ostrom's 1990 book, *Governing the Commons,* and the many studies cited in her long list of references. Ostrom's book, as well as any number of the other studies, includes sophisticated discussions of the characteristics associated with successes and failures. While these discussions are not without their disagreements, on the whole the evaluative literature on common pool resource situations is highly informative.

Summing Up

The quality of the evaluation of collective goods delivery in the US draws mixed reviews. In some of the smaller sectors — regulation and common pool resource situations — the evaluation literature seems quite informative. The nonprofit sector — also relatively small — has little formal evaluation although in large part (but not entirely) consumer patronage levels provide a fair amount of automatic evaluation.

For the two most important areas involved in collective goods delivery, however — governments and the professions — the assessment must be much less positive. Professions were completely left alone over much of this century in the period when the main features of the role they were to play in service delivery was being shaped and decided. More recently, the situation has improved, but the inertia of established institutional arrangements is great. The formal evaluation efforts of government services, never highly effective, have suffered conspicuous decline in the last two decades, although there is at least a glimmer of hope now that the situation is beginning to be reversed. The evaluation and study of institutional relationships within the regulatory sector has also been

[51]See, for example, Ostrom (1990, Chap. 3).

seriously lacking. There are a few bright spots in the area of external (double-loop) evaluation in the academic community, think tanks, and in government agencies such as the Congressional Budget Office and General Accounting Office. However, these efforts are not always heeded by governmental decision-makers (the two government agencies listed may do somewhat better in this respect), and the efforts themselves are too few and far between. In addition, as pointed out in the GAO statement quoted above, the evaluation of agency functions is not meant to be part of the missions of units such as the CBO and the GAO. The fact that they have been conscripted into doing so is itself a comment on the inadequacy of the evaluation functions being performed in the Federal government.

In a recent perceptive comment on the changing role of government and its relationship to the people of the US, Steuerle, Gramlich, Heclo, and Nightingale point out that in recent years the American political process has, at the same time, become more responsive to a number of public inputs of a superficial nature — polls, policy activists, media-based politics, and advocacy groups — while becoming less responsive to more substantive aspects of public thinking.[52] As they put it, the public is being courted, but not really heard or respected. This situation has not gone unnoticed on the part of the public, which in turn has given rise to increased cynicism on their part. If this is true, and their arguments seem to me persuasive, it could be that one important factor giving rise to greater superficiality and less substance is the lack of good, deep, believable, and objective evaluations of government service delivery programs and government oversight of non-governmental service delivery programs meant to further collective goals.

[52]Steuerle *et al.* (1998, Chap. 5).

Part 2
New Directions

The second part of this book, the following two chapters, is devoted to discussing possible new directions that might be taken to deal with the problems discussed in Part 1. Chapter 6 deals with the possibilities for building investigatory models where all human social goals are given equal consideration, while Chapter 7 considers possibilities for expanding procedures for gathering data on human subjective states.

Chapter 6

What Can be Done?

Science, rationality, objectivity can no more be captured, legislated, or demarcated than can the concepts of freedom or democracy because their existence hangs on both professional training and on an attitude that itself is bound up with freedom and democracy...If we really want to know what we can do to advance science, we can guarantee that this attitude, scientific rationalism — tolerance, honesty, commitment to the advance of science above personal advance and to the freedom to exercise criticism, a willingness to listen and to learn from others, and so on — is not violated and becomes entrenched as a tradition.

Deborah Redman
Economics and the Philosophy of Science, 1991

Economics is such a splendid science, such a beautiful model for social thinking, that it is a pity that most non-economists, irritated by the cultural barbarism of its practitioners, writes economics off as politically slanted rubbish. They lose a chance to think clearly about economic growth or social justice. The isolation is a pity for economists too. The conversations outside economics are so varied, so close to life as it is lived, that the economist who writes them off as emotion or nonsense or pictures at an exhibition will lose much..., in fact the same thing the outsiders lose: a chance to think clearly about economic growth or social justice.

Donald (Dierdre) McCloskey
Knowledge and Persuasion in Economics, 1994

It is a sad and often wilful misunderstanding of economic theory which seeks to portray it as heartless and incapable of dealing with actions which spring from emotional or altruistic motivations.

Patrick O'Sullivan
Economic Methodology and Freedom to Choose, 1987

Having devoted considerable attention in the preceding five chapters to problems, in this chapter, I will suggest some steps toward resolving them. Virtually all of the difficulties discussed in Part 1 can be successfully addressed by employing the methodology used to such advantage by economists for market-tradable goods and extending it to all human-scarce goods. I hope to show that this need not be as difficult as economists have always claimed. The whole exercise will be properly approached only in the spirit of Deborah Redman's "scientific rationalism:" with tolerance, honesty, and a willingness to listen and to learn from others.

The key foundation stone on which the argument in this chapter (and this book) rests is the importance of individual human motivation in social science. It is the *sine qua non.* All science requires a theory of causation which provides the basic dynamic upon which all the other scientific observations and predictions rest. In the natural sciences, these include heat, sunlight, gravitational force, magnetic force, and so on. In the human sciences, causation is provided by motivation — motivation of individuals toward whatever goals they may have, goals that were determined in the first place on the basis of perceived needs. Finally, human actions result as humans engage in making free choices in order to pursue goals.

The social science that has best used a model of free choice based upon goal motivation is economics and, therefore, I will begin this chapter with a review of the reasoning used in economic science.[1] But the economists, to reiterate yet once more, have only taken their approach part way and, therefore, my next task will be to give ideas on how the economics model can be extended to include collective goods.

[1]Trained economists may wish to skip some of this discussion.

The Economic Deliberate Choice Model

Economics is the science that deals with choices involving scarcity, but in application this is rather far-reaching, for almost all human policy decision problems involve scarcity. The economic (and policy) model of choice is, therefore, a model of *constrained* choice, meaning that the resources are never available to allow us to move completely to many of our goals. Economists represent this in a manner which can alienate critics of utilitarianism: a "utility function" represented in the following with a capital "U":

$$W = U(x_1, x_2, x_3, \ \dots x_n). \tag{6.1}$$

(Welfare comes from the utility a person gets from all of the items he or she consumes, or activity he or she enjoys.) In fact, critics should not be put off by this expression,[2] which is not one that suggests some classical approach with interpersonal utility comparisons, but merely a more general and (properly) noncontroversial statement that human welfare depends on human consumption. Thus, the expression (6.1) means simply that a person's welfare depends on what he or she consumes. Critics might prefer the alternative form of the expression:

$$W = \Sigma_i \, w_i \, x_i, \tag{6.2}$$

which means that welfare is equal to the sum of the distance that a person travels toward (or away from) each of his goals (the x_i) multiplied by the importance he or she puts on each (the w_i). The latter approach allows one to think of the choice problem in more practical and concrete terms, where the welfare aggregation for a single person begins with giving the preference intensity for a unit advance toward one of the goals a value of 1.0 (or 100, or whatever), and then setting all the other weights in comparison to that one.

---

[2]The fact that some of them are put off by this usage is a good illustration of the problems in moral philosophy and other social sciences discussed in Chapter 5, where practitioners in these disciplines refuse to use the economic choice model at all because economists sometimes use terminology associated with utilitarianism. This mistake has caused an incalculable amount of harm, including the writing off of economics as "politically slanted rubbish" as McCloskey puts it.

The economic choice model is completed when we add to it that aspect of human activity wherein persons strive to optimize their welfare by doing things which, in their own estimation, increases that welfare. In formal terms, this is done when a unit advance toward any goal yields the same welfare per dollar of effort as does a unit advance toward any other goal.[3] Individuals will have information problems in attempting to do this, of course, but they must do the best they can with whatever information is available. Finally, it is important to note that as economists apply this choice model to the world of market-tradable goods, they are completely value-neutral when it comes to deciding which commodities and services to include in the menu of possible choices. No good is excluded *ex ante*, no matter whether it's illegal, dangerous to one's system, or whatever. The choice model used by economists is completely fair and impartial, at least so long as it is not asked to go beyond the realm of market-tradable goods.

The Economic Choice Model as Subjectivist and Teleological

So, there are two fundamental approaches to social science methodology: *objectivist-behavioral*, where humans are treated as objects subject to study in behaviorist terms based on empirical observation as observed by other persons; and *subjective-interpretive*, where the social scientists treat individuals as having a subjectivist character, determined in part through their own self-conscious and free choices. In the latter approach, individuals are viewed "not as causally determined by any external stimulus, but rather as (engaging in) action, as (performing) the purposive execution of a project, as activity directed to a goal of which the agent is actually or potentially conscious."[4] As O'Sullivan points out, one could hardly imagine a better example of the subjectivist-interpretive methodological approach than the choice model used by economists just presented. It is a welfare maximization model which proceeds according to the motivations provided strictly by the agent's own goals, and so is a model

[3]While the metric of this is difficult, presumably this is what we do when we make our choices in a market. For further discussion of the choice model in economic theory, see O'Sullivan (1987, Chaps. 5 and 6) or consult any microeconomic theory textbook.
[4]O'Sullivan (1987: 58).

which is strictly teleological in character. While there is plenty of room for objectivist-behavioralist methods to be used in social science, the subjective-interpretive approach, built as it is on the basic foundation of human motivation, is fundamental to social science and, at the same time, is *completely* consistent with the mainstream microeconomic choice model of economic science. It is, as McCloskey puts it, a "beautiful model for social thinking," and it is a pity that economists have chosen not to take it any farther than they have.[5]

Extending the Economists' Model to Collective Goods

There is no reason that *all* human goals cannot be included in the economists' choice model. Many economists in their better moments subscribe to Lionel Robbins' dictum that "economics is the study of human behavior insofar as it is a relationship between ends and scarce means which have alternative uses." In the well-known essay where Robbins makes this remark, he makes it very clear that by this he means all ends where scarcity is involved, including, in particular, ones that are collective in nature.[6] I am merely asking economists to extend what they accept in their better moments to what they do in practice, and to use *that* model across all of the social sciences and for some aspects of moral philosophy. I also ask that the fair and impartial manner used by economists to include all market-tradable goods into consideration be extended to the broader domain of all market-tradable and collective goods. And finally, I ask that, when relevant, social scientists employ all possible methods for obtaining data, including methods involving high-

[5]"Economists are deaf to history or philosophy. Most of them yawn at geography or psychology; they do not take seriously anthropology or sociology. Although they want to speak to law and political science, they do not want to listen. They ignore remoter conversations altogether, and ignore too their own past conversations. The suggestion that the study of literature or communication, or even the nonliterary arts, might also speak to them would be regarded by many economists as lunacy" (McCloskey, 1994: 28; also see the chapter epigraph).

[6]"Economics is the science which studies human behavior as a relationship between ends and scarce means which have alternative uses..., there are no limitations to the subject matter of economics save this" (Robbins, 1984 (1932): 16–17). Also see the discussion of Robbins in Chapter 1.

quality polling and interviewing techniques, data uniquely required by subjective-interpretive models which are founded upon human teleology and choices.

To recapitulate from the methodological discussions in the Introduction and Chapter 1, economics has been a successful discipline because it has found a way to use a subjectivist methodology while also using — and claiming obeisance to — objectivist techniques. In a way, economists have been able to eat their cake and have it at the same time by using a subjectivist approach without doing the empirical work that a fully implemented subjectivist approach would require. This was achieved simply by adopting procedures which O'Sullivan attributes to a group of Austrian economists, but which, in fact, trace back much farther (see note 57 in Chapter 1), where the necessary motivation (and related goals) was obtained from employing common sense together with introspection, observation, and empathy. This resulted in an assumed motivational scheme, "cognitive rationality," driven solely by the human goal of selfish material gain.

If we are to extend the microeconomic model to all the other goals that assume importance — an approach that might be viewed as employing a "goal model" for social science analysis — there are two ways this could be done. They could be pursued separately, or each could be used to reinforce the other. The first way would involve pursuing methodology for collective goals similar to that suggested by the Austrian economists[7] for individual goods; the other would involve attempts to empirically investigate subjective views concerning the importance of alternative social goals.

An Austrian Approach for Collective Goods

If economists, following the lead of the Austrians, have been able to use a viable subjective methodology based on human motivation without doing extensive empirical work that would need to deal with the other-minds problem, we might ask whether such an approach is possible when

[7]While, as stated above, this methodology goes back much further, I will continue to term it "Austrian" since those economists discussed it the most explicitly.

dealing with *collective goods*. Indeed, one wonders why such a line of inquiry has not been followed before now. I believe that such an exercise is possible and, indeed, that it is close to the methodology I used in my earlier book on tax analysis.[8] In that book, I suggest that an investigator could construct a list of social goals which are of central importance in *any* society, and to do so without undertaking special empirical investigations. First, there is something of a literature on the topic of major social objectives, and the researcher can begin by consulting that. Next, the researcher can study statements concerning political and social ideologies of a sample of writers who range widely across the ideological spectrum in order to construct a list of all the social goals implicated in their statements. The polling and interview literature will yield relevant information. Finally, one can check to see whether the list of basic goals he has obtained can be used to describe most major aspects of any present, past, or imagined society. The resultant set of goals, pruned where possible to eliminate overlaps and relatively insignificant objectives, can then be cross-checked to see if it adequately represents the political and social ideologies of any other writer.

Using these methods, I obtained five major goal areas: *reward, efficiency, need, freedom,* and *equality,* which were then broken down further into more specific goals: *reward* into reward for effort, ability, luck, and so on.[9] The areas just described were meant to apply to broad social programs or policies. The same approach can be used for a more narrowly focused investigation, such as of a farm subsidy program, by using, besides the above, goals more closely related to the program being studied.

Thus, the investigator can isolate a list of social goals (collective goods) which most persons consider of some importance relative to the policy under examination. The next step for social scientists is to provide analysis by drawing upon all relevant theoretical and empirical knowledge, and to give the predicted opportunity costs (trade-offs) in terms of all the other goals for moving a unit closer to any goal (particularly a goal of central concern). No effort is made by the social science investigator to place weights on any goal different from weights placed upon other

[8]Kiesling (1992: 15, 119, 164, 209, 245, 292).

[9]See related discussions of the goal model in the Introduction and Chapter 7.

goals.[10] Note that this methodology has yielded considerable information that is highly useful to decision-makers without engaging in empirical investigations which require dealing with the "other-minds problem."

An Empirical Approach for Collective Goods

In order to understand what would be required for empirical implementation of a subjective-interpretive approach to policy analysis that includes collective goals, we can first investigate what such an approach would look like for microeconomic analysis as it currently exists.

As microeconomic analysis is currently performed, the motivation is *assumed* to be that of cognitive rationalism, that is, selfish material gain. The assumption is fully general, which means that this motivation is considered correct for everyone. Now, let us visualize adding to the model some true empirical testing in microeconomics. This would require investigations into the actual mental states of individual persons. The hypothesis would be that a given person, Henry Clyde, has significant motivations *other than* that of selfish material gain. Mr. Clyde would need to be administered a combination of questionnaires, polls, and interviews in order to discover any personal goals he may consider important, other than classical selfish gains.[11] To the extent that persons in the economy were found to have conflicting goals, the classical motivation assumption would need to be amended. An "other-minds problem" exists because Mr. Clyde could report, as a significant goal, providing funds for local charities (or whatever) when he has no such goal and is merely trying to impress the interviewer. It could happen. There is no foregone conclusion that it *will* happen.

Next, we can attempt to implement, empirically, a model of social action meant to include collective goals directly. This involves a change in focus from testing the classic assumption of cognitive rationality to empirical testing directly for allegiance to specific collective goals. The

[10]The reader might recall the RULE postulated in the Introduction above: "all values given either to the weights placed on social goals or the identification of the goals themselves are supplied by, and only by, the group's properly chosen decision-makers."

[11]No claim is made that efforts to provide other data by means of behaviorist investigations, such as checking Mr. Clyde's tax returns, could not be made. (Although the particular example I have chosen would no doubt involve a cooperation problem.)

model now begins with a statement of specific collective goals: an example would be the ten or so goals I used in my earlier book on tax analysis, plus other goals more directly related to the particular policy action under investigation. (It should be noted that economic marketplace efficiency is one important collective goal.) Other goals might come up in the conversation with the respondent as being important to him or her, and would be included. Some of the empirical investigation could usefully examine behavioral phenomena, but the empirical study would not be complete without examining "mental states" with the use of polls, questionnaires, and interviews. Questions designed to show the relative importance the respondent places on alternative social goals (the trade-offs he would make) would be the most useful approach to take here, I believe. For example, in my pilot interview study, I asked one of my respondents whether, from the standpoint of taxation, we should treat two persons earning the same amount equally if one worked many hours per week and the other did not. My respondent, Jane, answered that we (that is, the government) should not; it's none of our business. What I was attempting to ascertain was whether the state, in collecting taxes, should make a distinction between reward for effort and reward for ability. What I found out was that, for Jane, the social goal of maintaining personal freedom was of much greater importance than any such reward distinctions. Again, this methodology must deal with any errors caused by the "other-minds problem."

There are two ways in which interviewing and polling techniques can be used which correspond to the Austrian and empirical estimation approaches to motivation. First, they can simply be used to demonstrate to the researcher which social goals members of the public seem to consider important, without delving further into how important (in relative terms) they consider them to be. Thus, we can add an empirical dimension to the Austrian approach discussed above by asking individual respondents to indicate which social goals they consider important. I have found that an excellent way to do this is to pose the hypothetical: "If you were to choose what kind of society you most wanted to live in, what would it be like?" Much can be learned from respondents in lengthy interviews where the conversation revolves around questions of how much the respondent would be willing to trade off x amount of progress toward one social goal for y amount of progress toward another social goal.

Conversations involving trade-offs among social goals and between social goals and money would be required for empirical estimations of collective goods demands. Since collective goods accrue to everyone equally, the "demand," for collective goods or amount that the group would give up for a unit of a collective good, must be calculated by adding together the amounts —of money or another collective good[12] — which each member of the group would give up individually.[13] Since there are many collective goods and many possible levels of each, detailed demand estimates of this type —unless the number of group members and number of collective goods in question were small — would be next to impossible to achieve. More possible would be estimates for a recognizable level of a single collective good (or just a few of them), such as a situation where subsidized day care is made available to all working women and a sliding scale of subsidized prices is presented. The only way the numbers problem might be overcome would be either by using small samples of the population or by discovering a number of population groups whose members think alike.

Can Empirical Estimation Problems Involving Collective Goods Demands be Overcome?

I am suggesting polling and interviewing techniques could be used to good advantage either to establish sets of social goals considered important or, within limits, to yield insights on collective goods demands directly. Economists have traditionally argued that collective goods are to be avoided on grounds that empirical problems are simply too difficult to overcome. The time has come to make an appraisal of the economists' objections to empirical work in the area of collective goods.

[12]But eventually denominated in monetary terms.

[13]Suppose that a group of five persons had the following demands for a level of a service which will accrue equally to all of them: *A* feels it's worth $100, *B* $200, *C* $400, and *D* $1,000. *E* is against having the service and could only have his negative feeling assuaged if he were *paid* $600 (negative demands for collective goods are possible.) Adding the five individual demands together, we find that the group, as a whole, would pay $1,100 for that particular level (or it could be additional unit) of the service.

There are three aspects important to an empirical analysis of goods in the social sciences: how they are to be *defined*, how they are to be *measured*, and how *demands* for them are to be *estimated*. The question is whether there are unique problems specific to collective goods, and whether they are serious enough to preclude rigorous analysis by social scientists in ways required for good policy analysis. Many collective goods, such as national defense and moral virtues, are difficult to define and measure. But many individual goods are difficult to define as well — the services of a management consultant or of a psychologist, for example. Standard goods in microeconomic theory textbooks, such as bushels of wheat, are sure bets both for definition and measurement. Collective goods, such as the number of persons in poverty or the size of the poverty gap, are the same sure bets.

The key difficulty with measurement and definition of troublesome collective goods, as compared to troublesome individual ones (national defense versus the product of a psychologist), is due in large part to their sheer size. There is simply more at stake. If an individual cannot get it right concerning the product of a psychologist, there is only the misfortune of a single individual to concern us. If a nation finds it difficult to define and measure the quality of national defense, much more is involved. It may be that the qualitative nature of the problems involved is not all that different.

Numerous individual and collective goods are too complex to be represented by single measures. Such complexity makes analysis of such goods difficult, not impossible. In this respect, we can consider methodology often used by evaluators of complex activities, such as judges of sporting events, barbershop quartet singing competitions, and the like. The same kind of approach can be used to make manageable the analysis of complex products, including many collective goods. A good example is the methodology which has been used to analyze national defense problems — often termed "sub-optimization" — about which there is a fairly large literature (much of it produced by economists).[14] The overall problem of finding a measure or a definition for "the national defense" is most

[14]See, for example, Hitch and McKean (1960), Hitch (1965), Enke (1967), and Hoeber *et al.* (1978).

readily grasped if we ask: "What is a *unit* of national defense?" In fact, there are two aspects to a nation's defense, each equally unsuitable for precise definition and measurement. The quality of a nation's defense effort is a combination of the ability to keep a potential opponent from mounting aggression against it in the first place, and the ability to overcome any aggressive actions that *are* launched in the second place. How could one define a "unit" of either one of these?

On the other hand, it is possible to break down a nation's defense efforts into sub-categories which are much more definable and measurable when each is viewed separately. In effect, several collective goals are substituted for one. Instead of deterrent or attack capability in general, we can view the time it takes to deliver a given amount of offensive or defensive power to some region of the world by types of Air Force units, submarines, aircraft carriers, army units, and so on. If decision-makers (but not the analysts, normally) wish to aggregate these into a single measure of defense capability, they would need to develop a set of weights as to the relative importance of the constituent sub-components of defense activity.[15]

The most difficult area to define, and especially to measure, is that dealing with norms and morality. Some clues to how this might be done were presented above in the discussion of emotion in Chapter 3, and will be shown in the workings of commissions in Sweden later in this chapter. For the ethical domain, there is always the important question of which aspects are susceptible to social interventions in the normal course of events. Examples were given — usually in areas having to do with some dysfunction — where the practicality of social intervention seems indicated and measures are easily supplied (for example, the Head Start program or the mentoring of young at-risk children). Otherwise, in dealing with ethical values and norms, we may need to go into the field of social psychology, particularly with respect to personality development. This kind of inquiry would be especially valuable to students of collective goods because it is a key foundation to questions concerning demands persons have for collective goods, including how they relate to their demands for individual goods.

[15]And also for relationships *between* components, lower weights for greater imbalances, and so forth.

Preferences

The empirical estimation problem for collective goods that has most impressed economists is that having to do with preference revelation. As discussed earlier, with all group members sharing a collective good, there is no good behavioral device for ascertaining how much a unit of collective good is worth in the eyes of an individual consumer, a fact causing no end of difficulty. While all group members *must* share collective goods, at the same time they may (and usually do) place very different values on them. Group welfare would be maximized with a scheme in which all pay their marginal evaluation,[16] or barring that, at least reasonably equal shares —perhaps shares which vary according to income. Individual group members can maximize their gains by not contributing, but only if most others *do* contribute. They are "free riders."

There are at least two, quite separate, ramifications of the free-rider problem for us to consider. First, the free-rider problem is considered important to economists and others because of the effect it has on the ability to conduct human social affairs through voluntary cooperation. The existence of the free-rider problem is an important reason humans require governments having coercive powers. But while that is of great social importance, it is not of greatest importance to our discussion here, which is focused on data collection. For this second ramification of the free-rider problem, the crucial question is: to what extent will this problem make it impossible for social scientists to obtain accurate data concerning preferences for collective goods? Our central concern is whether individuals will cooperate with investigators to an extent great enough to yield accurate information concerning their preferences.

Economists who, after all, have traditionally concentrated on selfish behavior, have typically taken a rather cynical stance about the possibilities of cooperation where collective goods are concerned. But the situation

[16]For readers lacking training in economics, the *marginal evaluation* is that placed on the last unit consumed. This rule is typically more complicated for collective goods than for individual goods. For individual goods, the proper price payment is the valuation a person places at the margin, that is, on the last unit — if ten apples are consumed, the price paid is the same for all ten and is the marginal evaluation placed on the 10th. For collective goods, optimal pricing may require different payments, for example, the second unit of the good as opposed to the fourth unit.

is surely better for data collection; there is evidence that individuals are more cooperative social beings than the economists have thought. In his recent book, *Passions Within Reason*, Robert Frank presents reasons why varying degrees of altruistic behavior can be expected from humans.[17] While much of such behavior may be motivated by selfish concerns, Frank finds evidence to suggest that humans also engage in "genuinely unopportunistic behavior," that is, behavior implying almost completely altruistic motivation — such as performing rescues at high risk of personal danger. Frank argues that while several hypotheses could be consistent with altruism prompted by quasi-selfish motives, there is only one hypothesis consistent with both these and genuinely unopportunistic motives: what he terms the "commitment model" of behavior.[18]

The commitment model is based on the supposition that humans find themselves in social situations where there are great advantages to cooperative behavior, but where for any given individual there are even greater advantages from non-cooperative behavior when most other individuals are cooperating. Frank makes a convincing case that potential cheaters have a more difficult time of it than one might suppose, and for why the cooperators of the world are able to do a reasonably good job of identifying both each other and possible defectors. The evidence seems to show that, on average, persons who have character traits such as sympathy and concern for fairness, rather than being "softheaded losers," turn out to be successful *even in material terms*.[19] This suggests that economists are wrong with respect to "rational egoism" *even on their own ground*.[20] Thus, Frank points out that empirical studies show altruism as being positively correlated with socio-economic status, but do *not*

[17]Frank (1988).

[18]Frank (1988: 68).

[19]Not to speak of the utility they get from their altruistic behavior patterns. The following comment appears in Rushton (1980: 84) with respect to persons who score high on indices of altruism: "...he or she is more empathic to the feelings and sufferings of others and able to see the world from their emotional and motivational perspective...Altruists also behave consistently more honestly, persistently, and with greater self-control...Furthermore, the consistently altruistic person is likely to have an integrated personality, strong feelings of personal efficacy and well-being, and what generally might be called "integrity."

[20]Frank (1988: 235).

show a direct relationship between altruism and intelligence.[21] If correct, this finding is of key importance, since it shows that altruism is more responsible for socio-economic status (which, of course, is partly determined by income and wealth) than intelligence itself.

Another source of empirical information relevant to the free-rider problem comes by way of a large number of controlled laboratory studies conducted over the past two or three decades. A typical experiment would have a small group of subjects who are given perhaps $5.00 and informed that if they invest all of their $5.00 in a group investment good, and if all other members of the group do likewise, they will all receive a payoff of $10.00. If they invest and no other member invests, they will lose their $5.00, or at least most of it. But if they do not invest their $5.00 and all other members do invest, their payoff will be $15.00. Typically the subjects are not allowed to communicate with each other, either during or after the experiment. There have been many variations, for example, group size is varied, payoffs changed, and communication allowed.

By now, there have been hundreds, if not thousands, of studies of the kind just described. The following might be a fair assessment of what, on balance, they have shown. From the degree of cooperation shown, the rational egoist free-rider hypothesis, in simple form, is disconfirmed rather conclusively. There are some indications of genuinely unselfish other-regarding behavior, but the most consistent suggestion is that most subjects are quite willing and happy to cooperate and, up to a point, will cooperate even when others do not — either as an attempt to signal the others to cooperate or to reflect genuine other-regarding behavior — but beyond this modest degree of one-sided cooperation, subjects do not wish to be shown up as being "suckers." Most of the findings seem to betray a strong and lively moral sense of equity and fair play on the part of subjects, and also suggest that such fairness ideas are widely shared. Implicated throughout is a strong reciprocity ethic, or "tit-for-tat."[22]

---

[21]In a recently published book, Daniel Coleman (1995) gives considerable evidence that cognitive intelligence and "emotional intelligence" are two different things, with the latter more likely to be related to having a successful and happy life (also see Gazziniga, 1995).

[22]The following references provide a fairly good introduction to this literature: Caporeal *et al.* (1988; also see the many comments in the same journal), Miller and Andreoni (1991), Oliver and Maxwell (1988), Ostrom, Walker, and Gardner (1992), Sugden (1984), Walker and Williams (1994), Wickstrom (1985), and Yamagishi (1988).

Frank's work, and the laboratory experiments with respect to a person's preference for collective goods, suggests that the harsh version of the free-rider problem often suggested by economists is off the mark. Humans in most societies are basically cooperative creatures so long as they feel their fellows are cooperating as well. For the most part,[23] *individuals will not go out of their way to give false witness* with respect to their demands for public goods. This means that investigators can, in large part, depend on the cooperation of respondents in polling and interview studies.

The Goal Model Subjective Approach Summarized

Pulling the strands together, the procedure I am suggesting — the methodology used in the social sciences — is summarized as follows. The approach is meant for social policy analysis, but since arguably there is no question investigated by the social scientist — no matter how arcane — which does not bear directly or indirectly on social policy, the methodology is meant to be applied to all activities of all social scientists with few exceptions.[24]

For whatever analytical or policy issue at hand, the investigator begins by making a conscientious effort to identify all social (and if relevant, individual)[25] goals to which the issue may be relevant. Next, to the extent possible, the investigator attempts to find meaningful ways to measure progress toward the goals. Goals which prove difficult to define precisely and/or to measure, must be explicitly discussed anyhow, in the nature of "noting them in the margin," so to speak.[26] If some goals are considered too trivial to include, the reasons for excluding them need to be stated explicitly.

---

[23]Admittedly, a small number of anti-social persons may prove to be exceptions.

[24]If a social scientist is working with material not somehow related ultimately to social policy, one can question the usefulness of the activity itself. The *raison d'etre* of social science is social policy which improves the human condition.

[25]In some policy analysis, the fortunes of a single firm or investor or institution may be important. Also, for issues involving human freedom (a collective goal), it may be relevant that a single individual be allowed to do what he or she wishes.

[26]Such procedures are often used in benefit-cost analysis.

Having obtained the relevant set of criteria, along with measures, the next task for the investigator is to provide an analysis of all the ways in which it is possible to move closer to each goal (and particularly the goals of central concern) by drawing on all relevant theoretical and empirical knowledge in any of the human sciences, physical or social. (This may require interdisciplinary teams or consultation with experts in other disciplines besides the investigator's own.) Already, at this stage, the investigator has obtained information of considerable value to decision-makers.

The investigator is now ready to take the second step, which is to use all relevant theoretical or empirical knowledge to calculate the trade-offs (opportunity costs) in attempting to make progress toward the various goals, in particular the trade-offs between progress made toward those goals of central interest to policy-makers for the issue at hand and all the other goals identified as relevant. It should be noted, in this regard, that for some of the other relevant goals, opportunity costs can be, and often are, negative. That is to say, the goals are complementary to each other: getting closer to one goal has the beneficial side effect of getting the group closer to another one. Now the investigators have completed the majority of the work highly useful to decision-makers, and have done so in ways which are ethically unbiased and which do not require empirical investigations which run afoul of the "other-minds problem."

Finally, there is a third possible stage to the analysis — should it be deemed desirable — in which the investigator, through interview techniques, attempts to find the relative weights placed upon goals by individual (or perhaps small groups of) decision-makers. These are then analyzed from the viewpoint of their "preference functions," as Ragnar Frisch termed this approach (see the following). Again, it is to be noted that these are value weights supplied by the decision-makers, not by the social scientist. A variation on this theme would be for the investigator to construct sets of alternative preference functions in situations where there are only a few obvious alternative views, and to show which policy actions are suggested from each.

What I have in mind is an approach which can be used for explanation in social science, as well as for informing policy formulation. For this aspect, it must be added that the approach I suggest is one in which the analysis in social science is to be extended to "inner mental states," and that, contrary to the empiricist tradition, this can be done with the aid of polling and interview techniques sophisticated enough to inquire into the results of human introspection and recall of mental histories and experiences.

A Note on Honest Impartiality

There has been more than a tinge of cynicism in the past three or four decades among social scientists about the possibilities for approaching their work with an attitude of good old-fashioned objectivity. Some grounds exist for such gloomy thinking, no doubt. Blaug has discussed how value biases can enter social science even when the analyst attempts objectivity, such as from the way he chooses topics to study, the statistical tests he uses, and the data he gathers.[27] Some of the pessimism may be due to McCloskey's attempts to talk about how economists "persuade," interpretations which I believe are largely misplaced because of less than careful reading of what McCloskey really has to say. "Persuasion" would seem to imply bias, or unseemly attempts to get the reader to come around to one's own point of view.[28] Perhaps other forces are also at work, including examples from actual practice where there are, regrettably, numerous examples in which social scientists allow strong political and ethical biases to influence their analysis in ways that are quite transparent to more objective readers. Some of the public choice writers discussed in the previous chapter are excellent examples of this, but there are others. Some of this may also be due to the characteristics of the logical positivism tradition with its insistence, going back to "Hume's fork" (the strict separation of facts and values), that there is a large universe of ethical positions which is both not part of pure science and vast enough to be constantly luring true "scientists" away from the straight and narrow. Some of it may also be due to the position that economists should never

[27]Blaug (1992, Chap. 5).

[28]I suspect McCloskey does mean this literally, but only at the broadest level, far beyond the level of ideological bias. What McCloskey would argue, I believe, is that the writer in fact adopts the fairest, most honest, most objective analysis possible in the hope that the reader will give his work *credibility*. But see also note 2 in the Preface and Blaug (1998b).

work for political decision-makers purely as "technocrats," for fear that they may find themselves promoting evil causes.[29]

While there is no way to get beyond all of these problems completely, a good portion of this cynicism is misdirected, in my opinion. It should not be beyond human capability to find a fair and honest way to study human activities, including those involving policy decision-making. What is required is a professional ethic stipulating honest attempts to consider the strengths and weaknesses of all possible ways to achieve important social goals, including what needs to be given up in terms of other goals in order to make progress toward the goal in question. To reiterate from the simple model presented in Chapter 1, the goodness of policy actions (or human actions of any sort) is made a function of the distances traveled toward and away from relevant goals and the weights placed upon them. As in any impartial scientific investigation, the "experts" hold themselves aloof from taking positions either on the weights placed upon goals or on the choice of which goals to admit into consideration beyond an impartial attempt to show their relevance.

The expert needs to be an impartial advisor to decision-makers and to structure his or her research accordingly. Contrary to Blaug's pejorative dismissal of turning social scientists into "technocrats," in an important sense this is exactly what we are, and honorably so.[30] What is important in all this is a proper *attitude* — which is really McCloskey's and Redman's central point — of honesty, tolerance, and an attempt to explore competently the full ramifications of all the different ways to achieve goals. There are teachers in American classrooms (and surely elsewhere) — I have had

[29]An example of this thinking is Blaug (1980: 149; 1992: 128).

[30]Blaug's position, I believe, fails to give enough credit to the intelligence of social scientists by assuming that if they work for decision-makers in impartial fashion, there is a danger of becoming involved in evil causes. In Western democracies, there are few investigations that economists or other social scientists will be called upon to make which would involve them in truly evil causes. In those few instances, I have faith that they would have sense enough to notice this, and to demur from offering their services. Blaug's position is consistent with logical positivism, whose adherents hold that the realm of pure and good "science" is relatively small, and the realm of ethics and value judgments large and seductive to the pure-hearted "scientist." McCloskey (1994: 60) terms this the "five o'clock" view of art and science: "until five o'clock, we labor at science; afterwards, we play at art." (See McCloskey, 1994: 17 and Chap. 5 *passim*).

some of them — who are able to present sympathetically the arguments on multiple sides of controversial issues in a manner which does not give their students the faintest hint of their own personal views. If it is possible to do this in the classroom orally, it should be even more possible to do it in writings. The cynical view that objectivity should not even be aspired to because it is impossible to fully achieve. It is, at the same time, incorrect and dangerous. We can do better.

Precursors

The approach I am taking here has, of course, been anticipated to various degrees. While undoubtedly there are others, there are four writers I consider of key importance in this respect: two eminent personages from the era around the turn of the twentieth century, John Dewey and Max Weber, and two highly respected Scandinavian economists of more recent times, Jan Tinbergen and Ragnar Frisch. (A fifth might be added, the contemporary philosopher of social science Patrick O'Sullivan.) I regret that space does not allow me to give the work of these writers — Dewey, in particular — the attention they deserve.

John Dewey

Dewey is one of the towering personalities from the first part of this century. Psychologist, philosopher, and educationalist, his writings form an important foundation to my own efforts here, in that he anticipated and argued eloquently for many of the points I am making in this book. It remains one of the important academic historical mysteries of the twentieth century why Dewey's excellently reasoned advice has been followed as little as it has, despite the fact that he was widely accepted as one of the more important thinkers of his day.[31]

Of Dewey's many writings, for our purposes two might be considered most important: a transcription of his lectures from a course he gave at the University of Chicago over the three quarters of the 1900–1901 academic year (entitled *The Logic of Ethics*, *The Psychology of Ethics*, and

[31] I presume it is because of the great strength of the empiricist tradition.

Political Ethics, respectively),[32] and his 1922 book, *Human Nature and Conduct: An Introduction to Social Psychology*.[33] Also of interest is Dewey's remarkable presidential address delivered to the American Psychological Association in 1899, an excerpt from which is included in the epigraph to Chapter 4.[34]

Dewey envisioned social sciences — with social psychology taking a leading role — as being devoted to real-world practical and policy concerns, empirically based, and dealing in analysis where social goods are teleological. They are based on social goals which are, in turn, based on human needs, where desires originate from the motivation to attain goals and where human choice is the key element of human behavior. All morality originates in human belief, greatly influenced by early childhood training and emotional development. Dewey's emphasis on the empirical basis of morality strongly suggests the use of data collection with respect to subjective states and beliefs.

Dewey pointed out eloquently, in any number of places, the dangers of empiricism and scientism, including the remarkable statement in his 1899 presidential address about the danger of attempting to find an empirical basis of psychology only in the laboratory: treating the laboratory as a "final refuge" which, if done, can only give "artificialities, mere scientific curiosities." Many would argue that in mainstream psychology, this is exactly what has happened. Dewey argues that there is no such thing as fixed ends, meaning among other things that it is not possible to have truth with a capital "T" in matters of human goals (and, therefore, ethics), and that a Kantian, logical approach to the derivation of "correct" ethical principles is not viable.

Max Weber

Max Weber wrote at about the same time as Dewey and suffered a similar fate in that his writings contained a great deal of good advice which later went unheeded, at least in the mainstreams of the social sciences.

---

[32]Dewey (1991).

[33]Dewey (1922).

[34]Dewey (1991).

He is considered to be one of the founders of sociology, but his influence has not been, overall, as great in that discipline as writers such as Durkheim.[35] Weber subscribed to the overall approach taken by economists. However, unlike the economists, he wished to apply it to all social phenomena, holding that "nomological propositions in sociology must be formulated in terms of the rational, purposive actions of original persons."[36] Weber was critical of scientism, and thought that with introspection and the understanding of human motivation, the social scientist had a tool unavailable, and perhaps superior, to those used by the natural scientists.[37] Weber placed such understanding — termed *verstehen* — as central to the process of explanation and prediction in social science. While the basis of Weber's *verstehen* was quite obviously introspection, extended to fellow feeling, there seems to be some doubt as to how far this was carried over into knowledge gained from others from conversation, interview, and so forth. I would consider this to be a natural extension, although Gordon seems to conclude that Weber himself is somewhat "enigmatic" on this point in his writings.[38]

Weber also argued that much could be accomplished in social science through the use of the idea of "representative persons" (or institutions), for which he gave the term "ideal types."[39] One example of this, which Weber referred to explicitly, is the rational representative person who forms the basis of microeconomic theory. To reiterate, important in this is the existence of "fellow feeling" among humans, where many of them are similar in important respects to each other. Thus, Weber's use of the *verstehen* and ideal types concepts comes close to the shared value idea discussed in Chapter 3.

---

[35]Gordon (1991: 465 ff).

[36]Gordon (1991: 469). "Nomological" here means the reduction of apparent complexity to more general statements or explanations.

[37]"The main methodological distinction between the natural and the social sciences, in Weber's view, derives from a fundamental difference in the relation of the scientist to the phenomena he investigates. The natural scientist is an external observer of the material, but the social scientist lives within a social system and has the status, along with other humans, of a participant in social events." (Gordon, 1991: 469).

[38]Gordon (1991: 472).

[39]Although the "ideal type" argument may not be quite this simple, there is disagreement among scholars. See Gordon (1991: 473 ff) and the otherwise large literature on the subject.

Economist Precursors

The methodology I am suggesting has not been much used explicitly in economics. There are two noteworthy exceptions: the work of two Scandinavian economists (quite eminent ones, however, being the first economists to win the Nobel prize), Jan Tinbergen and Ragnar Frisch. Tinbergen's ideas were first published in his classic 1967 work, *Economic Policy: Principles and Design*, in which he specifically mentioned the need to include collective preferences in policy analysis.[40] He includes in his list of goals for economic and social policy,

> maintenance of international peace; maximum real expenditure per capita with "full" employment and monetary equilibrium; improvement of distribution of real expenditure over social groups and countries; emancipation of certain underprivileged groups, and as much personal freedom as is compatible with the other aims.[41]

Tinbergen also devotes a separate chapter to reforms and changes in foundations where he specifically includes additional collective goals into the list of target variables in his models, including, among others, social security schemes, redistributive elements, minimum incomes, and equalization of opportunities. Ragnar Frisch was an econometrician with a strong interest in how economics could be applied to broad policy questions. His ideas for policy analysis were presented in his 1970 Nobel Prize Acceptance Address and 1971 paper.[42] He suggested (1) selecting a preference function of variables relevant to the policy problem and then (2) using econometric techniques to do analysis, which allows for (3) exploration of relationships between the variables. Frisch anticipates these points as useful for social science investigation in his discussion of two aspects of policy analysis. First, the economic and social science analysis allows the investigator to explore relationships between the variables. This corresponds to the first and second steps outlined above. This is followed by the identification of "preference functions" which

[40]Tinbergen (1967: xiii).

[41]*Ibid.* Note that all the stated aims are collective in nature.

[42]Frisch (1970, 1971; both reprinted in Frisch, 1976).

provide the variables to be explored and/or the weights placed on them by decision-makers, thus corresponding to the third step. Frisch considered his preference function approach important, innovative, and overdue:[43]

> (My) purpose...is to make a plea for a new type of cooperation between politicians and econometricians. The new type of cooperation consists in formalizing the *preference function* which must underlie the very concept of *optimal* economic policy. A preference function is simply a function of some of the variables that enter into a description of the economy, the function being such that the *maximization* of it can be looked upon as the definition of the goal to be obtained in economic policy.[44]

Frisch is careful to maintain impartiality by dealing only with the preferences of political and other decision-makers. His "preference function" requires that policy-makers select the social goals to include as variables, as well as the weights to be placed upon each goal. It must also be noted that Frisch's procedures include very careful interviewing of decision-makers, and he takes pains to note that such interviewing should only be done by sophisticated analysts who are themselves highly informed about the econometric (and other technical) analysis:

> One way to approach the decision-maker is through *interview questions*. It is well-known that people will not always behave in an actual situation exactly the way they *said* in an interview question that they *would* behave in such and such a situation. But still, I think, it remains that valuable information may be obtained through interview questions, provided the questions are wisely formulated in a *conversational manner*, and not simply carried out by some youngster in the opinion poll trade. I have worked out a rather elaborate technique for such conversational interviews to be carried out by the econometric experts. And I have had the good fortune to test this out in conversations

[43]"It is my firm conviction that an approach to economic policy through a preference function contains the key to a much needed reform of the methods of decision-making in society at large in the world of today." (Frisch, 1976: 17)

[44]Frisch (1976: 41). Frisch's emphasis.

> with high-ranking politicians both in developing countries and in industrially developed countries. I have found that it is surprising how far one can reach in this field when the conversation is wisely steered.[45]

Ragnar Frisch did not belong in the empiricist or logical positivist traditions which hold that quality subjective interviewing falls outside of "science," although the only use of interviewing that Frisch specifically spoke of was for obtaining the preference functions of political leaders.

Finally, the young contemporary philosopher of social science, Patrick O'Sullivan, should be mentioned. His 1987 book, *Economic Methodology and Freedom to Choose,* is a well-reasoned argument for the fundamentally subjectivist nature of economic science. He provides philosophical foundations for the subjectivist-interpretive approach in some depth, including arguments for why the objectivist-behaviorist approach, if pursued alone, is faulty. The reader can see, from the number of times O'Sullivan has been cited in this book, the debt I owe to him.

Illustrative Examples

Some further illustrations of the use of the goal model approach in practice are discussed in this section. Since the policies subject to study in the social sciences vary greatly in breadth, so too must the goal sets chosen for any particular investigation vary accordingly. The set of goals relevant to a relatively focused investigation, such as the structure of a single type of price support, would not be very large. If the issue being considered is broadened, let us say to the entire system of farm subsidies, the applicable goal set becomes wider. For issues such as the farm subsidy program (in the US), an excellent way to identify relevant goals is to study sets of congressional hearings held whenever a major policy change is proposed. House and Senate committees typically invite (allow) all interested parties to testify, and by identifying all the concerns of the various parties, the investigator can identify a full set of relevant goals.

For broad-level social policies or general analytical models used in the social sciences, it is useful for the investigator to have at hand a set of major social objectives which describe the greater part of the goodness

[45]Frisch (1976: 24).

dimensions of *any society*. One must be careful, however, not to limit the goal list to only those — it must always be left open to all relevant concerns. If the reader will indulge a return to my taxation analysis, my interest there was a nation's tax policies considered from the broadest possible perspective. For this, based in part on earlier work by Scott Gordon and others, I derived a set of five basic goal areas: *reward*, market sector *efficiency*, *need*, *freedom*, and *equality*. It was argued that these five goal areas, when broken down into somewhat more detailed sub-goals, give reasonably good coverage of all the major attributes of a society. This may be obtained by asking people to describe the various attributes they think of in describing a good society, or by merely describing the key aspects of group existence itself, or even by analyzing the facets of political ideologies held by members of the population. I believe this list, especially when further broken down as follows, provides a good starting point for studying collective goods goals in general.

1. *Reward.* There are three main types of reward: for effort, ability, or good fortune. One way to provide measures for these is to note the percentage of a person's earnings due to each. A manual laborer working 60 hours per week exerts effort; a clever entrepreneur may earn a great deal through both effort and ability; someone who inherits a large fortune has a reward due to good luck. But rewards can be given for any activity the group deems meritorious.
2. *Efficiency.* Economists typically measure efficiency (in the sector of market-tradable goods) by the aggregate value of gross product a group produces, or the aggregate level of income (each of these measures is equal to the other.)[46]
3. *Need.* Need objectives can be divided into two general types: *general need,* having to do with the degree to which poverty is overcome; or *special needs,* having to do with special medical requirements, and the like. It is possible to roll all needs into one, which is the amount of money needed to obtain a "decent" standard of living.

[46]A somewhat more sophisticated measure is sometimes used: the aggregate value of "consumer surplus." This is a measure of the difference between the price a person would pay and the price he or she did pay. The value of gross product or income measures are more understandable, however, and also closely related to aggregate consumer surplus.

4. *Freedom.* Freedom goals are also of two types. The first is what the philosophers call "negative freedom," which is freedom from undue interference by others, such as freedom to worship and freedom of speech. Groups interested in such freedoms have constructed indices for how much religious, speech, and political freedom is allowed. The other type is termed "positive freedom," defined as the freedom to realize one's own lifetime potential. An index of positive freedom would show what percentage of persons at a given level of ability achieve satisfactory standards of living over their lifetime, or, conversely, the percentages of persons who do not so achieve. Criminals who have been forced into a non-productive lifestyle because of an inability to obtain satisfactory educational opportunities are examples where there has been a failure to achieve positive freedom.
5. *Equality.* Equality goals can be measured by absolute inequality measures (usually of income or wealth), or else by a measure of "ethically unexplained inequality," which would require measures of wealth not due to one's own efforts and perhaps also to the efforts of his immediate parents. Many absolute measures are often used: for example, the percentage of total income or wealth possessed by those in the top and bottom ten percent of the population.

Using this list of goals as goodness criteria, it is possible to arrive at a much broader and more satisfactory analysis of tax issues than traditionally accomplished by economists working in the tax area, to continue with the example I have been using (the analysis applies to any policy area, of course.) Tax economists have tended to focus on the second goal area above — efficiency — along with vague notions of "vertical and horizontal equity," as discussed in the introduction. Thus, I concluded that the traditional analysis resulted in biases due to neglect of such goodness criteria as some aspects of reward, the wealth distribution, and the ability of persons to realize their lifetime potential.

Policy research organizations

While the procedures suggested above have not been used very much in the academic social sciences, there are examples of analysis, somewhat similar to the approach suggested here, conducted by policy research organizations. Such organizations often deal directly with policies meant to satisfy collective goals, but they concentrate on the particular policy problem at hand and the social objectives most immediately relevant to it, and do not set out to identify all the relevant dimensions in the manner I am suggesting. Some organizations come fairly close, however, such as the Rand Corporation, the Institute for Research on Poverty at the University of Wisconsin, and the Urban Institute. But still, compared to all the social science work that goes on, and that should go on, these are sheer drops in a bucket. On top of that, many academic social scientists tend to think of applied policy analysis as beneath their dignity.

Governmental study commissions: The Swedish example

One area in which the approach suggested here has often been utilized is in the workings of governmental study commissions. Governmental commissions are typically given the task of thoroughly exploring the background and context of an issue, of sorting through the (often controversial) facts relevant to the issue, and then of arriving at an independent judgment as to what should be done, including giving alternative courses of action along with the strengths and weaknesses of each. In theory, the commissions approach, when well implemented, has a great deal to recommend it for providing high-quality impartial analysis of important social questions. The commission members typically have enough stature and prestige to keep from being unduly intimidated by sponsors. They are given enough time and financial resources to do quality research. The commissioners and staff are selected to represent a variety of points of view such that all important and relevant social goals are properly considered.

The particular example I wish to relate is how governmental study commissions have been utilized in Sweden.[47] Over many years, the Swedes

[47]Governmental commissions have been used in most other Western nations, and many individual studies have been exemplary. But for using the commission approach as an evaluatory *system* for any and all social concerns, the Swedes would seem to be far ahead of their nearest competitor. For further discussion of the use of commissions elsewhere, besides Sweden, see Rist (1974), Hall (1980), Rhodes (1980), Tunstall (1980), and Prest (1980).

have developed governmental study commissions that investigate most important (and many less important) social issues, particularly issues which might be subject to governmental legislation.[48] The tradition seems to be that whenever the Swedes notice a social need, or potential social need, they immediately set up a commission to study it. It is a tradition which has yielded highly worthwhile results.[49]

The commission system in Sweden is unique in the extent to which it is used: over the past half century, the number of commissions active at any one time has been in excess of 200, often near 300.[50] Investigations have been made and reports published on virtually every area of social concern with the single exception of foreign policy. Members of study commissions are typically chosen to represent diverse backgrounds and all major interests, including the points of view of all political parties of any importance. Some 20 or 30 percent of the members of major study commissions are members of parliament (the Riksdag), and perhaps 20 percent represent interest organizations.[51] The others are drawn from a variety of backgrounds, including academics and high-ranking civil servants. Some key commission members, as well as staff members, hail from the governmental department or departments most concerned with the issue being studied. Study commissions are well funded and have large and competent staffs. They are normally given ample time to make a careful study, often four or five years.[52]

The purpose for which study commissions are formed is normally to suggest legislation to deal with the issue, at least if the commission members feel there is something to be gained from government intervention. Often, such proposals are implemented, although in a significant minority of instances (Premfors gives the figure of 15 percent),[53] the advice is rejected. In addition, it is far from unusual for dissenting

[48]According to Premfors, *ad hoc* commissions have been an important feature of central policy-making in Sweden for almost two centuries. (Premfors, 1983: 625; see also Meijer, 1969)

[49]For discussions of the Swedish commission system, see among others, Furubo (1994), Premfors (1983), Foyer (1969), Meijer (1969), Anton (1969), and Petersson (1988).

[50]Premfors (1983: 624).

[51]Premfors (1983: 625).

[52]Premfors (1983); Meijer (1969).

[53]Premfors (1983: 626).

opinions to be included in commission reports; as many as one-fourth of them have such sections.[54] On the other hand, it is commonly assumed that one goal of commission investigations is that they will work as a mechanism to reach consensus, thereby reconciling a number of opposing interests. This seems to happen remarkably often, since about three-fourths of commission reports are unanimous.[55]

When a commission's report is finished, it is sent to all interested parties for comments and these comments often become part of the report as well. As a general rule, the commission mechanism is an important ingredient to legislation in Sweden. According to Premfors, about 40 percent of *all* Swedish legislation can be traced back to a commission report. As might be expected, there is a lessening of commission activity when the scope of overall government activity is cut back, but it is significant that commissions are widely used even in cutback periods, as the experience in Sweden since the 1980s has demonstrated. It is noteworthy that, by tradition, the key convenor of commissions is the Minister of Finance who, of course, has an interest in fiscal restraint.

While commissions are typically proposed by individual government departments (which, in Sweden, are relatively small), most commission investigations appear to be reasonably objective despite the fact that some of the commissioners, as well as key members of the staff, are often department members. There are a number of reasons for this. First, the commission members are typically knowledgeable persons of independent stature who are not easily intimidated. Second, committee members are usually selected from a broad spectrum of interests, including representation from all of the major and more important minor political parties. Third, if Premfors is correct, there is a tradition of objective scientific inquiry in the working of Swedish commissions.[56] Finally, since the practice of using study commissions is constantly ongoing, and because the commissions themselves are given ample time to do their work, there is seldom an air of social crisis about a social issue. This contrast with what happens elsewhere, particularly in the US.

---

[54]Premfors (1983: 628).

[55]An indication of the presence of shared values in what is, admittedly, a relatively homogeneous society.

[56]Premfors (1983: 629).

Foyer's comprehensive discussion of the Swedish Official State Investigations is now somewhat dated, but it is quite instructive with respect to the workings of study commissions.[57] They range widely, as Foyer puts it, from "great social and economic issues, some of which must be continually re-examined, [to] limited and highly specific questions."[58] Foyer gives as examples of the range of subjects examined in 1968,

> democracy in regional administration, the sex classification of intersexuals, health care in industry, the organization of research in transportation, the taxation of tractors, modern service arrangements for residential areas, sport fishing, and recommendations for sermon topics from the Old Testament...[59]

As the topic of the last study in the quotation indicates, and relevant to the discussion above in Chapter 4, the Swedes are not hesitant to involve moral and religious questions in their studies, although this is, in part, a natural outcome from the fact that there is a state church. Also of interest, and relevant to the chapter to follow, is the degree to which interviews — including interviews going into reasonably great depth — are used in commission research. Examples of studies using interviews discussed by Foyer include the importance of referenda in forming opinions, the impact of civil authorities in labor markets, conditions of employment in agriculture, the leisure activities of young people, the workings of nurseries and day-care, the existence of facilities for the aged, the degree to which musical tastes are met, and many others.

Finally, the Swedes sometimes use the study commission approach to look at major social issues considered in broadest terms. Petersson describes a study commissioned by the Swedish Government in 1985 of the workings of power and democracy in Swedish society.[60] This ambitious study was meant to deal with such broad questions as where power exists in Swedish society, whether individuals have power resources great enough to influence social change, and how the distribution of power and influence

[57]Foyer (1969).

[58]Foyer (1969: 184).

[59]*Ibid.*

[60]Petersson (1988).

in Swedish society might be changing. The study dealt at length with power concentrations in the business sector, interest organizations, the public sector, and opinion-making channels, and how all this interacted with the workings of political democracy. Associated with the project were thorough-going studies of a good many of the most important features of Swedish society.

Other Applications

Finally, I would like to suggest a few other applications for the goal model where I think it could be used to improve upon past practices in moral philosophy and the social sciences.

Moral Philosophy

Throughout this book, I have been arguing that the methods of social science could be brought to the study of moral philosophy, especially to empirical investigations. If the term "moral" is a social concept as Dewey argued, then all moral and ethical concerns can be modeled in terms of social goals. The comprehensive goal model I am suggesting, then, provides a construct for the empirical investigation of moral belief. (This does not at all eliminate the importance of logical deduction, which will always influence what persons believe about morals.) An extended example of how this might work is given in the following chapter, where important insights about my three respondents' key (and one could argue, controlling) moral beliefs are brought out as a result of lengthy in-depth interviews. Other empirical work in matters of ethics and morality could be accomplished through simple polling methods (a great many are already, of course) and introspection.

Social Psychology

One area where the goal model could make a contribution is in the sub-discipline of social psychology where, surprisingly enough, neither socio-cultural concerns or subjective interviewing has been widely used. Empirical social psychologists have dealt largely with the study of attitudes and the forces determining them (or at least variables correlated with them.) Many of these efforts have not been too successful, yielding findings such as "radicalism is somewhat associated with dissatisfaction" that are not especially instructive.[61]

An important critic of social psychology from inside the discipline has been H. Brewster Smith. He is widely respected in the field although he is viewed as being outside the mainstream.[62] Smith has shown the way to a broader goal model approach to attitude explanation based, in part, on careful subjective interviewing, although his approach does not seem to have caught on in his sub-discipline. Smith has done some good work with respect to the attitudes of American men toward the Soviet Union (and Soviet citizens) during the Cold War era, the attitudes of Peace Corps volunteers, and in other areas. Smith, however, feels that there is still something lacking in the way social psychologists view the role of opinions in their discipline, even when some of his own improvements are included. He affirms a version of the goal model here with the statement that his opinions received their strongest impetus from "object appraisal," meaning "the process whereby the person develops attitudes that are a creative solution to the problems posed by the existence of disparate internal demands and external or environmental demands."[63] But then Smith continues:

> Here I must admit to persisting puzzlement. The challenge is to find a meta-theoretical stance that meets the pragmatic test of putting our thoughts and findings in some defensibly consistent order and allows us to bring evidence to bear on understanding and humanizing politics.[64]

In my view, the comprehensive goal model might well provide the kind of "meta-theoretical stance" sought by Smith. Would not an approach which attempts to include all major human social goals and to study their interrelationships succeed in "putting our thoughts in a consistent

[61]This discussion follows Smith (1956: 10). Also see Smith's criticisms of contemporary social psychology in Smith (1991: 38 ff).

[62]Smith (1991: 40, 55) himself has commented on this in a number of places.

[63]Smith (1956: 112, 41).

[64]Smith (1991: 119).

order and bring evidence to bear on understanding and humanizing politics?" The goal approach used by economists to establish motivation may provide a reasonably good answer to Smith's question concerning what use a person has for his or her preferences and opinions. Preferences and opinions allow persons to decide which social and individual goals are the more important and so yield the greatest utility or satisfaction when they are reached (or more nearly approached). Humans use their preferences and opinions to most further their own happiness, which would seem to be "meta-theory" enough.

Developmental Psychology

With the exception of the clinical areas and anthropology, the one area in social science which has used the empirical investigation of the human experience most is developmental psychology. Developmental psychologists are often especially interested in the development of emotions and moral beliefs.

While there is a large literature in developmental psychology, I will merely concentrate here on the work of one nicely representative researcher: Carol Gilligan. Gilligan initially conducted long interviews with a group of college juniors and seniors — mostly females — about questions of morality involved in personality development. She then interviewed the same individuals five years later. She obtained a number of important insights using this approach, and her writings on questions of morality development, especially as they relate to differences between men and women, have been widely noted.

Perhaps Gilligan's most important finding from her interview studies is that individuals seem to take two very different approaches to morality, one involving more or less impersonal notions of justice, the other involving empathy toward others where care and personal interactions assume central place. One has the central focus on justice, the other on care. Gilligan's work has made an important contribution to our understanding of personal beliefs, especially those of women and the importance of love and compassion in morality questions. I have one comment, however, which I tender somewhat tentatively given that my own professional training is elsewhere. Gilligan seems to view the two approaches in either-or terms. Perhaps there are elements of conflict between the two approaches, but it may be possible for persons to pursue both approaches at the same time. A person with a fully developed moral agenda would have both kinds of morality in his or her moral tool kit. At least this seems a reasonable hypothesis; admittedly, it is only that. But I believe that one good way for this hypothesis to be tested empirically is with the comprehensive goal model.

Gilligan's research approach (which reflects that usually taken in her sub-discipline) has been to view morality questions strictly from the perspective of the individual. Persons are asked what morality means to them personally, or how they would personally deal with a moral dilemma in their own life, or even to simply describe "yourself to yourself." This is fine as far as it goes; after all, we are all only individuals. But, sometimes, in morality questions we need to take a slightly different perspective, that is, how would the person view an ideal society to live in? The goal model applicable to Gilligan's results would yield this perspective while at the same time making it possible to include the care approach, since the desirability of caring relationships can surely be included as an important social objective. By including both perspectives in the questions, one could explicitly view the trade-offs between alternative goals perceived by the respondents. Presumably, the relative weights placed on alternative goals would be, on average, somewhat different for men than for women if Gilligan is correct.[65]

The Study of Political Ideology

The comprehensive goal model applied to the study of political ideology, when implemented with high-quality interviewing techniques, could be

[65]A third area in psychology where the comprehensive goal model would make quite a direct contribution is that of a small but growing group interested in "goal-directed behavior," that is, taking the very approach I suggest in this book. Useful volumes of readings in this area include Frese and Sabini (1985) and Pervin (1989). These psychologists also express interest in the subjective personality since, while they speak of the desirability of dealing with all "action," they tend to define "action" as being broader than "behavior." This is a fine beginning, but unaccountably, up to now there does not seem to have been much in the way of empirical implementation of their theoretical approach. The comprehensive goal model would seem to be the obvious answer. These writers were also discussed briefly in Chapter 4 in the section dealing with rational choice motivation.

useful in adding precision to the literature dealing with political ideology. Most of the previous empirical investigation in this area has been based on large-scale polling studies. These are valuable up to a point, but often the questions used are ambiguous and open to alternative interpretations, thus making it difficult to be sure what the respondent meant precisely. This can be seen, for example, by studying many of the questions used in the national surveys Coughlin discusses in his study of welfare policy in a number of European and American nations.[66] The surveys abound with statements such as "Government should make sure that there are good opportunities for each person to get ahead on his own" or "Government should guarantee each person a decent, steady job." The chances here for diverse interpretation are legion. Is it enough for the government to provide a low unemployment rate as the opportunity for persons to get ahead on their own (if so, *how* low a rate?), or should it make sure that everyone can read and write well and has training in some viable job skill, or is it enough that the government ensure against illegal job discrimination? How is the word "decent" in the phrase "decent, steady job" to be interpreted? True, some questions do better than this, such as "Should the Government approve a national health plan?," but even here exactly what kind of national health plan did the interviewer have in mind?[67]

There seems to be considerable confusion in the political ideology literature about the very definitions of terms such as "liberal" and "conservative," as well as considerable debate about the dimensionality of the liberal-conservative distinction.[68] Without going into great detail, it would seem that the goal model with the simple set of objectives outlined above could go a long way to straighten out these issues even at the conceptual level, not to speak of what could be accomplished with empirical implementation. Thus, reward for contribution is associated with the conservative view, relatively high reward for ability *vis-a-vis* effort is more conservative, and vice versa for liberal. The conservatives place great emphasis on market sector economic efficiency and negative

[66]Coughlin (1980).

[67]In some situations, there may have been an active discussion taking place about a *specific* plan. Thus, such a question takes on an unambiguous meaning.

[68]See, for example, Lyons and Scheb (1992); Conover and Feldman (1981).

liberty goals, and the liberals on positive liberty goals and helping the needy, and so forth.[69] There would seem to be a place for using the goal model with careful interviewing in this area, not only to supplement the polling efforts, but also to obtain more in-depth results on ideological dimensions. The following chapter addresses how this might be done.

[69]Negative freedoms are freedom of the press, freedom of religion, and so forth. Positive freedom is the freedom to realize one's lifetime potential.

Chapter 7

Exploring the Human Subject

It is well known that people will not always behave in a given situation exactly in the way they *said* in an interview question that they *would* behave in such and such a situation. But still, I think, it remains that valuable information may be obtained by means of interview questions, provided the questions are wisely formulated in a *conversational manner*, and not simply carried out by some youngster in the opinion poll trade...I have had the good fortune of testing this out in conversations with high-ranking politicians both in developing countries and in industrially developed countries. I have found that it is surprising how far one can get in this field when the conversation is wisely steered.

Ragnar Frisch
Economic Planning Studies, 1976

...I conclude...that the standard approach to interviewing is demonstratively inappropriate for and inadequate to the study of the central questions in the social and behavioral sciences, namely, how individuals perceive, organize, give meaning to, and express their understandings of themselves, their experiences, and their worlds. Further, the traditional approach neglects to examine how their understandings are related to their social, cultural, and personal circumstances...

Variations among interviewers and across interviews...are not viewed here as "errors" but as significant "data" for analysis...In my view, such variation is endemic and unavoidable, and the documented failure of technical solutions reveals that the requirement of standardization cannot be fulfilled in practice...Within the perspective

> of interviews as speech events and speech activities, variations in how particular questions are asked, as well as variation in the overall course of interviews, become objects of inquiry.
>
> Elliot Mishler
> *Research Interviewing,* 1986

My main preoccupation in this book has been policy analysis, not with the building of scientific knowledge proper. I say this because with respect to the latter there has been, and continues to be, considerable debate among methodologists concerning the role of human mentation, a debate which I would prefer to avoid. The positivists and their descendants eschew mentation entirely on the empiricist grounds that only objective facts are admissible in the search for scientific truth — facts obtained through the senses and by third parties. Phenomenologists, on the other hand, feel that worldly phenomena can be understood only if reflection on one's mental impressions is part of the process.

The student of policy analysis need not become involved in the debate about science proper: at least this is true if the extreme positivist position is not entirely correct, a position which would require that we regard data obtained from humans about their own histories, opinions, and motives as absolutely worthless. Given our discussion of the goal model so far, such an extreme position is surely untenable. That we cannot usefully establish motives from social intercourse, not to speak of introspection, polls, and interviews, defies the bounds of common sense. Of interest here is the earlier discussion of relevance and how the human sciences cannot tolerate the degree of insulation common in the natural sciences.[1] The human sciences need to avoid insulation for the most part because they must deal with a broad spectrum of human actors pursuing their everyday roles in society. Whether or not the need for such a broad perspective is indicated for the academic social sciences, it is certainly needed in policy analysis. Science has to do with the solving of puzzles;

[1]See the methodology discussion in Chapter 1.

policy analysis (or a given policy problem) is not a puzzle at all because it does not have any set solution.[2]

Survey research into the subjective aspects of the human experience began with the rise of interest in the study of attitudes in the 1920s and 1930s.[3] After World War II, the use of survey research became more common and, in recent decades, it has progressed rapidly. According to Ladd and Benson, the number of polls conducted by US newspapers doubled and those by television stations tripled between 1976 and 1988.[4] Survey research has also been used a great deal in social science, although somewhat less in economics and social psychology.[5]

As with most human endeavors, there is, in survey research, a quantity-quality trade-off. As Schuman comments, surveys have their origin in

> two of our most natural intellectual inclinations. One is to ask questions of other people and treat their answers with some seriousness...The second inclination is to draw samples to represent a much larger universe.[6]

---

[2]Terwee (1990: 31) defines a "puzzle" as having a set, final solution. His discussion of insulation follows Kuhn (1970: 37, 160). Despite all this, some students of social science methodology are still quite hostile toward using subjective data, particularly from interviews. See Gordon (1991: 52 ff, 633 ff). While Professor Gordon sometimes admits to the usefulness of subjective data in his text (but interviews are never mentioned), in personal correspondence his views are more strident, having asked me to specifically point out to my readers that "there is a *fundamental* difference between us on how subjective judgments ARE and SHOULD BE included in public policy formation."

One argument Gordon makes in this respect is that, while giving causal status to "reasons" (motives) might be acceptable for explaining human actions, the methods of science would then require that we inquire into the *causes* of the reasons, and going back this far into the patterns of causation implies excessive determinism or lack of free will. In my opinion, such reasoning would hold only if we could establish causes of reasons without error, or without considerable error, which we cannot. In addition, the mere explanation of how a person came to have the reasons he has for his views does not imply a lack of free will in his obtaining them. He *chose* to accept those reasons as correct and to reject others (Gordon, 1991: 52).

[3]Converse (1984).

[4]Ladd and Benson (1992).

[5]According to Presser (1984: 96), the percentage of articles using polling in top journals in 1950 and 1980 was: sociology, 24 and 56; political science, 3 and 35; economics, 6 and 29; and social psychology, 22 and 21.

[6]Schuman (1982: 22–23, as quoted in Mishler, 1986: 2).

In gaining information through surveys, we wish to ask questions of persons concerning their life experiences in as much detail as possible, while at the same time we would like to obtain information for as broad a slice of the relevant populations as possible. Following through on both of these "inclinations" at the same time, while not impossible, is accomplished only at considerable cost.

Social scientists in the twentieth century, for whatever reasons, have chosen to solve the quantity-quality dilemma in survey research by opting mostly for the former. The interview approach which has become standard practice is that of the large sample public opinion poll or survey, where groups of interviewers conduct short personal interviews on the telephone or house-to-house and read pre-set questions in standardized ways, which usually means limiting interpretive comments to pre-set responses (if any.) The alternative is the longer (or "quality") interview, where the interviewer can feel free to ask follow-up questions, to probe in depth, to obtain background material, and to allow respondents explanatory comments to explain what they mean. Most survey research can be considered subjective, although some of this involves inquiries into strictly factual matters. A tiny minority involve interviews where more than a few minutes are devoted to any item.

When research budgets are limited, the arguments in favor of opting for large sample polling techniques seem obvious. In-depth interviewing presumably would not allow researchers to gauge the feelings and opinions of large populations except at considerable expense. Large numbers allow the use of sophisticated statistical and analytical techniques, and the use of pre-set questions and standardized interviewing methods arguably makes it possible to preserve scientific objectivity. These are the time-honored arguments, although they have been the subject of considerable criticism in recent years.

In a recent assessment of the state of survey research at the end of the twentieth century, Wolfgang Donsbach points to a number of problems. The extensive use of polls by the media has produced a situation where journalistic values take precedence over credibility, where there is "horse race coverage" of elections rather than "precision journalism."[7] Polls often produce misleading, invalid, or irrelevant data on the social and political

[7]Donsbach (1997: 20).

process, where there is bias and problems with respect to validity and reliability. He cites a recent paper by David Yankelovitch (1996) who states that the prevailing attitude today is simply that of "a poll is a poll is a poll."[8] With the recent surge in new public opinion researchers, many are of poor quality and non-professional — and poor quality drives out good quality. Existing methodological knowledge has become "diffuse and imprecise."[9] "Quantitative" research has been discredited in recent years, having come under attack by proponents of "quality" research. Indeed, "the new epistomological battle is a methodological one, and the camps are *quantitative versus qualitative research.*"[10] And, finally, according to Donsbach,

> we still lack a unified theory and we still have too much unexplained variance in opinions and behaviors...Too much effort has been spent on descriptions of the *state* of opinions and its short-term changes, too little on the forces and dynamics behind these states and changes. The majority of the people in the field are uninterested in striving for the general laws behind human cognitions and behaviors.[11]

Any perusal of the polling literature shows both a great deal of useful information, largely factual, and a large body of more superficial results which do not yield much in the way of useful underlying knowledge and understanding; to paraphrase Donsbach, information on the state of opinions, but not on the forces and dynamics that lie behind them. Some discussion of this kind of superficiality, with respect to political ideology, was presented at the end of the previous chapter. A positive answer to the query, "Do you pay too much Federal income tax?," tells us something, I suppose, but there is a large complex of subjective forces and opinions which underlie such a response, for which we are given no information. Here is where knowledge of how respondents viewed the various social

[8]Yankelovitch (1996).

[9]Donsbach (1997: 23).

[10]Donsbach (1997: 25).

[11]*Ibid.* Wolfgang Donsbach is the immediate past president of the World Association of Public Opinion Research and is the Managing Editor of the *International Journal of Public Opinion Research.*

goals in my "goal model" could make a large difference. One is reminded of the comment by Steuerle *et al.* (concluding section of Chapter 6), with respect to the operation of the American political process, as dealing with public inputs of a superficial nature which lack underlying substance.

As Donsbach states, there has in fact been increasing criticism of quantitative polling methods in recent years, and this has given rise to an unfortunate hostility between two opposing camps of pollsters. It would seem that the proper course, as has been argued persuasively by a number of writers, would be to combine methods and use the two of them together.[12]

One of the more thoughtful critics of quantitative methods and proponents of qualitative ones has been Professor Elliot Mishler who, in an important 1986 book,[13] argues both that standard methods have more weaknesses than commonly supposed, and that in-depth techniques can succeed in overcoming them. It will be useful to devote some attention to Mishler's arguments.

Mishler points out that the standard large-scale polling approach involves the assumption that interview situations can be reduced to isolated acts of unbiased behavior, an assumption in which interviews are considered behavioral, as opposed to linguistic events. The paradigm is that of stimulus-response, as in a formal experimental laboratory, an approach which "allows and, indeed, encourages interviewers and analysts to treat each question-answer pair as an isolated exchange."[14] This entire approach is highly mistaken, Mishler claims, in that it "removes from consideration the primary and distinctive characteristic of an interview as discourse, that is, as meaningful speech between interviewer and interviewee as speakers of a shared language:"[15]

---

[12]Two very good papers in this regard are Reichart and Cook (1979) and Ianni and Orr (1979). See also Foddy (1998).

[13]Mishler (1986).

[14]Mishler (1986: 11). The influence of the empiricist, scientist, tradition here can be seen: note the similarity of the idea that a question-answer pair is an isolated exchange and Kuhn's idea that a state of insulation is necessary for the puzzle-solving aspect of normal (physical) science (Methodology discussion in Chapter 1).

[15]Mishler (1986: 10–11).

> The difference between a conception of interviewing as a form of talk and a concept of "verbal interchange" or "verbal interaction" is far from trivial. It marks radically different understandings of the nature of the interview, of its special qualities, and of its problems...Situations and forms of talk have structures...that reflect the operation of several types of normative rules...(T)hese rules guide how individuals enter into situations, define and frame their sense of what is appropriate and inappropriate to say, and provide the basis for their understandings of what is said...Units of behavior, on the other hand, are arbitrary and fragmented and become connected and related to each other not through higher order rules, but through a history of past associations and reinforcements that vary from person to person.[16]

While proponents of standard survey techniques may feel that they have achieved objective and comparable research results with standard interview training and pre-set questions, Mishler argues that they are mistaken. In reality, there are serious problems with standard survey techniques introduced by variation among interviewers, unreliability of coding, and ambiguities and spuriousness among variables. Mishler buttresses his arguments with considerable empirical evidence, much of it generated by persons sympathetic to the mainstream quantitative approach. He describes studies in which tape recordings were made of interviews to determine the degree to which interviewers properly asked the questions appearing on the prepared interview instrument. In particular, four careful studies together yielded the finding that questions were improperly asked in 25 to 40 percent of the interviews. Interviewer derelictions were of a nature that the investigators deemed it likely that they seriously biased the nature of the responses obtained.[17] He also mentions studies that have shown difficulties in question construction, hypothesis specification, lack of attention paid to respondent's understanding, and other problems. From his empirical survey, Mishler concludes:

> ...The following generalization is warranted, I believe, as a statement of the level of understanding that has been achieved

[16]Mishler (1986: 11).
[17]Mishler (1986: 18–19).

regarding the effects of interviewer and question variables: some variables, and perhaps all of them, have some effects on some, and perhaps all, types of response under some conditions. Or, restated in somewhat different terms: each stimulus variable studied may influence some feature(s) of a response, the magnitude and seriousness of the effect being a function of various contextual factors...

This is a disturbing conclusion, all the more so because such a statement could have been made prior to making the studies.[18]

Many or most of the problems just discussed, Mishler claims, can be overcome with better quality interviewing. The obvious difficulty with longer interview methodology (besides time and resource requirements) is the seeming uncontrolled variation it introduces in interview and interviewer effects. But Mishler does not see this as a problem, or if it is a problem, he feels that it can be overcome by making verbatim transcripts of the interviews and studying them carefully. Indeed, he argues that such study can yield insights into the effects of interview and interviewer variations and, thus, add additional information to what is learned otherwise:

> Variations among interviewers and across interviews...are not viewed here as "errors" but as significant "data" for analysis. In the standard approach, differences on how interviewers ask questions are treated as technical problems that can be "solved" by obeying various rules and prescriptions for question wording and interviewer performance...In my view, such variation is endemic and unavoidable, (and)...the narrow technical approach...excludes from consideration the course of the interview itself,...the internal history of the developing discourse, which is shaped by prior exchanges between interviewer and respondent. Within the perspective of interviews as speech events and speech activities, variation in how particular questions are asked, as well as variation in the overall course of interviews, become objects of inquiry.[19]

[18]Mishler (1986: 15–16).

[19]Mishler (1986: 52–53).

A Pilot In-depth Interview Project

With Mishler's comments on quality interviewing as a basis, I can now present the results of a small pilot study in which I explore the possibilities of the in-depth interview as a device for determining collective goods demands.

The pilot study design

This being a first attempt, I chose only three subjects who were much more accessible than would be the population average (but not too unlike the nature of political decison-makers, perhaps). They were three members of the local (Bloomington-Monroe County, Indiana) chapter of the League of Women Voters. To supply the variation in views needed to make the exercise meaningful, I chose persons with differing political philosophies, one quite liberal, one middle of the road, and one moderately conservative. The conservative identifies herself politically as a Republican, the liberal as a Democrat, and the middle-of-the-road person thinks of herself as an independent who more often tends to vote Democratic. The names I have chosen to call them in this report are Jane (the liberal), Betty (middle-of-the-road), and Carol (the conservative.) Jane is in her mid-70s, a widow of a university professor. She is active in the League, her church, and sometimes in other civic activities. Betty is in her mid-60s, is divorced, and works part-time as a laboratory assistant at the university. She has been an active participant in doing League issue studies, and is currently participating on a state League study. Carol is in her 50s, is a well-regarded high school English teacher, is married to a member of the professional staff at the university, and is an active church member.

Individual questions used in the study were carefully designed and were accompanied with considerable factual material intended to give each respondent an informational basis beyond what she already possessed for answering the questions. In the dissemination of factual information, I attempted to keep my remarks impartial and objective. When I felt it necessary to outline different points of view about some issue, I tried to give each position equal amounts of sympathy while being as objective as possible. Similarly, in giving factual information that tended to support one political or ethical viewpoint, I attempted to counterbalance this with similar information for the opposite viewpoint, or at least indicate that such facts may well exist. The interviews were recorded and transcribed verbatim. Thus, it would be possible for the interviewer or other interested researchers to study the transcripts to check for possible sources of question bias (in the light of Mishler's comments, better descriptions might be "variations" or "idiosyncracies"), and then to make adjustments for them or, otherwise, learn from interactions between respondents and the interviewer.

In designing the interview schedules, I allowed myself some latitude for experimentation, at least for Betty. The main plan was to have four hours of interviewing, one hour at a time, with each subject. The first interview was to deal with general issues based on the goal model, while most of the last three were to deal with Federal, state, and local government programs. The second interview was more open-ended (but based on the summarizing and dissemination of large amounts of information), while the third and fourth were highly structured, where scenarios on three subjects were carefully prepared and read verbatim. For Betty, I tried reducing the schedule to two 90-minute sessions, an experiment which was not completely successful. With hindsight, I believe the first interview and the last two (the structured ones) to have been successful. The second interview was only partly successful for the reason that I was overly ambitious. A rather long interview with very careful preparation is needed to deal with just one level of government programs, and sometimes more than one interview would be needed. Nonetheless, I obtained a wealth of material about the respondents' views in these areas.

The goal model role in the pilot study as the guiding structure

My guiding motif throughout all the interviews was to anchor respondents' opinions and beliefs to social and individual goals they considered important. The primary list of goals I designed around and spoke about were:

1. Reward for effort, ability, and luck.
2. Economic efficiency (maintenance of incentives and well-working markets).

3. Avoidance of poverty.
4. Meeting special needs (for example, medical, or of a single mother with young children).
5. Freedom from interference by others.
6. Freedom to realize one's lifetime potential.
7. Avoiding income- and (especially) wealth-inequality, which is considered excessive.

Typically, I asked, at the end of a discussion, if there were any goals besides these the respondent might consider important, and which social goals they considered of key importance. I asked them to speculate on the qualities she would most like to see in a society they would consider ideal. From a respondent's answer, without going much farther, it is possible for a researcher to understand which social issues he or she considers of central importance.

While the goal model provided the central guidance for my questions, I seldom talked directly about goals. Instead, I structured questions to shed light on the importance the subject placed on alternative social objectives. One interchange that illustrates this is the following, with Jane:

Q. Think about taxation. And how people get returns to their effort and their ability and so on. If someone works hard, but he's not got very many brights and he makes, say, $12,000 per year, and then if someone doesn't work very hard but he's clever and he makes $12,000, would you treat them differently?

A. No, I don't think we can stick our nose in.

Q. How would you treat if someone has an income of $75,000 and he earns it all with his labor, and if somebody makes $75,000 and he gets, say, 30 or 40 of that from earnings from capital, would you treat those people the same?

A. I just can't see how that would work out.

Q. Because it's just hard to do?

A. I haven't given that very much thought, and somehow I don't like the idea because it's what we earn seems like it should be private.

Q. Makes any difference to you if his stocks and bonds were inherited as opposed to if bought with money he earned?
A. No. To me, anybody who has money, it's what he DOES with it that matters to me, and he ought to be rewarded if he does good things with it.
Q. Would you extend that to really wealthy people, like people who have 100 million dollars or 200 million dollars? That wealth really isn't taxed very much now. Also, there is the question of great wealth if or if not inherited.
A. Are we talking about Ross Perot and Jay Rockefeller, for instance?
Q. Well, Ross earned most of his, or so he says.
A. Yes, a lot of it was really due to good luck.
Q. Yes. Well would you tax a lot differently from...?
A. No, I don't think so. I just, to me that's getting, government interfering too much in life. I just don't think I'd go along with that.

What I found out in this interchange is that Jane has a strong libertarian streak. She may or may not be in favor of differential rewards — it remains to be found out — but when doing so comes into conflict with personal freedom, personal freedom wins hands down. I tried to explore her views on reward and, instead, learned a great deal about the weight Jane places on freedom. This is a good example of how the researcher often learns about the weights respondents place on goals, not always directly, but because of interactions and conflicts between goals, important facts are learned indirectly.

Introduction to Jane, Betty, and Carol

Before getting into a sampler on what it is possible to learn about how the respondents view social policies according to the goal model, it will be useful to give an overview of their fundamental approaches to their social world and how they relate to it as individuals. This will also allow me to show how much can be learned from the ideal society question.

Jane

Of my three respondents, Jane was the most other-regarding. Where some widows devote spare income to cruises and foreign travel, Jane devotes hers to charitable causes, admitting to having made contributions to some *80* groups at some time or another. She modestly explained this on the basis of "selfishness:" "I would rather give my money to the groups that I like and approve of the work that they do than pay it out in taxes."[20]

Jane's greatest social concern is the poor and unfortunate, especially the children. When I asked her to state what she thought would be the ideal society to live in, she responded:

A. I guess I would like to live in a society where problems of poverty, poor education, poor health, etc., are more a matter of the whole society in taking responsibility for helping everybody, not that everybody can possibly be alike or treated exactly alike, but it seems to me it would help if they were allowed a basic or base that everybody could work from.

Q. By "base" you mean some sort of a minimum level so they wouldn't have to starve or go homeless or things like that?

A. Yes.

Jane's good society is a communitarian[21] one, where the weakest are taken care of. She spoke of how she came to feel that way, from living in a small town and having a mother who was ever solicitous of the welfare of those less fortunate. While not being particularly religious, Jane had a strong social conscience. And speaking of conscience, one of Jane's more eloquent statements had to do with what she considered to be one of the more tragic of all social misfortunes: where young children in at-risk situations begin with a good outlook toward the world which is knocked out of them by poor environment, only to grow up as social liabilities. The following response is little short of eloquent:

> I think children have an inborn conscience, and the reason I think this is because I see in very young children signs of remorse when something happens to their little brother or sister or little friend that they happen to be with. It may not be something that they themselves have done to this other little friend. Maybe

[20]When I pointed out to her that at her income level, only a fraction of what she gave was financed by lower taxes, she considered the point unimportant.

[21]In the sense used, for example, by Etzioni (1993).

something, he fell and hurt himself, and the other child shows that he understands how that little person feels if he got this bloody knee, and later on if he does do something to his little sister, and she cries, he feels, and he recognizes that he has done something that was hurtful, and he feels a little bit hurt within himself, now that's what I call a conscience. And I think, I don't know how people lose their conscience, but that's what I think has happened to a lot of children and, therefore, people. I think it's happened to the parents who are rearing children or not rearing them, having them. They have no feeling because they've been so hurt and so downtrodden in their own youth that they have no feeling anymore for other people.

Jane's commitment to the financing of government through taxation to support social welfare programs was consistent with the rest of her thinking:

Q. Would you be in favor that social redistribution — now seven percent — be raised to ten percent if mostly for kids, poverty sorts of things?
A. I would. But see, I would almost be willing to go along for the amount of taxes that they pay in Scandinavian countries, because I think that if you don't pay it out in taxes, we're paying for it in other ways. We're paying for lack of health care, for lack of education, we are paying for too many children born to teenagers, we're all paying for it anyway. But we just don't call it that. So I'd rather be honest about it and say I'm willing to pay 35 percent of my taxes, or 35 percent more taxes for things that I think are essential.

Despite her willingness to have government take on greater social responsibility, Jane, like my other two respondents, is at a loss when it comes to deciding what to do with welfare problems, or with the key issue of teenage pregnancy. Jane also expresses frustration about the large and growing disparities in the income and wealth distributions, which she abhors. She is in favor of increasing the progressivity of the income tax (while realizing it should not be so progressive as to materially harm incentives) and she would be in favor of raising the effective rates of the estate tax (but perhaps lowering the tabular rates) by eliminating loopholes.

Although Jane is a communitarian, she possesses a strong libertarian streak. She is against high estate and inheritance tax rates on this basis, would not allow police to search a housing project for guns without a search warrant, and is staunchly pro-choice on the abortion question.

Betty

Betty's outlook on the world is not dissimilar to that of Jane. She is also a communitarian in important respects, as indicated in a comment she made on the subject of the right to do what one wishes with his or her private property:

> But the business about property, Herb, I don't believe in a lot of that business about "it's my property and I can do with it what I please." I think that you're a STEWARD for the land, and that you're just sort of keeping it for a while, and living on it for a while, and that business about uh, you ought to be able to do with it what you please goes against what I believe.

Betty feels there's nothing wrong with having government provide services if they are needed, although she is less strongly devoted to government intervention than Jane. Areas in which she thinks there was not enough government presence include Head Start type programs and day care, but more particularly in the areas of job training and job *provision* (in the manner, for example, of WPA programs), where she would expand the government's presence considerably. When I gave Betty my appraisal that it was quite difficult for governments to provide both jobs and job training and then asked what resources she would devote to such a project, she replied, "Whatever it takes."

With the exception of her job market ideas, Betty did not know whether the overall size of government should be changed, or in what direction. She is in favor of moderate tax increases to close the deficit and for programs to provide day care and aid the homeless. (With a "correct" jobs program, she was confident these things would be unnecessary.) She is in favor of tightening "loopholes" in the tax code which, she feels, are enjoyed by the wealthy. She approves of moderate income tax progression, with top marginal rates in the range of 50 percent, but by no means *ever* above 50 percent.

Betty is a staunch libertarian, whose views are quite similar to those of Jane. Like Jane, she is concerned about the increasing disparities in income and wealth. After I presented data concerning income and wealth distribution over the past half century showing increasing concentrations since the 1970s, she responded:

> Well. It's turning into a very bipolar society, I think that's terrible. Very poor and very rich. And uh, we're gonna be a Third World country after a while ...I don't know, its very strange ...I think you're right ...They're getting further and further apart ...Getting more poor and, what's the, I don't know what to do about it. But I think it's true. It's true.

Finally, Betty has a fundamental criticism of the American market-oriented social system as leading to an overemphasis on money and material goals at the expense of other goals of a more long-term or communitarian nature. When I asked her what kind of society she would most want to live in, she responded:

A. Well, oh shoot, I don't know. The thing that's so annoying to me is the bottom line being MONEY. If I could have it the way I'd like it, the bottom line would not necessarily be money. It would be, uh.., but that's really hard.
Q. Now's the time, if you have any overall reservations about the society you're in, or thoughts.
A. Right now? Oh, you mean, in general. Uh, well (long pause) the thing about the money that I could follow up on, is that, because of the money, uh, it's generally not, things generally aren't geared toward what's best for everybody. It's geared toward what's best for the person who's MAKING THE MONEY, you know, getting rich.

Carol

Of my three respondents, Carol turned out to be the true conservative, although not a very extreme one. She sees the country operating on the horns of a dilemma, one that she finds frustrating because the way to solve it does not appear obvious to her. On the one hand, there are obvious problems, which, much as she would like it to be otherwise, are *social* problems. On the other hand, the method for dealing with these problems so often proposed and tried over the past half century, using government intervention, is one she does not trust. Carol is not a bitter or rigidly doctrinaire opponent of government intervention. She is willing to admit that government solutions have often worked for some kinds of programs. Government would often be acceptable if it could get its administrative act together. On the other hand, she is well schooled in numerous examples where she feels government programs have failed. Added to this, Carol is a strong libertarian and feels that government regulations can quickly become excessive and counterproductive.

Carol is not the kind of conservative who fuels his or her distrust of government by denying the importance of existing social problems. Often, in our interviews, when I stated some problem, she would go into a fairly long discourse in which she stated it back to me in considerable, and perceptive, detail. The problem is, what to do about it? Numerous times in our interviews, she would end by admitting that she was completely at a loss as to what to do. High on her list for ways of dealing with problems were those using non-governmental initiatives (or perhaps using the government only as a financial catalyst). She would have firms be responsible for day care; churches and private foundations deal with homelessness; and so forth. But she also realized that for many of the most troublesome problems, such initiatives may not suffice.

When I asked Carol my question about what kind of society she would most like to live in, her answer centered upon mutual respect and freedom from regulation.

A. Well, whether it's local, or whether it's in my classroom, or the nation, I would like to live in a society where people treat each other well. And by "well," I mean that they *respect* other people, regardless of who they are, and I think the highest and best thing that one person can give another person is respect and honor. And the honor of the people by our treatment of them, and I believe that the best kind of society for me would be a society in which people honor other people, in which people respect other people. That means that we would treat one another well, where we respect who they are and who each person is and what each person does, and not make judgments on the basis of color or creed or any other artificial division among peoples, and that we would accept all people for their talent and for their abilities, and for who they are and not make judgments based on labels.

Q. Okay. Anything else?

A. Um, it appears to me that we need certain regulations, but not all regulations, and I think people need to have the freedom to interact with others without interference, and that we should have the right to travel and to do the kind of things that we normally have in the United States.

In a later addendum, it becomes clear that Carol's idea of respect does not preclude the idea of help, and ends with a statement of her distrust of government:

> But going back to your first question, what kind of society do we want? I want a society where people are respected and where people care and take care of each other. Those two things are essential to me, that we do that, and I know there are people..., we help our neighbors, we help the people that live around us, but the people with the most need are not those who live near us. The people with the greatest need live among the people who are also in great need, and there has to be found a way to support these people. I'm not always sure it should be government though; maybe the government ought to contract out some of it, because sometimes the government agencies ...

Carol's philosophy is one of mutual respect and honor (despite ethnic or other differences), and it is a philosophy in which each person would be afforded the *opportunity* to succeed, but where persons are seldom given resources (except in direst circumstances) which would encourage dependency. In Carol's ideal society, persons would widely take the initiative to help each other through difficulties without the need for government intervention, a society where altruism of the kind central to Frank's commitment model is much in evidence.

Like Jane and Betty, and because of her emphasis on equal opportunity, Carol is in favor of a program such as Head Start, which she feels is underfunded. (She would increase funding for Head Start, but *only* if the funding for other government programs is correspondingly decreased.) Carol claims that she does not mind being taxed, although she adds the significant proviso: "particularly when I feel the money is being used well, and when I feel the services that come back are of good quality." As already indicated, she often feels that this proviso goes unmet. When I pointed out to her that of the industrialized nations, the US is a relatively lightly taxed nation, she countered with the observation that her accountant told her that some of her summer income was being taxed 47 percent at the margin.

Other findings by goal area

The following is a brief sampling of some pilot study findings by goal area:

Reward

Reward is an ethical concept important to most, but reward distinctions did not seem to matter much to any of my respondents when I asked them to relate them to taxation, perhaps the most relevant institution where reward is concerned. All three women thought rewards functioned reasonably well (Jane was a bit of an exception) and all thought freedom more important than tinkering with rewards. Carol emphasized that reward should follow hard work and considered the income tax too progressive for that reason. Jane indicated that rewards in life could be capricious. In her interview about old age pensions, she had the following to say about the earnings approach (versus the membership approach):[22]

A. So, this other plan, that their pension should be related to their LIFEtime income, (pause) seems to me, to be unfair. But, uh, whoever said life was gonna be fair? You know that old adage, we all know that, that's certainly not something that we all believe by any means. I remember my husband saying, "You know, people do pick the wrong, uh, field to go into sometimes. A fellow has to pick teaching (chuckles).

[22]Where persons are rewarded simply by virtue of having membership in a group (see next page).

So now whether society agrees that that's a very worthwhile way to earn one's living, they don't show it by paying you...(H)igh earnings may not necessarily depend on the person's talent or anything else (chuckle)."

In addition, all three respondents had reservations about whether some of the low wages and high salaries/incomes in the American economy were justified by reward notions (see next page.)

Economic efficiency

While I hoped to inform the respondent, I did not attempt to provide instruction about technical efficiency questions beyond reminding them once or twice that economists think that well-working markets are efficient. In addition, all three ladies seemed to understand the importance to efficiency of maintaining incentives.

One area where I could gauge their feelings about economic efficiency was that involving the progressivity of the Federal income tax. Carol, in particular, brought up the question of incentives in discussing progression, especially substantial progression for which she was unenthusiastic. She touched on the point several times over the course of the interviews; the following are two examples. When we were discussing the prospect of increasing progression, she agreed that perhaps it could be done somewhat, "but not enough to curb incentives." Then she added, "Sometimes, when I realize that half of what I earn when I'm self-employed[23] is going to the government, I wonder if it's worth it. Wouldn't I just be better off not doing it?" Another time, when I was asking her about the possibility of raising effective collection rates[24] on the estate tax, given the fact that they were now quite low, she responded:

A. I would, but not a huge amount, because I think it's part of the..., I don't believe the government's role is to take money and redistribute it, take the money from productive people and redistribute it, and

[23]Carol had been told by her accountant, whether correctly or not, that taxes on her summer income from self-employment amounted to almost half of the income.

[24]As I explained to the respondent, by "effective rates" I meant average (as opposed to marginal) rates.

leaving the top wage-earners demoralized. I don't want to see us do that. I think the top earners do have a responsibility to pay more than low earners, but I don't think it should be to the point where those people feel that the government has taken ...

Q. Right.

A. I don't want to see those people demoralized. So I don't want the government just to take as much as they can get from them and then give it to those who don't have anything.

Jane, who was in favor of substantial progression, gave, in stating a somewhat confused argument about the workings of the economy, the limit beyond which marginal income tax rates would be too high, although whether she had incentives in mind is hard to tell:

Q. How progressive should the income tax be, do you think, should the top rate be...?

A. As progressive as you can possibly make it.

Q. 50 percent? 70 percent?

A. Fairly high rates. I realize we need huge amounts of money (the economy) and it needs to be moved around rapidly and all that. So I don't suppose it would be too smart. To tax beyond, I don't know what the top would be.

Betty merely spoke of marginal tax rates above 50 percent as being too high, without giving a reason, although she seemed to feel that one ought to be allowed to keep at least half of any dollar earned. Whether she had incentives or fairness in mind, I don't know. Here is where a follow-up question should have been asked, and in an actual data collection effort (as opposed to a pilot study) this could easily have been done.

One of my questions dealt with whether the respondent had any comments or criticisms about the workings of the American market-oriented economy. In answering this, as well as in other points in the interviews, Jane, Betty, and Carol made comments which could be interpreted as dealing with efficiency, usually at the macro-economic level. The most pervasive and cutting criticism of this kind had to do with the subject of jobs. I will not take the considerable space needed to present the relevant comments about jobs, but all three women had major concerns about both the lack of jobs and, especially, the widespread prevalence of jobs which do not pay enough for a decent existence. Carol spoke of the inability often for a family to get by on a single paycheck; Betty pointed out that she personally knows people who hold two jobs and are barely making it. Jane pointed out that "lots of jobs don't pay enough" and wished for a raise in the minimum wage.[25] Both Betty and Carol also pointed to a lack of suitable job opportunities for educated persons.

A related concern is the distribution of salaries at the other end of the spectrum. Both Jane and Carol explicitly suggested that salaries at the top were too high. This is most often thought of as an equity complaint, but it could have an efficiency aspect as well. Here Carol, my most conservative respondent, questions both the salaries and wealth at the top:

A. I'm a little bit concerned about some of the [inaudible, probably "high"] salaries. I've been reading the *Wall Street Journal*...

Q. Oh yeah, they're really something else.

A. And stockholders are now beginning to look at those, and beginning to ask questions. People are looking at doctors' salaries and things...But people are beginning to question this. The value of this person's service and the value received. Are they equitable? And I'm not so sure they are. The *Forbes* 500 list, another eye-opener. How much money these people are estimated to have.

The value and value received comment can be interpreted as an efficiency criticism.[26]

Need

The weights people place on social goals when dealing with persons who cannot, or even will not, make a decent living are very important for understanding their overall pattern of demand for collective goods. Dealing with need requires relatively great effort in any society since it requires resources taken from those who contribute. In my basic goal list, I defined

[25]This interview took place before the increase in late 1996.

[26]According to economic theory, in efficient markets the value of marginal product is equal to price, or the value of marginal product of a worker is equal to his marginal compensation.

two types of need goals: general need (poverty for whatever reason) and special need (due to physical or mental disabilities). There is also a third distinction that can be made, although it's hard to maintain in practice: the differentiation of the needs of children from the needs of adults. Assuming for the moment that we can find a way to separate the two, the needs of children is a goal which almost entirely overlaps another goal on our list, "positive freedom," that is, being allowed the ability to pursue one's own lifetime potential without hindrance.

All three respondents placed high weights on all goals involving needy children. This was most pronounced with Jane, as we already saw in our sketch of her overall philosophy above. Jane takes the view that the entire society should assume responsibility for problems of poverty and poor education, whether for children or adults. But much of the driving force behind Jane's philosophy, I believe, is the plight of disadvantaged children. Jane would *greatly* add to the funding of Head Start, to counseling and tutoring programs for at-risk children, to the funding of parenting classes, and to helping families with young children in general.

I collected many comments concerning the social welfare problem in general (which all three respondents found rather intractable), and it would not be profitable to go over these, although I did find something of a contradiction in how the problems of the poor are viewed. On the one hand, first, they are seen as problems mostly beyond the control of poor persons taken as a whole. From this point of view, Jane and Betty have strong suggestions for government help with the problem: through social welfare programs on the one hand, and job provision and training on the other. Carol is much less sure of what to do. She would provide lesser levels of social welfare as a last resort and, perhaps, also modest government payments or tax breaks to stimulate private agencies to provide job training (to persons who show they truly want it), training in parenting skills, providing shelters for the homeless, food kitchens, and the like.

Secondly, the poverty problem among the adult population is seen as being associated with persons failing to take responsibility for their own lives, in particular welfare dependency and teenage pregnancy. From this standpoint, all three respondents seemed at a complete loss as to what to do.[27]

---

[27]These interviews occurred before passage of the Welfare Reform Act of 1996.

Negative freedom

As the philosophers use the term, "negative freedom" means the freedom not to be interfered with, to be able to do what one wants in his or her "own space." The guarantees in the US Bill of Rights include negative freedoms, freedom of religion, speech, assembly, to move, and to choose one's own occupation. That all three of my respondents placed high weights upon the negative freedoms (were strong libertarians) was already established above. Here, I shall merely include a few of their representative statements.

Jane: [With respect to searching for handguns without search warrants in a housing project known to have many guns and where the inhabitants seem in favor of doing so.] I suppose if the police could prove to me that they have sufficient evidence that they were going to find something and that they were sufficiently worried about what these guns were going to be used for, but I think it would have to be a very special thing.

Betty: [With respect to requiring long-term contraceptive shots.] Uh, I don't like long-term contraceptive shots, I don't think. (Chuckles.) I wouldn't be for that. No.

[About the abortion question and the right of religious groups to affect the school curriculum in questions like sex education.] Well, I am very, very much for a woman's right to choose. She may choose one way or the other, that's her business. But she has the right to choose.... And I don't, as far as freedoms are concerned, I'm against the freedom of someone telling ME what to believe.... That's, I'm very much against that. And they can believe what they please, but they're not gonna force ME to believe it.

Carol: It appears to me that we need certain regulations, but not all regulations, and I think people need to have the freedom to interact with others without interference, and that we should have the right to travel and to do the kind of things that we normally have in the US.

[With respect to the police not using warrants in a housing project (see above)] Uh, I'm not in favor of government taking people's rights. If you look at the constitution, one of the rights guaranteed us is that your home is your castle, and I do not believe that I would want anyone coming in here and searching my home without a warrant, and without just cause at any time. So to me, it was shocking that they could go in these projects and search without a warrant. But on the other hand, the people who lived there thought it was a good idea, at least from what I saw on TV. Whether they all felt that way, I don't know.... But they didn't interview anybody who said that that was a violation of rights. I'm not in favor of taking any of our constitutional rights away from us.

[Concerning religious groups affecting the school curriculum with respect to sex education and parenting education.] I believe that the schools should offer the education and those who do not want their children to have that have the right to have them excused. Excusing them from it means it's not gonna keep others from getting that education if they really want it.

Excessive inequality

The last social goal area on my list is that dealing with the view held by many, if not all, persons that a good society should not have "excessive" inequality, somehow defined. The conception of inequality I used in these interviews is that where a person feels that, no matter what else is true, the economic disparity is simply too great. A person might feel that while having the top ten percent of the wealth-holders owning half the wealth might be acceptable, having the top one percent owning half the wealth is not. This is presumably the kind of feeling the great writer on taxation, Henry Simons, had when he stated a case for highly progressive taxation, on the basis that the existing distribution of income and wealth is "distinctly evil or unlovely."[28]

---

[28]"The case for drastic progression in taxation must be rested on the case against inequality — on the ethical or aesthetic judgment that the prevailing distribution of wealth and income reveals a degree (and/or kind) of inequality that is distinctly evil or unlovely" Simons (1938: 17).

Another approach takes the form of thinking of "unexplained inequality." After one has proceeded to give what seems to be acceptable reasons for existing inequality, by citing differences in ability and effort, allowing reasonable amounts of gifts and bequests, and so forth, does he or she feel that there is *still* substantially more inequality than these

I found a considerable amount of the Henry Simons type of inequality thinking in all three respondents. They were quite concerned that the US was, and seemed to be becoming more so, a nation of haves and have-nots. Upon hearing the information about the income and wealth concentration, Carol observed: "So we really ARE a nation of haves and have-nots," as if this confirmed a suspicion that she had already had.[29] Jane agreed that the increasing concentration of wealth was worrisome and added that this had happened "while the poor have gotten poorer." After having been presented with the data on income and wealth concentration, Betty remarked that the US was changing into a "bipolar society, very poor and very rich," and feared that we are going to "turn into a Third World country after a while." (See above.)

Interview findings for government programs

Phase 2 of the study, consisting of three interviews, was devoted to establishing the demands for (or at least the opinions of) collective goods typically delivered by governments.[30] In these, efforts were made to use

factors warrant? We find persons making judgments concerning this kind of inequality all the time. While I attempted to get at this kind of perceived inequality in some of my questions, I failed to find much identification with it on the part of my respondents.

[29]As one reader pointed out, another possible explanation is that Carol had heard my statements but did not believe them, whereupon my data surprised her.

[30]Economists had made some effort to gather data through personal interview techniques on a subject known as "contingency valuation." This is an interesting idea that persons might be willing to pay for changing the condition of some national resource even though they personally do not have plans to visit it (although they might do so some day.) A number of efforts have been made to get responses of this kind, with mixed results. See the volume of papers on the topic by Hausman (1993).

Based on this, as part of my own study, I asked one of my respondents, Jane, a series of questions about whether she would be willing to pay anything to keep persons from doing things that would pollute the Grand Canyon, or for other actions of this kind — such as logging in national woodlands. After at first complaining about my insistence on coming up with a number ("That's the trouble with economists!"), in the end Jane reluctantly volunteered that "Well, yeah, I'd pay a hundred dollars, I'd add that to my annual tax." (for avoiding logging). While interesting, this result from my few questions does not begin to address some of the problems mentioned in the Hausman volume. Still, I would guess that one could get more meaningful responses of the contingency valuation type in long interviews of this kind than economists have obtained in shorter interview formats.

the scenario approach, that is, to give respondents enough information about the respective programs to allow them to give informed answers. The first hour was devoted to a survey of the respondent's feelings about government programs at local, state, and federal levels along with efforts to get detailed responses about some programs. As already indicated, this was overly ambitious, although still highly instructive. The second and third hours were devoted to an experiment using very highly structured interviews where the scenarios were carefully prepared and read verbatim. For reasons of space, I will not report the considerable information gained in the first hour (an indication of some of the results is given below), nor go into much detail with respect to two of the three structured interviews given. However, a presentation of the results from one of the structured interviews should give a reasonably good idea of what can be accomplished with the scenario-type methodology.

The experiment in the highly structured interviews was to see what would come of a more focused and detailed inquiry into some issue areas than what was done in the first two interviews. This required narrowing the subject matter to one or a few manageable public policy areas. Accordingly, I narrowed this part of the study to selected problems involving the elderly: retirement pensions, health care, and services for the frail elderly. Two interviews were then devoted to these topics, of which the first dealt with pensions, the second with the other two areas (the "services for the frail elderly" interview was fairly short). For each area, I constructed a short polling instrument in which I attempted to explain the essential issues of the problem and give the respondent enough factual and historical information to allow her to answer my questions in an informed manner. The polling instrument was read to the respondent verbatim, and she was carefully instructed to stop me and ask me to read again any passage that she did not fully understand. The area I have chosen to report on in more detail is that of retirement pensions.

Interview findings for retirement pensions

My questionnaire for the retirement pensions area was five double-spaced pages in length. In addition, I had a set of tables giving key aspects of actual pension plans in six nations: Germany, the Netherlands, Sweden, Switzerland, the United Kingdom, and the United States. Each of these had 15 entries of data concerning the retirement plans in each country. Finally, I had a set of sample pensions and their costs which I could refer to when necessary. As part of the interview, I went over four of the six country schemes carefully.[31] I only referred to the cost chart to give an overall view of cost requirements of different plans or to answer any questions that arose. Costs were reported in terms of size of a required tax on earnings.[32]

I began my presentation on retirement pensions with a statement of what it would take for persons with reasonable lifetime earnings patterns to provide for their own retirement pensions without outside help (save and invest eight percent of their earnings throughout their earning career).[33] Next, I explained that industrialized nations have found that this often does not happen, for various reasons (including situations where a person's lifetime earnings are too low to generate adequate pension funds), so that they have seen the need to institute national pension programs. I then outlined the two main philosophical approaches toward pension design: *membership*, where the controlling idea is that membership in society is the important consideration; and *earnings*, where the key consideration is lifetime earnings. I also discussed how pensions were designed in the six countries included in the table and pointed out the various aspects of pension design that are important, such as minimum levels, maximum levels, percentage of earnings taxed, and percentage of funds taken from the general treasury. Much of this was done as I ran down the information in the country information tables. Finally, I asked respondents for their ideas on how they would design the pension system they would like best if they had unfettered power to do so. I suggested that they might begin by giving thoughts "off the top of your head," and then to perhaps think about some of the country schemes and what they considered good and bad aspects of them. I concluded with the statement: "I just want your idea of the fundamentals or basics of what you would consider the best way of handling the problem of providing retirement income and where, in the process, you think the government would have to get involved."

---

[31]The pension schemes in the other two countries were redundant.

[32]I would be happy to share the questionnaires and other materials with interested readers.

[33]Approximate figure developed with reference to Winklevoss (1993, Chap. 1).

Responses

The pension designs preferred by all three respondents were substantially different from the current US scheme. It is also interesting that one of the first observations made by all three was to indicate their approach to pensions design in the US was affected by the fact that all of the comparison nations had universal health care systems and the US did not.

Jane's ideal pension design had a Dutch flavor. She liked the membership idea and only added earnings because she seemed to think she would be under great social pressure to do so.[34] She wants a minimum pension of 120 percent of poverty level paid to everyone without exception and a maximum payment of 250 percent of poverty. This reproduces the Dutch system. The idea of this is that middle- and high-income people would be expected (and encouraged) to participate in supplementary private pension plans. Finally, Jane indicated that she would hope to limit the cost of this program to a 15 percent tax on earnings and this, unfortunately, judging from the Dutch experience, does not seem as if it would be enough to pay for it. When this was explained, Jane indicated she would resolve the problem by making compromise adjustments, such as raising the earnings tax a bit, lowering the guarantee level some, and perhaps taking some funds from the general treasury to help pay for those persons whose contributions are not enough to cover their pensions.[35]

While Jane leaned toward the Dutch approach, Betty leaned more toward that of Sweden. In addition, Betty indicated that perhaps a good idea would be a compulsory savings retirement plan, which could reduce the scope required in the formal retirement scheme. In any event, Betty opted for a minimum level: 120 percent of the poverty level for everyone. She would base pension payments above that level mostly on earnings, but also, to some extent, on years of participation, as it is in Sweden.

[34]See the reproduction above of Jane's observations to the effect that "high earnings may not necessarily depend on the person's talent or anything else."

[35]Since my efforts were in the nature of a demonstration project for methodology, and not a detailed investigation of substantive beliefs in detail, I did not ask Jane follow-up questions to resolve this. In comparing the Dutch cost figures with those from other nations, Switzerland in particular, I also suspect that the cost figure given for Holland is somewhat overstated, but again, substantive detail was not my objective.

She would have a payment cap at a fairly generous level (compared to Jane's): three or four times the poverty level. Betty hoped not to exceed an earnings tax of 20 percent, and again I explained this is likely not enough to cover the cost of her scheme whereupon she indicated that she understood the need to make compromises.

Carol's preferred plan is, beyond a minimum payment, based wholly upon earnings and has an interesting wrinkle. She would also have a generous minimum payment for everyone of about 120 percent of the poverty level, and she indicated that an important reason for her generosity in this respect was because the US did not have universal health coverage. Her pensions would then be based entirely upon lifetime earnings and would be capped at the level of median income, or perhaps slightly higher than that. Again, the idea is that well-heeled people are supposed to purchase their own supplementary retirement insurance. A very interesting aspect of Carol's scheme, about which she was quite definite, was that persons with very high incomes would be asked to contribute their full percentage share of all their (labor) income (Carol's plan has no contribution cap), and then not collect *any retirement pension at all*. Her justification:

> Those people [persons with very high incomes] have what they need to secure themselves. The government doesn't need to give them a hand ...But they need to give other people a hand, and so, I would say, that we would tax everybody, but they would not be on the recipient end of this. I don't think that people who are extremely wealthy need to be collecting social security ...Uh, and I think that's something they would pay back to the nation in response to the kind of life they have been able to achieve for themselves. And I don't think the rate is that high that it's gonna affect them, that much.

Services interview findings for the frail elderly and interview finding for health care: summary comments

In the structured interview dealing with the frail elderly, I asked questions about what the respondents would like to see done with respect to services for those of the elderly who have difficulty in providing for themselves in various ways. These include counseling, meals, transportation, and assistance in taking medicines, amongst others. I gave information on the size of such programs ($4 billion, three-fourths from the federal government) and read statements of the Senate Committee on Aging and a state administrator to the effect that unmet demands were going up. The question I asked was simply whether they were in favor of keeping the funding at the same level, doubling it, tripling it, reducing it, or what. Jane would at least double it; Betty said it should be doubled at most; and Carol stated she did not wish to see it reduced but would need to have more information before she would support increases. All three were in favor of actions to increase the use of volunteers and Carol was in favor of collecting a higher percentage of funds from the recipients themselves.

In the health care interview, I went over considerable information about systems of health care and asked questions in four health care areas, of which the two most important involved suggestions for adjusting the existing medicare system and how they would design a health care system if they were starting from scratch. Jane and Betty were in favor of extending Medicare into long-term care, at least in part, while Carol indicated she thought the present system was working pretty well.

As for overall design, Betty was flat out for a universal single-payer system.[36] Jane also flirted with single-payer but was aware that it had some drawbacks. Jane also liked a tax credit approach where federal tax credits (not deductions) would finance significant parts of the purchase of private health insurance. Carol was in favor of a single-payer plan (extending the present Medicare to everyone), but with a calculated use of co-payments to preserve incentives and to keep costs down. All three were firmly in favor of universalized care and critical of the present US situation.

How would Jane, Betty, and Carol vote?

It is difficult for me to communicate satisfactorily the wealth of information about the moral and political beliefs of Jane, Betty, and Carol that I obtained in these interviews (in particular, the first two, who had the

[36]In single payer plans, a single entity, usually the central government, is the source of all payments to the medical community. A good example is the current Canadian health system.

full four-hour sequence.) As a mental exercise, I sometimes amuse myself in speculating, when there are bills in the US Congress, or the state legislature, or the county council, how my three respondents would vote on them. Almost always, I decide that I could accurately predict their votes, and can think of passages in the interview transcripts that would entitle me to conclude so. Jane's votes for social welfare measures, in particular those involving children, are positive; her votes for the Department of Defense and the space program are marginally negative; her votes for agricultural support programs and the CIA are negative. Carol's votes for increases in most federal programs (except for the Headstart variety) are negative; her votes for decreases in many of them positive. Betty's votes for increases and decreases would be sprinkled between aye and nay (I have a good idea as to which), except for the funding for job training and job provision programs which she would support full out. Jane would raise taxes; Carol would not. Betty would only raise taxes to fund job programs.

I should not need to belabor the point as to how useful this kind of information could be if obtained for representative samples of citizen populations. As an example, if my questionnaire-interview (or a refined version) on retirement were given to a representative sample of Americans, we would, for the first time, have a good idea about what Americans would really like to see for a retirement system. These techniques not only establish what respondents think about issues and programs, but their reasons for doing so.

Concluding Comments

In the past half century, we have seen public opinion polling become a staple in the mass media and used widely in the social sciences as well. This activity has yielded considerable useful knowledge. Recently, however, large polling methods have come under increasing criticism, both because of technical difficulties and because of the superficiality of the information it provides, giving users little understanding of the "general laws behind human cognitions and behaviors." As Donbach puts it, "too much effort has been spent on descriptions of the state of opinions and short-term changes, too little on the forces and dynamics behind these states and changes."

The solution to these superficiality problems, as an increasing number of critics are pointing out, is for social scientists and the mass media (in particular, the former) to explore public opinion in greater depth — to actively seek the "forces and dynamics" which lie behind the answers given in the polls. Polling and interviewing must delve directly into beliefs and the reasons people have for holding them. This involves additional expense, but the information obtained would justify the added costs, and it may be possible to explore the reasoning behind opinions and beliefs at reasonable expense. Observers of polling methods are increasingly suggesting that, instead of having a situation where proponents of quantitative and qualitative polling are at war with each other, ways can be found to combine the two approaches that would yield much more informative overall polling results.

Despite the hostility of some traditional empiricists, it seems to me, and I believe to a number of others who are better informed, that much of the underlying explanation of polling results that is so sorely needed can be provided by interviews. There may always be an "other-minds problem," no doubt, but with suitable effort ways can be found to minimize it for most purposes. Repetition can be utilized, as well as cross-checking. The dangers of bias can be reduced by producing verbatim accounts of interviews.

Gathering useful public opinion data that provides both understanding of large poll results and systems of motivation needed in social science explanatory models requires an underlying investigatory structure. As Brewster Smith put it, needed is a "meta-theoretical stance that meets the pragmatic test of putting our thoughts and findings in some defensibly consistent order and allows us to bring evidence to bear on humanizing and understanding politics." Wolfgang Donbach asks for a "unified theory" and "general laws behind human cognitions and behaviors." In this book, I have suggested that such a "meta-theoretical stance" that can produce "general laws behind human cognitions and behaviors" can be provided with a comprehensive goal model of human social and individual striving. For any human social problem, I have suggested that a set of goals can be produced with which the fundamental features of the problem space can be described. These, then, become the goals which provide the most important motives behind human policy actions with respect to the social problem, as well as the basis of judgment criteria in the appraisal of such actions. In this, the paradigmatic approach of the professional economists is used, except that it is extended to all relevant goals and done so impartially (hence the set of goals used can never be considered closed).

My objective in conducting the modest interviewing project discussed in this chapter was twofold: to get some idea of how much can be learned from, and the problems encountered in, in-depth interviewing techniques; and to test the working of the comprehensive goal model. With respect to the second objective, I continue to think the goal model to be a highly useful approach to social science. I feel that in structuring my questions and discussions around the eight or ten major goals first, and then having a long enough interview to allow respondents to wander into other concerns (goals) they might have, I have put my finger on a powerful research tool. For investigations at the macro-policy level, the eight to ten goal structure proved highly satisfactory (again, when respondents are allowed to wander into their own concerns); for investigations at more micro-policy levels, a combination of general and more focused goals can be equally useful, as shown by the results obtained in the more structured interviews on pensions, health, and problems of the elderly. The general goal model, in my opinion, yielded information in considerable depth concerning the moral, social, and political beliefs of my respondents.

As for the first part of my objective, two things can be said. First, as suggested by the above comments on results from the goal model, it would appear that much is possible from the use of quality interviewing techniques, that is, from the quality approach to public opinion polling. Secondly, with respect to the practicality of the approach, the jury is still out. For small samples, the approach seems feasible enough, and it may be that considerable explanatory insights behind larger poll results can be obtained from smaller samples. But can the approach work for large samples? Can the funds be found, can interviewer bias be overcome, and can the "other-minds problem" (including that stemming from strategic behavior) be overcome?

One possible strategy for dealing with the size question would be to pick a fairly large random sample for the administration of "foundation" interviews, similar to the first interview given to Jane and Carol. With an ongoing effort, a fairly large sample of these could be built up over a period of time, several years perhaps. Then, as individual issues come up, sub-samples of this larger sample could be randomly chosen for the administration of shorter interviews.

The interviewer bias issue would be dealt with partly by selecting large samples (and assigning multiple interviewers), partly by careful selection and training of interviewers, partly by careful construction of the interview instrument, and partly through the careful study of verbatim transcripts. It will not be possible to exclude the interviewer's personality from wide-ranging interviews; this is less a problem with structured interviews. Interviewers will need to be well-trained; with large numbers of interviewers, biases will tend to cancel out. If Mishler is correct, we need not be frightened of interviewer and interview variations if we can study verbatim accounts of interviews; indeed, they may prove a source of information.

Finally, let us return to the important topic of strategic behavior. Is the "free-rider problem" as serious as economists have claimed? I found no evidence of it at all in my small study, but otherwise the jury is still out. Important to the possibility of strategic behavior is for respondents to come to know and trust their interviewers, and also perhaps, when relevant, to realize the exercise is "academic" in nature, far from the halls where tax policies are being decided. The nature of the topic would matter; some topics would be more threatening to respondents than others. Many respondents might find a general philosophical discussion about social and moral issues somewhat enjoyable. Moderate amounts of compensation would likely enhance the degree of cooperation. To the extent that many respondents subscribe to the "commitment model" discussed by Robert Frank, they would tend to participate with their interviewer in a cooperative spirit. But some strategic behavior would always be a danger, especially since neutral and negative responses may or may not result from genuine neutral and negative demands for the collective good in question, and it will not always be easy to tell when this is the case. But it seems likely that researchers could suitably allow for the problems caused by uncooperative and hostile respondents; indeed, a lack of cooperation and hostility are themselves a form of information.

Social scientists have a wonderful and unique source of data not available to the physical scientists: the experiences, thoughts, and views that all persons have in abundance. This rich source of information has not been tapped more, in large part, because of the methodological problems discussed in this book. It seems a great shame.

Postscript

...Feminist psycho-social theorists, having linked the insistence on the private and nonpolitical nature of feelings with the absence of women and women's concerns in social theory, with reasonable consistency analyze the role of passions in social relations.

Cynthia Burack
The Problem of the Passions, 1994

But when reporters tracked down Vickrey [William Vickrey, who had just won a Nobel prize in economics]..., he insisted on talking about practical ideas for reforming the subways, the electoral system, the budget deficit, and much else besides. A *Times* reporter tried to pin him down, but Vickrey quickly dismissed his prize-winning 1961 paper as "one of my digressions into abstract economics." And he went on to say, "At best, it's of minor significance in terms of human welfare."...Here is a world-renowned theorist confirming what many outsiders had long suspected — that a good deal of modern economic theory, even the kind that wins Nobel prizes, simply doesn't matter much.

John Cassidy
The Decline of Economics, 1996

The spontaneous individual optimization that drives (theories of economic growth) is important, but it is not enough by itself. If spontaneous...bargains, whether through *laissez faire* or political bargaining and government, eliminated socially wasteful predation and obtained the institutions that are needed for a thriving market economy, then there would not be so many grossly inefficient and poverty-stricken societies.... Some important trends in economic thinking, useful as they are, should not blind us to a sad and all too general reality: as the literature on collective action demonstrates, individual rationality is very far indeed from being sufficient for social rationality.

Mancur Olson
Big Bills Left on the Sidewalk: Why Some Nations are Rich, and Others Poor, 1996

(There is) a struggle between the language of science and the language of morality for hegemony in describing what it means to be a person,...a struggle that the language of morality is losing.

Barry Schwartz
The Battle for Human Nature, 1986

There is a good chance that future historians will have different things to say about the progress of the natural and human sciences, respectively, over the twentieth century. For the one: wonderful progress; for the other: fair progress but many missed opportunities.

Many of the missed opportunities in the social sciences have been related in one way or another to collective goods, and in Part 1, I discussed some of the ways in which inadequate treatment of social goods has led to mischief. There have been two fundamental mistakes: the mistake of underemphasizing the social experiences of humans as opposed to their individual experiences, and the mistake of insisting on studying humans only from the outside as opposed to studying them from *both* the outside *and* the inside. The underlying reason for both mistakes has been misbegotten attempts by social scientists to mimic the successful methodology used in the physical sciences: the error of *scientism*.

Physical scientists are able to form and test hypotheses, using data gathered through objective observation through the five senses. When hypotheses are confirmed, they allow precise predictions, which again can be tested. Physical scientists, for the most part, can test hypotheses in portions of their respective disciplines which are "insulated," or walled off, from the rest of their discipline and from the rest of the world, which allows for controlled experiment and makes life pleasant in other ways as well. It would be marvelous if social science could be conducted this way, but it cannot. While social scientists should use the logical approaches, which have been successful in the natural sciences, as much as they can, the interactions that exist in human affairs make "insulation" impossible.

The natural scientists treat the subjects of their studies as *things*, which they are, or beings lacking the power of language in any case. As O'Sullivan points out, mainstream economists (and it holds true in the mainstream of the other social sciences — except anthropology — as well) have aped the hard sciences by also treating humans as "things:" the "objectivist-behaviorist" approach. The idea has been that

> "the human sciences can progress in their understanding of man only by following the same methods as the natural sciences. For this purpose, man must be treated as only another object in nature subject to efficient causal natural laws: as a sophisticated and complex organism but nothing more. All references to subjectivity, to human consciousness, freedom, and intentional activity must be banished because such subjective states are strictly unobservable and so have no place in a rigorous human science."[1]

Objectivism in social science, in pure form at least, is an idea that has been misplaced. The objectivist approach errs in neglecting a virtual gold mine of empirical data that exists due to the extraordinary amount of information humans possess because of their ability to empathize with others, engage in introspection, and interpret and remember their own experiences.[2]

The results of these failures, which lead to the neglect of collective goods in some form or another, were the subject of the first part of this

[1]O'Sullivan (1987: 53).

[2]"In the struggle for survival, it is of great advantage to organisms both to be able to detect deception amongst their fellow species members and to empathize with them. In *Homo sapiens,* these critical and empathic attributes are developed to an extraordinary degree." (Koertge, 1988: 476).

book. Economics, while fine as far as it goes, is too narrow in scope, dealing only with the individual, the material, and the selfish, leaving social objectives to one side. The other social sciences, in their mainstream methodologies and with the possible exception of anthropology, attempt to emulate the natural sciences and in so doing neglect social goals or else admit them into consideration in highly selective and biased ways. The inquiries into human motivation required for fully admitting collective goods into social science are avoided as not being the methodology of card-carrying natural scientists. The "instrumental" view of rationality used by economists to reinforce their narrow conceptualization of motivation is erroneous because it requires external arbiters who simply do not exist. The spiritual, the moral, and the emotional are falsely excluded from the domain of "true science," as well as from moral philosophy, on grounds that emotion is "irrational," not the proper subject of social policy. And finally, it appears that the many ways in which collective goods have been unduly neglected has led to inadequate evaluation practices of collective goods service delivery.

The omission of collective goods from the analytical procedures in whichever social science we choose to consider surely has had an adverse effect on policy analysis. The following quotation from Wertsch aptly describes this result for psychology, but its application to the other human sciences surely follows:

> "We have many isolated, often arcane pieces to a larger puzzle, but we have no coherent, integrative picture of the whole. We can answer detailed questions about neuronal activity or neonatal reflexes, but we have very little to say about what it means to be human in the modern world (or any other world for that matter)...One of the most striking manifestations of this weakness is that psychology has become increasingly less capable of providing insights into the major social issues of the day."[3]

In the two chapters making up Part 2 of the book, I turn to the question of what might be done to overcome the difficulties discussed in Part 1. The suggestion is made that empirical techniques which examine humans "from the inside" might be viable after all, at least if we do

[3]Wertsch (1991: 2).

not insist that science of any type, particularly social science, be perfectionistic. A model was suggested for social science inquiry which affords equal consideration to all human goals, at least the important ones. The required approach begins with the individual and aggregates from there, but by no means does it neglect the kind of macro-social influences so long discussed by sociologists. Information about goals important to persons in groups, for which the analysis is relevant, will be sought in any way possible, not excluding the high quality interview. For good policy analysis, it is not particularly necessary to have a complete list of goals (it will often be obvious which goals are the "important" ones), nor to have the weights placed upon them by group members to whom the analysis is relevant. All that is required is a list of goals thought important by a representative cross-section of the group. On the other hand, investigations which take into cognizance actual goals and the weight possessed by important political leaders, in the manner of analyses Ragnar Frish claims to have done, could be very useful.

The approach I suggest is characterized in Goldthorpe's recent important paper as either an extension of the economists' approach along lines suggested by Robbins (which it is), or one he suggests as possibly proper for sociologists which "treats as rational both holding beliefs and acting on these beliefs where actors have "good reasons" for so doing."[4] Goldthorpe characterizes the economics-Robbins approach as "economic imperialism," and so it could be viewed, I suppose, but as I see it economists could implement it only by recruiting the active assistance of specialists in other disciplines.[5] There is no reason the team leader for any analysis could not be a member of another discipline besides economics. Indeed, it is likely that implementation of the approach I suggest would require cooperative efforts by more than one of the existing social science disciplines, at least as conducted by their mainstream practitioners.

[4]Goldthorpe (1998: 179).

[5]There will come a day when the production of bad social science for reasons involving "turf" will have to end, and it should be sooner rather than later. Either teamwork will need to be employed directly, or researchers must become adept at adapting work in other disciplines to their own use. All this would be greatly facilitated if social scientists got into the habit of considering all the social goals relevant to their research problems.

I have a vision for how the social science academic and research programs in leading universities would be structured. What are now the individual social sciences would become sub-disciplines in an overarching administrative unit: the "School of Human Sciences." Graduate and undergraduate students would be responsible to the School, with concentration in one or more sub-disciplines, but with additional work required in the others. All students in the School, especially the graduate students, would be required to take a series of core courses which have a social problem orientation, taught in interdisciplinary fashion by instructors highly familiar with the subject matter of at least two sub-disciplines (or at least they know enough about the subject matter in other sub-disciplines to show how their subject matters can be related to policy problems). The overall perspective taken would be that of the goal model I suggested in Chapter 6, or something similar. All students would be required to take a course which deals in some depth with the theory in all the sub-disciplines, and another course which combines econo-, socio-, and psycho-metrics. Part of the combined metrics course, or else a separate course, would be devoted to polling and interviewing techniques. Core courses would occupy most of each graduate student's first year of study and have similar emphasis for undergraduates.

There would be two divisions in the School of Human Studies: a Division of Policy Studies and a Division of Theoretical Studies. The latter would contain courses similar to the central theoretical courses in the present social sciences. Students would be encouraged to take work in both Divisions, but most would have a strong policy component. Students would concentrate in one sub-discipline but would be required to take a "strong minor" in at least one other sub-discipline. Double concentrations would not be discouraged.

The Division of Policy Studies would have a number of departments, each organized along lines of some policy problem, health studies, tax studies, poverty studies, and so forth. Most (but not necessarily all) dissertations would be generated in the Division of Policy Studies. Departments in the Division of Policy Studies would be staffed by policy area experts whose respective training was in more than one discipline and, when possible, in more than two disciplines. There would be a teamwork approach in both instruction and research.

If the social sciences in academic disciplines were reorganized along these lines, and if students were given to understand material similar to that contained in this book, Goldthorpe's fears about "imperialism" would be overcome and the social sciences could begin at last to take their place alongside the natural sciences as disciplines making deep and lasting contributions to human welfare. Finally, on a more mundane and practical level, I strongly suspect that the new School of Human Studies would attract many more students, both undergraduate and graduate, than the separate social science disciplines have been able to do in recent decades.

References

Ackoff, G.A. (1990) Interview with Richard Swedberg. In *Economics and Sociology*, ed. R. Swedberg. Princeton University Press

Ackoff, R. (1962) *Scientific Method*. New York: John Wiley & Sons

Alchian, A. & Allen, W.R. (1967) *University Economics*, 2nd edn. Belmont, CA: Wadsworth

Alston, W. (1967) Emotion and feeling. In *Encyclopedia of Philosopy, Vol 2*, ed. E. Edwards. New York: Macmillan pp. 479–486

Anderson, B.M. (1911) *Social Value*. Boston: Houghton-Mifflin

Anderson, E. (1993) *Value in Ethics and Economics*. Cambridge, Mass.: Harvard University Press

Anton, T.J. (1969) Policy-making and political culture in Sweden. *Scandinavian Political Studies*, **4**, 88–102

Argyris, C. (1982) *Reasoning, Learning and Action*. San Francisco: Jossey-Bass

Aristotle (1980) *Nichomachean Ethics*. Translation by D. Ross. Oxford: Oxford University Press

Arnold, M.B. (1960) *Emotion and Personality* (in 2 vols.). New York: Columbia University Press

Arrow, K.J. (1963) *Social Choice and Individual Values*, 2nd edn. New York: John Wiley & Sons

Barnes, B. & Bloor, D. (1982) Relativism, rationalism, and the sociology of knowledge. In *Rationality and Relativism*, ed. Hollis and Lukes. Oxford: Basil Blackwell pp. 21–47

Baron, J.N. & Hannan, M.T. (1994) The impact of economics on contemporary sociology. *Journal of Economic Literature*, **32**, 1111–1146

Baumol, W.J. & Blinder, A.J. (1985) *Economics, Principles, and Policy*, 3rd edn. New York: Harcourt Brace Jovanovich

Beardsley, M.C. (1967) History of aesthetics. In *Encyclopedia of Philosopy, Vol. 1*, ed. E. Edwards. New York: Macmillan pp. 18–35

Beauchamp, T. (1982) *Philosophical Ethics*. New York: McGraw-Hill

Bell, D. (1982) Models and reality in economic discourse. In *The Crisis in Economic Theory*, ed. Bell and Kristoff. New York: Basic Books

Bell, D. & Kristoff, I. (ed., 1981) *The Crisis in Economic Theory*. New York: Basic Books

Bellah, R.N., Madsen, R., Sullivan, W.M., Swidler, A. & Tipton, S.M. (1985) *Habits of the Heart: Individualism and Commitment in American Life*. New York: Harper and Row

Bemelmans-Videc, M.L., Eriksen, B. & Goldenberg, E.N. (1994) Facilitating organizational learning: human resource management and program evaluation. In *Can Governments Learn?*, ed. Leeuw, Rist & Sonnichsen. New Brunswick, N.J.: Transaction

Benham, L. (1972) The affect of advertising on the price of eyeglasses. *Journal of Law and Economics*, **15**, 337–352

Benham, L., Maurizi, A. & Reder, M.W. (1968) Migration, location, and remuneration of medical personnel: physicians and dentists. *Review of Economics and Statistics*, **50**, 332–347

Benn, S. & Montimore, G. (ed., 1976) *Rationality in Social Science: Contributions to the Philosophy and Methodology of the Social Sciences*. London: Routledge and Kegan Paul

Bennett, J. (1976) *Linguistic Behavior*. Cambridge: Cambridge University Press

Bentley, A. (1908) *The Process of Government*. Chicago: University of Chicago Press

Bergson, A. (1938) A reformulation of certain aspects of welfare economics. *Quarterly Journal of Economics*, **52**, 310–334

Bernholz, P. (1993) Public choice theory: some items for a research agenda. *Public Choice*, **77**, 29–38

Bessette, J.M. (1994) *The Mild Voice of Reason*. Chicago: University of Chicago Press

Blaug, M. (1980) *The Methodology of Economics*. Cambridge: Cambridge University Press

______ (1992) *The Methodology of Economics*, 2nd. edn. Cambridge: Cambridge University Press

_____ (1998a) Disturbing currents in modern economics. *Challenge*, **41**, 11–34

_____ (1998b) The problems with formalism. *Challenge*, **41**, 35–45

Blum, W.J. & Kalven, Jr., H. (1953) *The Uneasy Case for Progressive Taxation*. Chicago: University of Chicago Press

Booth, W. (1995) Florida seeks to end rule by the book. *Washington Post*, 14 March, pp. 1

Boulding, K.E. (1972) Towards the development of cultural economics. *Social Science Quarterly*, **53**, 267–284

Bowen, H. (1943) The interpretation of voting in the allocation of economic resources. *Quarterly Journal of Economics*, **58**, 27–48

Breton, A. (1993) Toward a presumption of efficiency in politics. *Public Choice*, **77**, 53–66

Buchanan, J.M. (1960) *Fiscal Theory and Political Economy*. Chapel Hill, University of North Carolina Press, 1960

_____ (1968) *The Demand and Supply for Public Goods*. Chicago: Rand-McNally

_____ (1975) *The Limits of Liberty: Between Anarchy and Leviathan*. Chicago: University of Chicago Press

_____ (1986) *Liberty, Market, and State*. New York: New York University Press

_____ (1993) Public choice after socialism. *Public Choice*, **77**, 67–74

Bulmer, M. (ed., 1980) *Social Research and Royal Commissions*. London: George Allen and Unwin

Burack, C. (1994) *The Problem of the Passions*. New York: New York University Press

Burns, E. & Burns, T. (ed., 1973) *Sociology of Literature and Drama*. Middlesex, England: Penguin

Cairnes, J.E. (1888) *The Character and Logical Method of Political Economy*, 2nd. edn. London: Macmillan

Caldwell, B. (1982) *Beyond Positivism*. London: George Allen and Unwin

Caporael, L.R., Dawes, R.M., Orbel, J.M. & van de Kragt, A.J.C. (1989) Selfishness examined: cooperation in the absence of egoistic incentives. *Behavioral and Brain Sciences*, **12**, 683–679.

Card, D.E. & Krueger, A.B. (1995) *Myth and Measurement: The New Economics of the Minimum Wage*. Princeton, N.J.: Princeton University Press

Cassidy, J. (1996) The decline of economics. *The New Yorker,* 2 December, pp. 50–60

Churchman, C.W. (1966) On the intercomparison of utilities. In *On the Structure of Economic Science,* ed. Krupp. Englewood Cliffs, N.J.: Prentice-Hall

Clague, C. (ed., 1997) *Institutions and Economic Development.* Baltimore: Johns Hopkins

Clammer, J. (1985) *Anthropology and Political Economy.* New York: St. Martin's

Clarkson, G.P.E. (1963) *The Theory of Consumer Demand: A Critical Appraisal.* Englewood Cliffs, N.J.: Prentice-Hall

Clifford, D.L. & Sherman, P. (1983) Internal evaluation: Integrating program evaluation and management. In *Developing Effective Internal Evaluation: New Directions for Program Evaluation,* ed. Love. San Francisco: Jossey-Bass pp. 23–45

Cole, M. *et al.* (undated) *Ecological Niche Picking: Ecological Invalidity as an Axiom of Experimental Cognitive Psychology.* New York, Rockefeller University, Laboratory of Comparative Human Cognition and Institute for Cognitive Human Development

Coleman, D. (1995) *Emotional Intelligence.* New York: Bantam

Coleman, J. (1990) *Foundations of Social Theory.* Cambridge, Mass.: Harvard University Press

Comptroller General of the United States (1988) *Program Evaluation Issues.* Washington, D.C.: General Accounting Office

Conover, P.J. & Feldman, S. (1981) The origins and meaning of liberal/conservative self-identifications. *American Journal of Political Science,* **25**, 617–645

Converse, J.M. (1984) Attitude measurement in psychology and sociology: the early years. In *Surveying Subjective Phenomena, Vol. 2,* ed. Turner & Martin. New York: Russell Sage

Cook, T.D. & Reichart, C.S. (ed., 1979) *Qualitative and Quantitative Methods in Evaluation Research.* Beverly Hills, CA.: Sage

Corsine, R.J. (ed., 1994) *Encyclopedia of Psychology.* New York: John Wiley & Sons

Coughlin, R.M. (1980) *Ideology, Public Opinion, and Welfare Policy.* Berkeley, CA.: Institute of International Studies

Davidson, D. (1980) *Essays on Actions and Events*. Oxford: Clarendon Press

——— (1986) Judging interpersonal interests. In *Foundations of Social Choice Theory*, ed. J. Elster and A. Hyland. Cambridge: Cambridge University Press

Denver Post (1995) Corrections. 26 October, A2

de Jasay, A. (1989) *Social Contract, Free Ride*. Oxford: Clarendon Press

de Sousa, R. (1987) *The Rationality of Emotion*. Cambridge, Mass.: MIT Press

Dewey, J. (1922) *Human Nature and Conduct: An Introduction to Social Psychology*. New York: Holt & Co.

——— (1925) *Experience and Nature*. Chicago: Open Court

——— (1991) Lectures on ethics: 1900–1901. In *John Dewey: Lectures on Ethics, 1900–1901*, ed. Koch. Carbondale, Ill: Southern Illinois University Press

Donsbach, W. (1997) Survey research at the end of the twentieth century: theses and antitheses. *International Journal of Public Opinion Research*, **9**, 17–28

Downs, G.W. & Larkey, P.D. (1986) *The Search for Government Efficiency*. Philadelphia: Temple University Press

Dunleavy, P. (1992) *Democracy, Bureaucracy, and Public Choice*. New York: Prentice-Hall

Earley, J.E. (ed., 1989) *Individuality and Cooperative Action*. Washington, D.C.: Georgetown University Press

Edwards, E. (ed., 1967) *Encyclopedia of Philosophy*. New York: Macmillan

Elster, J. (1989) *Nuts and Bolts for the Social Sciences*. Cambridge: Cambridge University Press

Elster, J. & Hyland, A. (ed., 1986) *Foundations of Social Choice Theory*. Cambridge: Cambridge University Press

Elster, J. & Roemer, J.E. (ed., 1991) *Interpersonal Comparisons of Well-Being*. Cambridge: Cambridge University Press

Encyclopedia of the Social Sciences (1942) New York: Macmillan

Enke, S. (ed., 1967) *Defense Management*. Englewood Cliffs, N.J.: Prentice-Hall

Etzioni, E. (1988) *The Moral Dimension*. New York: Free Press

——— (1993) *The Spirit of Community*. New York: Simon & Schuster

Evans, R.G., Parish, E.M.A. & Sully, F. (1973) Medical productivity, scale effects and demand generation. *Canadian Journal of Economics*, **6**, 376–393

Fein, R. (1967) *The Doctor Shortage: An Economic Diagnosis*. Washington, D.C.: The Brookings Institution

Feldstein, M.S. (1970) The rising price of physicians' services. *Review of Economics and Statistics*, **52**, 121–133

_____ (1976) On the theory of tax reform. *Journal of Public Economics*, **6**, July/August, 77–104

Foddy, W. (1998) An empirical evaluation of in-depth probes used to pretest survey questions. *Sociological Methods and Research*, **27**, 103–133

Foley, P., Shaked, A. & Sutton, J. (1981) *The Economics of the Professions: An Introductory Guide to the Literature*. London: London School of Economics

Foyer, L. (1969) The social sciences in Royal Commission Studies in Sweden. *Scandinavian Political Studies*, **4**, 183–203

Frank, R. H. (1988) *Passions Within Reason: The Strategic Role of the Emotions*. New York: W.W. Norton

_____ (1992) Melding sociology and economics: James Coleman's foundations of social theory. *Journal of Economic Literature*, **30**, 147–170

Frese, M. & Sabini, J. (ed., 1985) *Goal-Directed Behavior: The Concept of Action in Psychology*. Hillsdale, N.J.: Lawrence Erlbaum Associates

Frey, B.S. (1993) From economic imperialism to social science inspiration. *Public Choice*, **77**, 95–106

Friedman, M. (1953) The methodology of positive economics. In *Essays in Positive Economics*. Chicago: University of Chicago Press

Friedman, M. & Kuznets, S. (1945) *Income from Independent Professional Practice*. New York: National Bureau of Economic Research

Frisch, R. (1970) From utopian theory to practical applications: the case of econometrics. *Economic Planning Studies*, 1–39

_____ (1971) Cooperation between politicians and econometricians on the formalization of political preferences. *Economic Planning Studies*, 41–86

_____ (1976) *Economic Planning Studies*. Dordrecht: D. Reidel

Furubo, J. (1994) Learning from evaluations: the Swedish experience. In *Can Governments Learn?*, ed. Leeuw, Rist, and Sonnichsen

Gauthier, D. (1986) *Morals by Agreement.* Oxford: Clarendon Press

Gazzaniga, M.S. (1995) Success and happiness: a high I.Q. is not the key. *New York Times,* 7 September, B3

Geertz, C. (1973) *The Interpretation of Cultures*. New York: Basic Books

Gilligan, C. (1982) *In a Different Voice.* Cambridge, Mass.: Harvard University Press

Glass, J.F. (1972) The humanistic challenge to sociology. In *Humanistic Society: Today's Challenge to Sociology*, ed. Glass and Staude. Pacific Palisades, CA.: Goodyear

Glass, J.F. & Staude, J.R. (ed., 1972) *Humanistic Society: Today's Challenge to Sociology*. Pacific Palisades, CA.: Goodyear

Goldfarb, R.S. & Griffith, W.B. (1991) Amending the economist's "rational egoist" model to include moral values and norms — Part 2: alternative solutions. In *Social Norms and Economic Institutions*, ed. Koford and Miller. Ann Arbor: University of Michigan Press

Goldthorpe, J.H. (1998) Rational action theory for sociology. *British Journal of Sociology*, **49**, 167–192

Gordon, H.S. (1954) The economic theory of a common property resource: the fishery. *Journal of Political Economy*, **62**, 124–142

——— (1980) *Welfare, Justice, and Freedom*. New York: Columbia University Press

——— (1991) *History and Philosophy of Social Science*. New York: Routledge

Griffin, J. (1991) Against the taste model. In *Interpersonal Comparisons of Well Being*, ed. Elster and Roemer. Cambridge: Cambridge University Press

Griffith, W.B. & Goldfarb, R.S. (1991) Amending the economist's "rational egoist" model to include moral values and norms — Part 1: the problem. In *Social Norms and Economic Institutions*, ed. Koford and Miller. Ann Arbor: University of Michigan Press

Groot, A.D. de (1969) *Methodology. Foundations of Inference in the Behavioral Sciences.* The Hague: Mouton

Hall, P. (1980) The Seebohm Committee and the under-use of research. In *Social Research and Royal Commissions*, ed. Bulmer. London, George Allen and Unwin

Handy, R. (1969) *Value Theory and the Behavioral Sciences*. Springfield, Ill.: Charles Thomas

Hardin, G. (1968) The tragedy of the commons. *Science*, **162**, 1243–8

Harsanyi, J. (1982) Morality and the theory of rational behavior. In *Utilitarianism and Beyond*, ed. Sen and Williams. Cambridge: Cambridge University Press

Hausman, J.A. (ed., 1993) *Contingent Valuation: A Critical Assessment*. Amsterdam: North-Holland

Hedstrom, P. (1996) Rational choice and social structure: on rational-choice theorizing in sociology. In *Social Theory and Human Agency*, ed. Wittock. London: Sage

Held, V. (1970) *The Public Interest and Individual Interests*. New York: Basic Books

Hitch, C.J. (1965) *Decision-Making for Defense*. Berkeley, CA.: University of California Press

Hitch, C.J. & McKean, R.N. (1960) *The Economics of Defense in the Nuclear Age*. Cambridge, Mass.: Harvard University Press

Hobbes, T. (1960) *Leviathan or the Matter, Form and Power of a Commonwealth Ecclesiastical and Civil*. Oxford: Basil Blackwell

______ (1962) *Leviathan or the Matter, Form and Power of a Commonwealth Ecclesiastical and Civil*. New York: Macmillan

Hoeber, F.P., Kassing, D.B. & Schneider, Jr., W. (1978) *Arms, Men, and Military Budgets*. New York: Crane, Russak, and Company

Hogarth, R.M. & Reder, M.W. (ed., 1987) *Rational Choice: The Contrast between Economics and Psychology*. Chicago: University of Chicago Press

Hollis, M. (1982) The social destruction of reality. In *Rationality and Relativism*, ed. Hollis and Lukes. Oxford: Basil Blackwell

______ (1994) *The Philosophy of Social Science*. Cambridge: Cambridge University Press

______ (1996) *Reason in Action*. Cambridge: Cambridge University Press

Hollis, M. & Lukes, S. (ed., 1982) *Rationality and Relativism*. Oxford: Basil Blackwell

Holtman, A. & Idsen, T. (1991) Why nonprofit nursing homes pay higher nurses' salaries. *Nonprofit Management and Leadership*, **2**, 3–12

Horton, R. & Finnegan, R. (ed., 1973) *Modes of Thought: Essays on Thinking in Western and Non-Western Societies*. London: Faber

Hospers, J. (1967) Problems of aesthetics. In *Encyclopedia of Philosophy, Vol. 1*, ed. E. Edwards. New York: Macmillan

House, E. (1986) Internal evaluation. *Evaluation Practice,* **7**(1), 63–64

Hume, D. (1978) *A Treatise of Human Nature*, 3rd edn., ed. L.A. Selby-Bigge (Revised by P.N. Nidditch) Oxford: Oxford University Press

Ianni, F.A.J. & Orr, M.T. (1979) Toward a rapprochement of quantitative and qualitative methods. In *Qualitative and Quantitative Methods in Evaluation Research,* ed. Cook and Reichart. Beverly Hills, CA.: Sage

James, E. & Rose-Ackerman, S. (1986) *The Nonprofit Enterprise in Market Economics*. London: Harwood

Johnstone, Q. & Hopson, D. (1967) *Lawyers and Their Work: An Analysis of the Legal Profession in the United States and England.* Indianapolis: Bobbs-Merill

Joskow, P.L. & Rose, N.L. (1989) The effects of economic regulation. In *Handbook of Industrial Organization, Vol. 2,* ed. Schmalensee and Willig. New York: Elsevier

Kagan, J. (1984) *The Nature of the Child.* New York: Basic Books

Kaplow, L. (1989) Horizontal equity: measures in search of a principle. *National Tax Journal,* **42**, 139–154

Kaufman, F.X., Majone, G. and Ostrom, V. (ed., 1986) *Guidance, Control, and Evaluation in the Public Sector.* New York: Walter de Gruyter

Kayaalp, O. (1988) Ugo Mazzola and the Italian theory of public goods. *History of Political Economy*, **20**, 15–25

Kessel, R.A. (1958) Price discrimination in medicine. *Journal of Law and Economics*, **1**, 20–53

——— (1970) The A.M.A. and the supply of physicians. *Law and Contemporary Problems*, **35**, 267–283

Kiesling, H. (1992) *Taxation and Public Goods: A Welfare-Economic Critique of Tax-Policy Analysis*. Ann Arbor: University of Michigan Press

King, D. (1998) The politics of social research: institutionalizing public funding regimes in the United States and Britain. *British Journal of Political Science*, **28**, 415–444

Kirchgaessner, G. & Pommerehne, W.W. (1993) Low-cost decisions as a challenge to public choice. *Public Choice,* **77**, 107–116

Koch, D.F. (ed., 1991) *John Dewey: Lectures on Ethics, 1900–1901*. Carbondale, Ill: Southern Illinois University Press

Koertge, N. (1980) Rosenberg's unkind remarks about social science. *Inquiry*, **25**, 471–477

Koford, K.J. & Miller, J.B. (1991) Introduction. In *Social Norms and Economic Institutions*, ed. Koford and Miller. Ann Arbor: University of Michigan Press

______ (ed., 1991) *Social Norms and Economic Institutions*. Ann Arbor: University of Michigan Press

Krupp, S.R. (ed., 1966) *On The Structure of Economic Science*. Englewood Cliffs, N.J.: Prentice-Hall

Kuhn, T.S. (1970) *The Structure of Scientific Revolutions,* 2nd edn. Chicago: University of Chicago Press

Ladd, E.C. & Benson, J. (1992) The growth of news polls in American politics. In *Media Polls in American Politics*, ed. Man and Orren. Washington: Brookings Institution

Lees, D.S. (1966) *Economic Consequences of the Professions*. London: Institute of Economic Affairs

Leeuw, F.L., Rist, R.C. & Sonnichsen, R.C. (ed., 1994) *Can Governments Learn?* New Brunswick, N.J.: Transaction

Lerner, A. (1944) *Economics of Control*. New York: Macmillan

Lindenberg, S. (1990) Homo socio-economicus: the emergence of a general model of man in the social sciences. *Journal of Institutional and Theoretical Economics*, **146**, 727–748

Lipsey, R.G. & Courant, P.N. (1996) *Microeconomics*, 11th edn. New York: Harper Collins

Love, A.J. (1983a) Editor's notes. In *Developing Effective Internal Evaluation: New Directions for Program Evaluation*, ed. Love. San Francisco: Jossey-Bass

______ (ed., 1983b) *Developing Effective Internal Evaluation: New Directions for Program Evaluation*. San Francisco: Jossey-Bass

______ (1991) *Internal Evaluation: Building Organizations from Within*. Newbury Park, CA.: Sage

Lukes S. (1973) On the social determination of truth. In *Modes of Thought: Essays on Thinking in Western and Non-Western Societies*, ed., Horton and Finnigan. London: Faber

______ (1982) Relativism in its place. In *Rationality and Relativism*, ed., Hollis and Lukes. Oxford: Basil Blackwell

Lyons, W. (1980) *Emotion*. Cambridge: Cambridge University Press

Lyons, W. & Scheb, II, J.M. (1992) Ideology and candidate evaluation in the 1984 and 1988 presidential elections. *Journal of Politics*, **54**, 573–584

Magat, W.A., Krupnick, A.J. & Harrington, W. (1986) *Rules in the Making: A Statistical Analysis of Regulatory Agency Behavior.* Washington, D.C.: Resources for the Future

Man, T.E. & Orren, G.R. (ed., 1992) *Media Polls in American Politics.* Washington, D.C.: Brookings Institution

McCloskey, Donald N. (1994), *Knowledge and Persuasion in Economics.* Cambridge: Cambridge University Press

McCulloch, J. (1870) *Principles of Political Economy with Sketch of Rise and Progress of the Science.* London: Murray

McKean, M. (1992) Success on the commons: a comparative examination of institutions for common property resource management. *Journal of Theoretical Politics*, **4**, 247–281

MacLeod, H.D. (1875) What is political economy? *Contemporary Review*, **25**, 871–893

Maloney, J. (1985) *Marshall, Orthodoxy, and the Professionalisation of Economics*. Cambridge: Cambridge University Press

Margolis, H. (1982) *Selfishness, Altruism, and Rationality*. Cambridge: Cambridge University Press

Margolis, J. & Guitton, H. (ed., 1969) *Public Economics*. New York: St. Martin's

Mathison, S. (1991) What do we know about internal evaluation? *Evaluation and Program Planning,* **14**(3), 159–65.

Mazzola, U. (1890) *I dati Scientifici della Finanza Publica*. Rome (Partially reprinted in Musgrave and Peacock, 1964)

Meijer, H. (1969) Bureaucracy and policy formulation in Sweden. *Scandinavian Political Studies*, **4**, 103–116

Mill, J.S. (1926) *Principles of Political Economy*, ed. W. Ashley. London: Longmans Green

Miller, J.H. & Andreoni, J. (1991) Can evolutionary dynamics explain free riding in experiments? *Economics Letters,* **36**, 9–15

Mishler, E.G. (1986) *Research Interviewing: Context and Narrative*. Cambridge, Mass.: Harvard University Press

Mitchell, W.C. (1993) The shape of public choice to come: some predictions and advice. *Public Choice,* **77**, 133–144

Mueller, D. (1989) *Public Choice II.* Cambridge: Cambridge University Press

______ (1993) The future of public choice. *Public Choice,* **77**, 145–150

Murdoch, I. (1970) *The Sovereignty of Good.* London: Routledge & Kegan Paul

Murry-Smith, J. (1997) *Honour.* Sydney: Currency Press

Musgrave, R.A. (1959) *The Theory of Public Finance.* New York: McGraw-Hill

______ (1969) Provision for social goods. In *Public Economics*, ed. Margolis and Guitton. New York: St. Martin's

Musgrave, R. & Peacock A. (ed., 1964) *Classics in the Theory of Public Finance.* London: Macmillan

Musgrave, R. & Musgrave, P. (1989) *Public Finance in Theory and Practice*, 5th edn. New York: McGraw-Hill

Myrdal, G. (1955) *The Political Element in the Development of Economic Theory*. Cambridge, Mass.: Harvard University Press

Nash, D. (1993) *A Little Anthropology*, 2nd. edn. Englewood Cliffs, N.J.: Prentice-Hall

Newhouse, J.P. (1970) A model of physician pricing. *Southern Economic Journal*, **37**, 174–183

New Palgrave Dictionary of Economics (1987) London: Macmillan

Noll, R. (ed., 1985) *Regulatory Policy in the Social Sciences.* Berkeley, CA.: University of California Press

______ (1989) Economic perspectives on the politics of regulation. In *Handbook of Industrial Organization, Vol. 2*, ed. Schmalensee and Willig. New York: Elsevier

North, D.C. (1993) What do we mean by rationality. *Public Choice,* **77**, 159–162

Nye, Jr., J.F., Zelikow, P.D. & King, D.C. (ed., 1997) *Why People Don't Trust Government.* Cambridge, Mass.: Harvard University Press

Odegard, P.H. (ed., 1967) *The Process of Government: Arthur F. Bentley.* Cambridge: Harvard University Press

Oliver, P.E. & Maxwell, G. (1988) The paradox of group size in collective action: a theory of the critical mass. *American Sociological Review,* **53**, 1–8

Olson, M. (1965) *The Logic of Collective Action.* Cambridge, Mass.: Harvard University Press

______ (1982) *The Rise and Decline of Nations*. New Haven: Yale University Press

______ (1989) The role of morals and incentives in society. In *Individuality and Cooperative Action*, ed. Earley. Washington, D.C.: Georgetown University Press

Ortuno-Ortin, I. & Roemer, J.E. (1991) Deducing interpersonal comparisons from local expertise. In *Interpersonal Comparisons of Well Being*, ed. Elster and Roemer. Cambridge: Cambridge University Press

O'Sullivan, P. (1987) *Economic Methodology and Freedom to Choose*. London: Allen & Unwin

Ostrom, E. (1990) *Governing the Commons*. Cambridge: Cambridge University Press

Ostrom, E., Walker, J. & Gardner, R. (1992) Covenants with and without a sword: self-governance is possible. *American Political Science Review*, **86**, 404–417

Ostrom, V. (1986) A fallibilist's approach to norms and criteria of choice. In *Guidance, Control, and Evaluation in the Public Sector*, ed. F.X. Kaufman, G. Majone & V. Ostrom. New York: Walter de Gruyter

______ (1993) Epistemic choice and public choice. *Public Choice*, **77**, 163–176

Paldam, M. (1993) Public choice: more of a branch or more of a sect? *Public Choice*, **77**, 177–184

Paloma, M.M. (1979) *Contemporary Sociological Theory*. New York: Macmillan

Patton, M.Q. (1986) *Qualitative Evaluation Methods*. Beverly Hills, CA.: Sage

Pervin, L.W. (ed.,1989) *Goal Concepts in Personality and Social Psychology*. Hillsdale, N.J.: Lawrence Erlbaum Associates

Petersson, O. (1988) The study of power and democracy in Sweden. *Scandinavian Political Studies*, **11**, 145–158

Poole, K.T. & Romer, T. (1993) Ideology, "shirking," and representation. *Public Choice*, **77**, 185–196

Premfors, R. (1983) Governmental commissions in Sweden. *American Behavioral Scientist*, **26**, 623–642

Presser, S. (1984) The use of survey data in basic research in the social sciences. In *Surveying Subjective Phenomena, Vol. 2*, ed. Turner and Martin. New York: Russell Sage

Prest, A.R. (1980) Royal commission reporting. In *Social Research and Royal Commissions*, ed. Bulmer. London: George Allen and Unwin

Proshansky, H.M. (1978) Applications of social psychology: perceptions and misconceptions. In *Psychology: The State of the Art, Vol. 309*, ed. Salzinger and Denmark. New York: New York Academy of the Social Sciences

Rawls, J. (1971) *A Theory of Justice*. Cambridge, Mass.: Belnap

Redman, Deborah A. (1991) *Economics and the Philosophy of Science*. New York: Oxford University Press

Reichart, C.S. & Cook, T.D. Beyond qualitative *versus* quantitative methods. In *Qualitative and Quantitative Methods in Evaluation Research*, ed. Cook and Reichart. Beverly Hills, CA.: Sage

Rhodes, G. (1980) The younger committee and research. In *Social Research and Royal Commissions*, ed. Bulmer. London: George Allen and Unwin

Rosefielde, S. (ed., 1981) *Economic Welfare and the Economics of Soviet Socialism*. Cambridge: Cambridge University Press

Riley, J. (1988) *Liberal Utilitarianism*. Cambridge: Cambridge University Press

Rist, R.C. (1974) Polity, politics, and social research: a study of the relationship of federal commissions and social science. *Social Problems*, **21**, 113–128

Robbins, L. (1984) *An Essay on the Nature and Significance of Economic Science*, 3rd edn. New York: New York University Press

Rogoff, B. (1990) *Apprenticeship in Thinking: Cognitive Development in Social Context*. New York: Oxford University Press

Rorty, R. (1989) *Contingency, Irony, and Solidarity*. Cambridge: Cambridge University Press

Ross, D. (ed., 1980) *Aristotle: The Nicomachaen Ethics*. Oxford: Oxford University Press

Rowley, C.K., Schneider, F. & Tollison, R.D. (1993) The next twenty-five years of public choice. *Public Choice*, **77**, 1–8

Rubin, Z. (1970) Measurement of romantic love. *Journal of Personality and Social Pschology*, **16**, 265–273

Rushton, J.P. (1980) *Altruism, Socialization, and Society*. Englewood Cliffs, N.J.: Prentice-Hall

Salamon, L.M. & Anheier, H.K. (1996) *The Emerging Nonprofit Sector*. Manchester: Manchester University Press

Samuelson, P.A. (1954) The pure theory of public expenditure. *Review of Economics and Statistics*, **36**, 387–389

——— (1969) Pure theory of public expenditure and taxation. In *Public Economics*, ed. Margolis and Guitton. New York: St. Martin's

——— (1981) Bergonsonian welfare functions. In *Economic Welfare and the Economics of Soviet Socialism*, ed. Rosefielde. Cambridge: Cambridge University Press

Samuelson, P.A. & Nordhaus, W.D. (1985) *Economics*, 12th edn., New York: McGraw-Hill

St. Pierre, R.G. (1982) Management of federally funded evaluation research: building evaluation teams. *Evaluation Review*, **6**(1), 94–113

——— (1983) Editor's notes. In *Management and Organization of Program Evaluation: New Directions for Program Evaluation*, ed. R.G. St. Pierre. San Francisco, Jossey-Bass

Salzinger, K. & Denmark, F.L. (ed., 1978) *Psychology: The State of the Art, Vol. 309*. New York: New York Academy of the Social Sciences

Sarason, S.B. (1981) *Psychology Misdirected*. New York: Free Press

Scanlon, T.M. (1991) The moral basis of interpersonal comparisons. In *Interpersonal Comparisons of Well Being*, ed. Elster and Roemer. Cambridge: Cambridge University Press

Schmalensee, R. & Willig, D. (ed., 1989) *Handbook of Industrial Organization* (in 2 volumes). New York: Elsevier

Schuman, H. (1982) Artifacts are in the mind of the beholder. *American Sociologist*, **17**, 21–28

Schwartz, B. (1986) *The Battle for Human Nature*. New York, Norton

Sen, A. (1987) *On Ethics and Economics*. Oxford: Basil Blackwell

Sen, A. & Williams, B. (1982) *Utilitarianism and Beyond*. Cambridge: Cambridge University Press

Senior, N. (1827) *An Introductory Lecture on Political Economy*. London: J. Mawman

Simon, H.A. (1987) Rationality in psychology and economics. In *Rational Choice: The Contrast Between Economics and Psychology*, ed. Hogarth and Reder. Chicago: University of Chicago Press

Simons, H. (1938) *Personal Income Taxation*. Chicago: University of Chicago Press

Simpson, P. (1987) *Goodness and Nature*. Dordrecht: Martinus Nijhoff

Singleton, S. & Taylor, M. (1992) Common property, collective action, and community. *Journal of Theoretical Politics*, **4**, 309–324

Smelser, N.J. (1990) Can individualism yield a sociology? (Review of James Coleman's *Foundations of Social Theory*) *Contemporary Sociology*, **19**, 778–783

Smith, A. (1976) In *An Inquiry into the Nature and Causes of the Wealth of Nations*, ed. R.H. Campbell & A.S. Skinner. Oxford: Oxford University Press

Smith, B.L.R. (ed., 1984) *The Higher Civil Service in Europe and Canada: Lessons for the United States*. Washington, D.C.: The Brookings Institution

Smith, D.H. & Shen, C. (1996) Factors characterizing the most effective nonprofits managed by volunteers. *Nonprofit Management and Leadership*, **6**, 271–289

Smith, M.B. (1956) *Opinions and Personality*. New York: John Wiley & Sons

______ (1991) *Values, Self, and Society*. New Brunswick, N.J.: Transaction Publishers

Smythies, J.R. (1968) *Biological Psychiatry*. New York: Springer-Verlag

Snow, C.P. (1971) The two cultures and the scientific revolution. In *Public Affairs*, ed. Snow. New York: Charles Scribner's Sons

______ (1959) *Public Affairs*. New York: Charles Scribner's Sons

Sonnichsen, R.C. (1994) Effective internal evaluation: an approach to organizational learning. In *Can Governments Learn?*, ed. Leeuw, Rist & Sonnichsen. New Brunswick, N.J.: Transaction

Stanley, D.T. (1984) Lessons for the United States. In *The Higher Civil Service in Europe and Canade: Lessons for the United States*, ed. Smith. Washington, D.C.: The Brookings Institution

Stuerle, C.E., Gramlich, E.M., Heclo, H. & Nightingale, D.S. (1998) *The Government We Deserve: Responsive Democracy and Changing Expectations*. Washington, D.C.: Urban Institute

Steurle, C.E. & Hodgkinson, V.A. (1998) And just who will meet our needs? A note on the resources of the independent sector and government. In *Nonprofit Organization and the Government: The Challenge of Civil Society*. Washington, D.C.: Urban Institute

Strongman, K.T. (1978) *The Psychology of Emotion*. New York: John Wiley & Sons

Sugden, R. (1984) Reciprocity: the supply of public goods through voluntary contributions. *The Economic Journal*, **94**, 772–787

______ (1986) *The Economics of Rights, Cooperation, and Welfare*. Oxford: Basil Blackwell

Swedberg, R. (1990) *Economics and Sociology*. Princeton: Princeton University Press

Taylor, M. (1987) *The Possibility of Cooperation*. Cambridge: Cambridge University Press

Terwee, S.J.S. (1990) *Hermeneutics in Psychology and Psychoanalysis*. New York: Springer-Verlag

Tinbergan, J. (1967) *Economic Policy: Principles and Design*, 4th revised printing. Amsterdam, North-Holland

Tresch, R.W. (1981) *Public Finance: A Normative Theory*. Plano, Texas: Business Publications

Tullock, G. (1993) Public choice — what I hope for the next twenty-five year. *Public Choice*, **77**, 9–16

Tunstall, J. (1980) Research for the royal commission on the press, 1974–7. In *Social Research and Royal Commissions*, ed. Bulmer. London: George Allen and Unwin

Turner, C.F. & Martin, E. (ed., 1984) *Surveying Subjective Phenomena, Vol. 2*. New York: Russell Sage

Tyler, P.E. (1995) Scientists urge Beijing to stop its persecutions. *New York Times*, 16 May, A1

Ullman-Margalit, E. (1977) Coordination norms and social choice. *Erkenntnis*, **11**, 143–155

U.S General Accounting Office (1992) *Program Evaluation Issues*. Washington, D.C.: U.S. Government Printing Office

Viscusi, W.K., Vernon, J.M. & Harrington, Jr., J.E. (1995) *Economics of Regulation and Antitrust*, 2nd edn. Cambridge, Mass.: MIT Press

Wagner, R.E. (1993) The impending transformation of public choice scholarship. *Public Choice*, **77**, 203–212

Wertsch, J.V. (1991) *Voices of the Mind: A Sociocultural Approach to Mediated Action*. Cambridge, Mass.: Harvard University Press

Wertz, F.J. (1998) The role of the humanistic movement in the history of psychology" *Journal of Humanistic Psychology*, **38**, 42–70

Weisbrod, B. (1988) *The Nonprofit Economy*. Cambridge, Mass.: Harvard University Press

White, H.C. (1990) Control to deny chance, but thereby muffling identity. (Review of James Coleman's *Foundations of Social Theory*) *Contemporary Sociology*, **19**, 783–788

Wickstrom, B. (1985) Free riders and band wagon: on the optimal supply of public goods. In *Public Goods and Allocation Policy*, ed. R. Pethig. Frankfurt: Peter Lang

Wildavsky, A. (1979) *Speaking Truth to Power: The Art and Craft of Policy Analysis*. Boston: Little Brown & Company

Winden, F. Van (1993) Some reflections on the next twenty-five years of public choice. *Public Choice*, **77**, 213–223

Winklevoss, H.E. (1993) *Pension Mathematics with Numerical Illustrations*, 2nd. edn. Philadelphia: University of Pennsylvania Press

Wittock, B. (ed., 1996) *Social Theory and Human Agency*. London: Sage

Wolman, B.J. (ed., 1977) *International Encyclopedia of Psychology, Psychoanalysis, and Neurology*. New York: Van Nostrand Reinhold Co.

Wrong, D.H. (1972) The oversocialized conception of man in modern sociology. In *Humanistic Society: Today's Challenge to Sociology*, ed. Glass and Staude. Pacific Palisades, CA.: Goodyear

Yamagishi, T. (1988) Seriousness of social dilemmas and the provision of a sanctioning system. *Social Psychology Quarterly*, **51**, 32–42

Yankelovitch, D. (1996) A new direction in survey research. *International Journal of Public Opinion Research*, **8**, 1–9

Zaloudek, M. (1996) Queen of pain. *Sarasota (Fla.) Herald Tribune*, 30 April, 1E

Zander, M. (1968) *Lawyers and the Public Interest: A Study in Restrictive Practices*. London: Weidenfeld & Nicolson

Zeraffa, M. (1973) The novel as literary form and as social institution. In *Sociology of Literature and Drama*, ed. Burns and Burns. England: Penguin

Subject Index

Author Index